BARBELL
BUDDHA

BARBELL
BUDDHA

THE COLLECTED WRITINGS OF CHRIS MOORE

OOO MAIDA VALE PUBLISHING

AN IMPRINT OF EYEWEAR PUBLISHING, LONDON, ENGLAND

First published in 2016
by Eyewear Publishing Ltd
Suite 333, 19-21 Crawford Street
Marylebone, London W1H 1PJ
United Kingdom

Typeset with graphic design by Edwin Smet
Author photo, divider art Natalia Baker
Cover art Lisa Mac
Printed in England by TJ International Ltd, Padstow, Cornwall

ISBN 978-1-908998-48-4

*The author's estate has requested that we retain American spelling and
grammatical usage for this text, though this is a British edition; Eyewear has
gladly agreed.*

EDITORIAL NOTE
*The text of this collected writing is based on various blogposts, essays, and
books published while Chris Moore was alive. Every attempt has been made
to collect and present the work as seamlessly as possible. However, it was
necessary to silently correct some errors that crept into earlier versions not
published by Eyewear; and amend a few passages for copyright reasons.
The editors (Davio & Swift) have attempted to preserve as much as possible
of the style and voice of the original, and 99.9% of this text is what one might
call "raw Chris Moore". As such, we have, at times, maintained a few tics
of expression or spelling that were the author's own.*

WWW.EYEWEARPUBLISHING.COM

CHRIS MOORE

TABLE OF CONTENTS

GET CHANGE

SPECIAL THANKS TO
THE EYEWEAR TEAM, CHARLOTTE MILES,
MATT MCDANIEL, SHEREEN MYERS BIENZ,
ABBY JOFFRE EIJKEN, CHRIS NORMAN,
AND THE BARBELL SHRUGGED TEAM
FOR HELPING MAKE THIS BOOK HAPPEN.

LOVE, CHRIS' FAMILY

PROGRESS

USE YOUR VOICE

A few years ago, I drove over to Little Rock to listen to Henry Rollins speak at this little venue called Juanita's Cantina. It wasn't my first show, but it was easily my favorite. The stories were rich and engrossing. The pace was forceful and unrelenting.

I left that show with something very important. I realized that I didn't need to be the smartest guy in the room to make my mark, nor the most talented speaker, writer, or whatever. The only thing in this life that really mattered was whether I was prepared to jump on top of opportunity, work my ass off, and use *my* unique voice as often as possible. I needed to be intensely, unapologetically me. I will never let go of that. I hope the same for you.

PREFACE

The other night I was having a bit of a rough time. A stack of filled pages waited patiently on my desk to be edited. A fresh, blank one stared back at me from my computer screen, that little cursor blinking non-stop like a ticking watch. This is how it goes sometimes. The fire will not light, so you just keep staring at that wood, tossing matches.

You might have some very romantic ideas about writing, art, or whatever, but let me say that this sort of scene is not uncommon. Listening for the Muse can be a bit like waiting at the bus stop. Some days you catch it right at the moment you show up with your lunch box. Other times, it just seems like all you can do is sit and wait.

Fortunately, the bus just about always comes. This night was a particularly long wait. The juices were just not flowing. My mojo seemed to be no more. During times like these all you can do is get the work out of the way for a minute and dick around on the Internet a bit. The premise is that you'll find a spark somewhere out there. Some fresh news story, funny meme or viral video will surely jostle you out of that rut and get you leaning into the wind again. Sure it will. In reality, this is just run-of-the-mill procrastination. It would probably be better to just stand up and walk for a few minutes, returning to that chair shortly thereafter, meat hooks glued to that keyboard. But I got lucky this night. I happened to actually stumble upon this quote that, when clicked, brought me to a site devoted to nothing but quotations. I cannot remember the line, so it must not have been that great. It hardly matters though, but what I found there does. Down in the bottom right of the window was this perfect quote from someone I've never heard of before, Bruce Barton. Now, I know almost nothing about Bruce, other than that he was an early twentieth-century author, businessman and politician. The quote is this: "Action and reaction, ebb and flow, trial and error, change – this is the rhythm of living. Out of our over-confidence, fear. Out of fear, clearer vision, fresh hope, and out of hope, progress."

I was surprised. To my left, I had this stack of paper that essentially was getting at the same thing. The topic: progress. I could not have expressed my own feelings on the matter any more perfectly. Sure, it was just a tiny occurrence of happenstance, but it was more than enough to jostle this flesh loose from its rut. I won't go so far as to say I was meant to see the words. I can't get all the way behind that. But, I cannot accept that it was purely a happy coincidence, either. Perhaps this was the way the Muses wished to work this day, who knows? In any case, it's good to remember that good things usually come to those who are willing to stick around for a while.

You never know when your bus will be coming in.

OUT IN THE GARAGE

"Progress is impossible without change, and those who cannot change their minds cannot change anything." – George Bernard Shaw

I once read a very elegant explanation of the theory of relativity. It was actually a quote attributed to its famous author, Albert Einstein. Maybe you've heard of him? If I may paraphrase here a bit, he reasoned that if you placed your hand onto a hot stove for a few moments it would feel like an hour. No argument there. However, if you spent an hour in conversation with a beautiful woman on a park bench, that time would seem to pass in just a few minutes. "That's relativity," he concluded. It's quite beautiful to explain an abstract and rather complex idea with such elegance. If you have ever found yourself engrossed in deep discussion, sport, or when practicing your chosen craft, then I'm sure you can relate.

But of course our perception of time also changes as we age. We slip deeper and deeper into a temporal illusion with every turn of the calendar. Days, weeks, months and years seem to fly by at an ever-accelerating rate. I'm sure you've noticed. Interestingly, there seems to be a very simple explanation for this.

Just about every experience from our youth is novel. Think back to your first days at school, your first little league soccer practice, a first date and kiss, perhaps even your first fight. These moments strike our brains like asteroids, leaving little consciousness craters that subtly shape all of our remaining days. But with time this novelty seems to grow, well, rare. Our days become less and less about discovery and growth, and more and more about completing a long and dulling series of checklists and to-dos.

This is how you are welcomed to the machine. All of these thoughts came into clear focus one chilly February evening out in my garage. It's here that I realized a lifetime goal of building my very own home gym. No, it is nothing fancy. The weight plates are a bit  mismatched. My power rack exhibits equal parts paint, bare metal and rust. These stacked barbells don't quite spin like they used to. In fact, I'm quite sure that most of this stuff would be considered junk not suitable for the typical chrome-plated, heavily sanitized health spa and its domesticated, aimless clientele. But that is precisely what I love about it!

It has taken me over a decade to build this collection that now fills the room with stories and experiences. The earliest pieces were purchased way back in my college days. Yes, I had a perspective that was terribly shallow at the time, something we all could admit to. Why else would I choose to buy a very expensive barbell, for example, instead of replacing that broken pair of glasses or that well-worn assemblage of oversized tee-shirts and cargo shorts I called my wardrobe? I was simply paying tribute to something that I loved absolutely. It was a very good thing to do, because right at this moment I can reach out with chalked, callused hands and grasp that same barbell. It was an enduring investment. I place it into the rack with care, not wishing to add any additional marks that are not first earned through toil. The ever-sharp knurling of the steel digs deep into my hand, triggering familiar sensory loops and reinforced paths within my memory. In an instant those first training experiences back in grade school come flooding into my mind. That initial feeling of empowerment, fulfillment, and instant addiction was transformational. I can also see the moment when my primary motive turned from simply having fun towards stretching my flesh and bones as far as they could possibly go. No, I do not regret chasing the performance dragon for so long. I've learned so many lessons and have accumulated more than a few well-earned scars that I would not trade. But still, there's the present to deal with. I'm guilty of letting those early, special experiences grow ordinary and routine. I let it all get boring.

This is a time for reviving and cultivating those initial passions.

Yes, time grows shorter as the demands of the day increase. Circumstances change. I owe it to my family to be there for them, fully present and attentive. And no, I cannot help but be pulled towards professional aspirations and long-term goals that are rapidly forming outside of these garage walls. But it's also impossible to forget the feeling of all those training hours passing by as mere moments. The deep satisfaction that comes with hard-earned and well deserved progress cannot be replaced. So, when all affairs are attended to and finished, I will continue to carve out a precious hour or so from the margins of the day. I will always make time for paying tribute out in the garage. And what's more, I will do my best to share these lessons with others, so that regardless of their pursuit or purpose, they will know how important it is to train, grow and discover themselves fully.

I want you to remember that the barbell is a tool for keeping oneself sharp, not for impressing others or measuring up to an artificial, needlessly imposed benchmark. This is the perspective that enables real, meaningful progress.

So how do you do that? How do you keep that perspective? How can you maintain a balance between seeking performance and fulfillment in training? Listen, I won't try to convince you that it is easy, but it is certainly possible. You just need to put together a clear map. You need to carefully identify what it is that you want and – what's often overlooked – what it is that you *don't* want! It's those boundaries that keep you focused on the goal at hand. They make it possible for you to establish clear milestones that will stretch your edges on a daily basis, pushing your forward a step at a time. Further still, a good map will remind you that you cannot do this on your own. You need influence, support, and honest feedback from those around you to keep you on track and accountable. You need help when circumstances are far from ideal, or when resources and your bloated schedule only serve to stand in your way. And yes, you need to know when to start a new journey with a totally new destination.

You don't need any more rules, procedures, or cookie-cutter programs. In fact, I would encourage you to break as many of those rules as possible. The only truth you need is this: there are many promising paths from which to choose. All will take you somewhere very interesting. What you really need are focus and an ever-expanding perspective. After all, from this new vantage point, you will see exactly where you must go. And progress favors those who are prepared to see.

THIS HISTORY

I'll be honest. I've never seen much value in doctor visits. Sure, exceptions have to be made when you find yourself coughing up a lung, or when you notice a novel burning sensation or angry looking blemish on your back. But other times it just seems to be an exercise in wasting time. At least, that has been my experience. I can close my eyes and hear the shuffling feet of the physician as he paces back and forth in the hallway. He could be very busy out there, maybe. Or, he could simply be making the most of these billable hours.

I do my best to clearly communicate the pain. In return there's only the cold touch of the stethoscope coupled with a generic concluding recommendation to stop what I'm doing. A muted thanks slips from my lips but I defer the offer of a pain-killing prescription.

It's usually a good thing to accept such offers. Consider it better living through chemistry. However, sometimes a band-aid or crutch cannot masquerade as a true remedy. That's what I was after.

There was something different about this latest visit. It was refreshingly thorough and focused. The assessment itself felt more like a mixed-martial arts submission maneuver than a diagnostic tool. The doctor grasped my right elbow firmly, drawing it in tight to his body for maximum leverage. "Just relax and let that arm hang, OK?" I complied to the best of my ability, but it's hard not to brace in anticipation of something unpleasant. He might as well have been slipping on a boxing glove. "Just close your eyes. I promise you won't feel a thing!" His right hand seized my wrist as his left manipulated the joint with considerable force. The experience reminded me of butchering a chicken, where you dig around those tiny joint spaces with a knife looking for a vulnerable entry point. Luckily for me he didn't find one!

The lack of any acute pain or instability was reassuring at first. For a moment I was confident this problem wasn't progressive. But that changed when the X-ray results came in. There, highlighted by bright light, was clear evidence of the burgeoning arthritis sabotaging my performance. This would have been troubling news ten years ago. Thankfully, I've matured just a bit in that time. I realize that a radiograph can deliver far worse news than, "I'm sorry, Mr. Moore, but you'll never bench press seven-hundred pounds again!" I had been there and done that. There was no sense in a serious comeback. But still, I couldn't help but think back. Were those old goals worth this manifest wear and tear? What would I have done differently if I had acknowledged early on that the chase could lead to surgery and that slippery slope of degeneration? Yes, the wise path is always easier to see in hindsight, but it would have been much more clear had there been a better plan in place long ago.

Can you remember the first time you lifted weights? I'm sure you can. In fact, we probably share the same experience. It likely involved a friend's backyard and some concrete-filled plastic weights purchased from the local department store. What they likely didn't come with, however, was prudent guidance or oversight. Luckily those old plates were far too light to present a real risk, even if I had managed to drop them right on my fucking throat! What's more, I was too weak and under-developed to consider heavier options But still, these early sessions were enough to install a life-long pilot light. For the next few years, and all throughout high school, I was preoccupied with pursuing a better, stronger version of myself. Did I know what I was doing? No, of course not! But this might have been an advantage. I can look back and see a few clear goals. I wanted to be stronger with time. That meant moving not only more weight, but doing so frequently and for a lot of repetitions. I also was interested in balance. There seemed to be no point in focusing heavily on just a few movements or abilities. Why not be really good at more? How else am I going to impress the gym class girls as they pace through the weight-room? And hell, let me make it clear that training was always fun! I never wanted to give it up. I certainly preferred it to going to football practice, to class, home, even Friday night keg parties.

Through every one of those bizarre and volatile teenage years, the barbell served as a great steadying influence, an outlet and a teacher. It was everything for a while.

I can see now where things started to go downhill. Sport was soon my highest priority. But not necessarily by choice, mind you. In the world of high-level collegiate athletics, you had to spend the better part of the year preparing at all hours just to have a chance on the field. There was no shortage of athletes who could lift more, run faster, jump higher, and perform better. Imagine an intense, constant pressure to meet and exceed all standards. You could feel the cold glare of those goddamn coaches if you weren't constantly putting up great numbers and times. Some folks thrived, but I quickly lost my appetite for it.

I returned to the barbell full-time in the years that followed, only now as a competitive Powerlifter. This newfangled motive was simple: this was a sport that played more to my natural interests and abilities. And if I'm to be honest, it offered a shot at redemption. I never quite got over my failure to make an impact in American Football. And no, I never really came to peace with my decision to leave it prematurely. There was that sad moment when I realized my parents would never walk out onto that field with me before my last game; to see an appreciative crowd applaud for those hard years of service. But at least now there was the chance to excel in some other way. I could become one of the strongest lifters in the country!

So, I turned myself over fully, training longer and harder than ever before. Every part of life that could possibly interfere with the mission was stripped right down to the bone. But that was the fatal mistake. This was supposed to be about passion and love. Should a passion ask for you to give up so much?

This wasn't about seeking balance. It wasn't for love. It was obsession. I had repeated a list of large numbers over and over again in my head until the point I could close my eyes and see the targets etched in bright red font. Nothing could stop that march, not even the emergence of a nagging little pain in my right arm. The choice had been made. When it was time to train, that arm got coated in analgesic equestrian liniments and then wrapped up tight. The goal seemed to be within reach, but I failed to consider the cost of the pursuit.

I did manage to reach many of my targets. I set more than a few national records. There was some measure of redemption. But it shouldn't be a surprise that my sense of fulfillment began to evaporate as soon as it had appeared. It's that old cliché. If a little bit gave me a taste of satisfaction, surely grabbing more would fill my belly. I'd like to say that I got wise quickly, but no, I chased that dragon for the better part of a decade.

The wiser path seems clear in hindsight. Let me point it out for you now: there's absolutely nothing wrong with setting big goals that fall well outside of your reach. In fact, it's essential if you want to achieve anything special. You have to be stretched at the edges to keep growing. It will draw out what you are not prepared to offer on your own. But the very moment you give up your balance and passion, the moment you turn downhill, you will quickly realize that your goal has started to take away a whole lot more than it gives back.

You should recognize that this price is far too steep.

KIND OF LIKE WAR

One of the most fascinating characteristics of strength competitions is how closely they are aligned with combat. Sure, you could say the same thing about other sports. Coaches of all stripes commonly weave wartime elements into bombastic pre-game pep talks. The turf itself is framed as a battlefield, with the coach and players acting out their roles as general and army. I suppose this approach has its effect and charm.

However, in my experience, the story is distilled and amplified to greater effect in Strongman, Powerlifting, and, to a lesser extent, Olympic Weightlifting. Here there's just one athlete locking horns with a savagely heavy barbell or implement. It's a *two men enter, one man leaves* sort of scenario. Intolerable decibels of death metal fuel the fight. Knurled metal scrapes against shins, tears hands, and draws blood. Lifters snort and shout. The losers internalize the defeat while the winners hoist cheap knock-off swords and battle axes as awards.

It's quite the scene. If you are at all curious, a few moments spent on YouTube will reveal all you need to know.

There is tremendous value in the daily training grind – in sharpening yourself in preparation for a competition. All of the hardcore angles of these sports can be a bit dramatic, sure, but it's only intended as tribute. It reinforces a relatively positive identity in the athlete. The promise is that, in the gym, you can be more than just a lifter. You can be a warrior!

OK, so maybe that's one step too far. Just typing the words makes me a little uncomfortable. Who wouldn't find themselves embarrassed to make such a claim in front of an actual veteran?

It's one thing to be bold with the barbell, quite another to do so once the armor and swords come out.

Yes, it's silly, but the association between combat and training is very easy to explain. It has its roots in recent human history. Spartan soldiers prepared for war by training with heavy stones and crude implements, very often exceeding the capabilities of modern Strongmen by a few hundred pounds. Disks more than four times the size of their contemporary track and field counterparts were hurled about routinely. Competitions like the ancient Olympics were the next logical step in this progression. In times of peace, why not compete in something, eh? Why waste all of that hard-earned brawn?

For those who may be interested, you can find all the detail behind those engrossing accounts of human performance from the anthropological record in Peter McAllister's excellent book, *Manthropology.*

This is all amazing, really. Strong social and mortal incentives can result in incredible performances and unparalleled rates of progress, no fancy programming or expensive modern equipment required. Of course, I'm of the opinion that you should not utilize the impending threat of severe injury, evisceration, or death to fuel your workouts! Rather, it's enough to realize one powerful truth: it's not only *how* you train that matters, but also *why*. If you want to become the fittest, leanest, strongest, or most efficient version of yourself, then you need to raise your expectations. You need to believe that this is possible.

That's the closest thing to a real war you will experience.

Yes, that historical link between sport and combat is genuine. And while we are not talking war here, it might be useful to acknowledge just how intense a true maximal effort can be. The risk of serious injury is very real. Your pulse climbs quickly as the load is prepared. The barbell begins to bow as each successive plate is added. After a spin of those safety collars, the platform is all yours. The approach is slow and respectful, as it must be. Chalked hands reach out and take hold of the knurling, squeezing hard to drive those tiny metal spikes into the skin. With the body settled and aligned, the crushing load is slowly drawn from the rack. Many have experienced a heavy attempt in the gym, but rarely with this kind of pressing weight. It's heavy enough to wrap that metal right around the back and hands as if it were small-

diameter plastic pipe. The knees shimmy and buckle. The skin grows bright purple as the blood pressure spikes. The lungs struggle for breath. Abdominal muscles brace a core that is on the edge of collapse. This is a stressful fight-or-flight moment to be sure. Years and years' worth of these attempts can leave their mark, especially on a dinged elbow joint. Yet, a successful lift always serves to invigorate.

Call it thrill-seeking, an attempt to reconnect with a warrior ancestry, or perhaps just deviant masochism. Regardless, I suppose you can see why this sort of thing *can* be an addiction. It's a showcase of the ego. That's all fine, but in recent years I've grown to favor another view. Consider this: if the warrior trains for battle, then in contrast it might be fair to say that the martial artist trains to learn more about himself. While war remains a possibility, it's never the desired outcome. Rather, every strike is first and foremost an opportunity to learn a new technique, master a familiar one, identify weaknesses and faults, and inspect one's motives. The daily training grind we so value has little to do with what we will become or our present capabilities. Rather, it's about the act of becoming, in and of itself. We must fight to remember that.

THE GREAT PIE IN THE SKY

"If you have built castles in the air, your work need not be lost; that is where they should be. Now put the foundations under them." – Henry David Thoreau

I laugh every time I think of the story.

My buddy Matt has been a tremendous friend and a trusted advisor for about ten years now. It's hard to say exactly what cements a friendship for that long. We do share the same politics and basic worldview. It could also be that we shared a few years laughing together like idiots over crude cartoons back in graduate school. Or maybe I've just always appreciated the way he can effortlessly cut through bullshit with that slight country drawl of his.

The exact details of the memory escape me, but I recall a discussion over dinner with some other friends. The topic was an interpersonal encounter that didn't go as planned. Matt, his southern drawl cocked and loaded, said, "Tell me, if you didn't want to go to Chicago, why'd you get on the train?" I must have spit out whatever I was drinking right then and there. I found the line so funny I've never forgotten it.

The lesson here is simple. Don't get on the wrong train! Without a well defined destination, there is no clear ending, and no real way of measuring progress. Sure, you might improve in some ways, but relative to what? Common goals sputtered about include getting stronger, leaner, faster, or fitter. Others might state a little more specifically, and boldly, that they want to win the largest competition, or become notorious for their physical prowess. Let me tell you, you couldn't pick a more shitty goal! You might as well just poke the first sunny locale you spot and jump on the train. You haven't planned the trip, what stops you plan to make along the way, or where exactly you will end up. In the years ahead, I might offer you my best southern drawl, this time with a strong sarcastic pitch. "Oh, you didn't get what you where after? Who would've see that coming?"

We need a bold but clearly defined outcome. We need to define the steps that will bridge the gap between that place and this starting line right at our feet. So put a stake in the ground.

If your goal is to be competitive, then everything that follows on our road map must serve to hone the body and prepare you for some highly specific and pretty intense demands. The lifter's primary focus is practicing the competitive lifts with a heavy-ass barbell. On another plane, the aspiring CrossFitter will also have to develop their maximal strength, but they'll also have to get really comfortable putting in huge amounts of work while their body screams for mercy and threatens to capitulate! What's more, there's the added twist of having to cultivate that adaptation many times over during a wide array of complex movements. This is a good time to point out that if you've ever heard someone disparaging the value of a CrossFit workout or competition, you can be assured that they've never given it a serious go. For any burgeoning competitor, you must be prepared to lay yourself fully upon the altar. If you cannot justify the price that needs to be paid, then friend, I recommend you seek a purely recreational path. There's no shame in it, but this is just the reality.

If you choose to buy in and make the commitment, then put your goal to paper now. That act alone will stir up your insides like a confetti machine, kick-starting this journey. Is it a silly short-term sugar high? Yes! Does this first little exercise guarantee that you will succeed? Shit, no! But you should understand something: if you do not write the goal down you're simply wishing. You're aimless. You're looking to play the lottery, not to take fate into your own hands. Further still, I would accuse you of voluntarily taking the same bullshit path of countless other failures and goddamn poseurs that have come before you.

Do not wish, plan.

As an aspiring athlete, choosing your goals is actually a pretty objective process. Regardless of the sport, there will be several types of competitions to choose from. Local events are always the most inviting, as the competition is less stiff and the barriers to entry will be lower. That doesn't mean these competitions are inferior in any way. On the contrary, I would bet that this is where you'll have the most fun. Take your time. Learn what it takes to compete successfully. Get an understanding of your weaknesses and your strengths. Build relationships with local competitors with whom you can train and grow. After a year or two of the pursuit you'll be a whole new person, unrecognizable to your former self. And sure, you might even be ready for a larger, more highly competitive regional event. That's when things get really interesting. Here, you have the luxury of more data. You can search through past events and compare your performance against other high-level athletes. You can project, seeing how you'd like to finish and what key milestones you'll need to meet in order to get there. Who knows, with a good plan, hard work, and a bit of luck, you might even qualify for a national level event. I know that seems far outside of your reach now, but this is exactly what a good map should look like. It should stretch beyond what you deem currently possible, but not without showing you the intermediate steps that are required to get there.

I want to assure you that this journey *is* worth it, but don't expect those goals to come free or easy. Draw your line, commit, and see the plan through. You will find success and will be better off for it. How long you keep up this chase is completely up to you. However, I think you'll find plenty of tools and stories in the coming pages that will empower you to answer that question for yourself.

Speaking of questions, there are now a few obvious ones to consider. What if you have no interest in competition? What if your competitive days are now behind you? How do you set fulfilling stretch goals that will create new growth? How do you redefine progress? Well, I think you start by looking in the mirror. I hope you don't mind another quick story.

My father gave me this great lesson when I was in grade school. Back in the day, before I ever had any concept of nutrition, I had a favorite after-school snack. I would take an entire sleeve of saltine crackers and carefully lay each one perfectly aligned around the face of a large dinner plate. Once satisfied with the arrangement, I would carefully place a square of American cheese on top of each cracker. After a few minutes under the trusty broiler, rolling banks of cheese would be making their way over the subtle, smoky-brown cracker edges. It's delicious, but completely devoid of any essential micronutrients. I might also add that it'll quickly fill your boyish frame with plenty of flab. The perfect dish for a picky, clueless kid.

I remember when I first recognized the connection between my rapidly expanding waistline and those crackers. My father seemed to notice. He could have ignored me, writing off this behavior as the goofy actions of a kid, but he didn't. He just paused for a moment and shared his lesson. "You know, I reckon you can figure this out for yourself. All you need to do is strip all of your clothes off and go stand in front of a mirror. If you're happy with what you see, then that's all that matters."

First, let me make this point. I never took his advice literally. The very thought of such a self-analysis is paralyzing, even now. But this is beside the point, because my dad knew what he was doing. He communicated this simple plan. *Where there is a question, there is no question.* The very fact that I was communicating this uncertainty, the unease with which I took the advice was all the answer I needed. But there is a deeper lesson here, one that I doubt my father intended.

We all set wildly varying goals, oftentimes based on a standard that is not our own. The way we look and dress. The level at which we perform. The decisions around what we buy and why. We are always looking outward. But in reality, the only opinion that matters is our own. You must be able to look into that mirror and answer the questions for yourself. Without that, nothing else matters. So if you are taking the recreational path, then embrace your own standard. How strong do *you* want to be? How fast? How lean? How fit? With those answers you'll be on your way, and better still, you'll sleep like a fucking baby knowing that you're taking steps towards making some dream real.

YOU DON'T WANT THIS

You have no doubt heard the phrase, "jack of all trades, master of none." Go ahead, say you haven't. I'll be forced to label you as a damn dirty liar! Even if the exact phrase has escaped your cognition, you know the idea very well. It's said that if you spend your time trying to become good at lots of different things, then you may indeed get *good,* but you'll never be become great at anything. Rather, that outcome seems to take big measures of focus and dedication, and of course it comes at the expense of other skills. Feel free to interject the romanticized view of a true craftsman, spending year after year and countless hours honing those skills, cultivating a love affair with the art, the trade.

It's a lovely idea that we can all appreciate. Whether it's true or not is a little more murky.

The funny thing about that "jack of all trades" line is that it actually ends with "but better than a master of one." Well, which is it? Can we have our cake and also eat it? Or, are we operating purely on assumption and misquoted proverbs here? Is it actually better to have some basic, conversational understanding of many different things, forgoing proficiency all together? Well, of course the answer is highly subjective and not as easy at it seems. The solution is not the same for everyone, and even within one's own experience, the right approach can change with time. That has terribly important implications when it comes to making progress, because the fundamental definition of what progress represents to us can shift from beneath our feet like sand at the beach. And, as humans, we often don't know what the hell we're talking about, or what it is we actually want!

Some plasticity is quite helpful.

Amongst a long list of other things, I blame a shit education system for our lack of clarity around goal-setting. What is school during those initial, formative twelve years if not a confusing jumble of generic and often inaccurate lessons forced down your gullet by uninterested, overworked, and undercompensated teachers? At the height of our childhood curiosity, we are broken down and rebuilt so that we become *more* average, forced into that goddamn bell-curve shaped mold within which we all must fit. The choice is not our own. Pursuing one's passion, especially for those foolish enough to love the arts, is simply not feasible.

The story hardly improves once you get to college. Here you typically coast through a few more years of required general education courses before you feel the heat of the real world start to breathe down your neck. So you do what seems natural...you pick the first career path that makes sense, often wasting the next twenty to thirty years of a startlingly finite life span in pursuit of a dream you'll never quite catch up to. You're left rationalizing to yourself that it *sure seemed like a good idea at the time!* It's a shame that no one really takes the time to ask you what you really want out of this ride.

I would submit that one of the greatest sins of our society is that it works so damn hard to produce more boring, aimless adults on this planet. That's a shame, when what we really need is more bright and brash young minds who want nothing more than to challenge assumptions and tell entrenched authority figures to eat shit from time to time. We need more people interested in making real change. Hell, that smells like the American dream to me! But the reality is that this system's failure is all by design. It's much more convenient for all those involved if you would just shut up, fork over the tuition, take the job, then hitch your fate to the nearest passing credit offer.

My first real perspective shift around goal-setting came during graduate school. After years of this institutionally enforced aimlessness, I rather enjoyed immersing myself in a single topic of interest. The schedule was brutally simple. If I wasn't in the laboratory doing the research, then I was studying the theoretical angles of my topic in the classroom. My only real reprieve was my Powerlifting training, which, incidentally, took place just a few footsteps down the hallway from my lab. There was no such thing as a weekend. The days were long, stretching from dawn to dusk and often beyond. Among my academic crew there was simply no excuse for not getting things done. We had limited time to make progress toward a very specific collective goal. And I must say, those four years changed me forever. They displaced the old version, setting the rest of my life in a completely different context and trajectory. I was now armed with some fantastically powerful scientific tools. But in an odd twist I slowly lost my appetite for using them for their intended purpose. Did I really want to spend the rest of my life intensely studying within such a narrow view? Would I be happy forfeiting a seemingly endless list of potential career opportunities? Was achieving that master status worth it in the end? No. For me, this represented the second sharp edge of the sword. If aimlessness and a lack of focus was bad, surely too much of those things was just as detrimental.

We all must learn the importance of balance, of ebb and flow. We need brief periods of intense immersion to trigger a real change in our physical abilities and perspectives. But we also must understand that these times of focus must be followed by general pursuits that provide plenty of opportunities for applying those hard-earned lessons. From that place, brand new ideas can be linked with the old, building sparkly new associations and creating new opportunities. The sport scientists and strength coaches among us will likely recognize some elements of periodization in this description, which is just a fancy word for focusing a training effort in a specific direction. I would simply state that this is how you can learn to narrow your view and improve your chances of realizing your goal.

This is your next step towards success.

While I usually champion the destruction of all assumptions, I'm going to make one now for the purpose of closing the point. I'm going to assume that you've had your fill of balance for the moment. My guess is that you've been working hard on lots of different things for a while now, with varied levels of success. Sure, you've learned quite a bit about nutrition and supplementation. You've pursued a somewhat well-reasoned strength and conditioning program. You're learning about mobility and general maintenance of your physical body. I might even step further out on this limb and state that, hopefully, you're pursuing new ideas and opportunities for personal improvement every day. Isn't that what brought you my way? Of course it is. With that assumption comes another: if you've written down that one key stretch goal, along with a few sub-goals that will lead you to that destination, then you've identified what's important to you. So, you're now prepared to decide what is *not* your goal, right? Trust me, that's often more challenging.

I ask the question because this is where everybody, everybody, fucks up from time to time. Perhaps one of these scenarios sounds familiar. Your primary goal is weight loss and improving body composition, yet you grow depressed and bitchy when your performance begins to decrease. It's as if the physics of a calorie deficit should not apply to your physiology.

You say you want to spend eight weeks getting as strong as possible, yet you spend half of your time performing punishing metabolic conditioning sessions. Why? Do you want to hold onto that bird while you also go after the two in the bush? Or, if I may hit a little closer to home on this example, you state that mobility and range of motion are what's most important, yet you get nervous when the load on the barbell predictably goes way down. You do not trust that the adaptations will happen and that the strength will quickly return. No, you just get antsy, bail on the plan, and then fall back into the engrained bad habits. That's a damn shame.

Here's what we *all* must realize. When it comes to achieving a big goal and making a huge, lasting change in our lives, we need immersion. We need a few months to stretch ourselves in a very specific way, so that the stretch will stick! So, our present exercise is simple. Right after we clearly define our primary goals, we need to define what's out of scope. We must decide what we *don't* want. Write it all down. This doesn't mean that you neglect these things. Hardly. You simply keep those dishes warm on the back burner while you fry your big fish up front. Doesn't that make sense?

Weight loss requires an understanding that optimal performance can resume once your body has adapted to its new, svelte form. That takes time. Maybe even years. If the goal is to gain strength, then you should be happy with performing a few light conditioning sessions per week, which will preserve your fitness while not sabotaging your ability to recover from the weekly, brutal barbell beatdowns. And if you need to spend time on your mobility and movement patterns, then for Christsakes, have a little patience and give it a chance to happen! You know the story about Rome. I'm not sure how many days it took to build, but it sure as fuck wasn't one!

Answer this question for yourself. Right now, what can you do without?

DAMN HABITS

"We are what we repeatedly do. Excellence,
then, is not an act, but a habit." – Aristotle

I've heard someone say, "show me what you eat and
I'll tell you what you are." I could make a similar
assessment based upon how you treat waiters,
what jokes make you laugh, how much you read, the
drugs you choose or choose not to imbibe, and most
importantly, your daily habits. There's nothing more
accurate than this – with time you become *exactly*
what you practice.

This should be obvious to us.

I'm left with the question, "So, what does that
make me?" The preferred answer is that I do all that
I should, and because of that I am all that I can be.
I show up every day ready to learn and create. I eat
what I need, and in the amounts that are necessary. I
take measured, daily steps towards my goals, making
certain that no weakness goes hidden and unturned.
And of course, I make sure that all of this is performed
with a certain amount of panache, complete with
sprinkle of piss and vinegar for good measure. Life is
short after all. Best not to take it too seriously.

Yes, I wish this were all true, but unfortunately
it's bullshit.

The genuine answer is that many days are a
struggle. Creation comes only after repeated self-
coercion, not romantic inspiration. I've spent one too
many months disregarding what I consume. Granted,

I'm lucky that my dietary sins are not characterized by chronic glut and excess. However, getting too little of the right things is just as bad. And yes, my steps have often been staggered and without clear direction, with no real focus on progression. My weaknesses have been coddled and withheld from view. Perhaps you've experienced something similar.

The frustrating thing is that this was all willful. Without diligence, even the most entrenched positive habits can start to lose their footing. Once that happens, there is nothing left but for the bad ones to gain ground. It's easy to fight back at the start, but these habits are patient. They know that, in time, you'll grow comfortable with the notion of dullness. Sure, you could call it getting older, but I'll call it giving in to old-age inertia.

It's alarming to wake up to the realization that you've let things slip, but at the same time, I feel blessed. I remain eager to act, so there's little wrong from a long-term view. I'm reminded that life doesn't unfold in a straight line. If our trajectory *was* consistent and upward, then success would simply be another cheap commodity. It would be reduced to something that you felt was owed. I'm glad this is not the case. Passion is linked to ebb and flow. The blessed high points bring ecstasy, while those low points actually serve to remind you of what you love the most. It's just that sometimes it takes a little while for that passion to spark anew. We have to be reminded.

For me, that passion is strength. It's knowing that I'm working towards a better version of myself. At one time that motive would have been based upon an outward projection. A market assessment of where I needed to be based upon what others were capable of. And to be honest, this is a still struggle almost every day, but luckily I've become quite good at introspection (the benefits of years of futile practice, I suppose). My primary goals are not centered on maintaining an active, mobile, and pain-free life. But still, I need to feel heavy barbells grow lighter. It's just deeply fulfilling.

If being strong by one's own measure remains a physical possibility, why the hell would you choose to be weak?

The path is simple. I've now chosen a few key barbell exercises that are really important to me the press, squat, and deadlift. This is not to say that other movements are invalid, but rather the most important thing anyone can do is choose their focus. If I've got one ass, I shouldn't try to ride every horse at once.

The loading plan is just as clear. I must start by being honest with myself. That means picking the right load, not the most impressive one. From there we fight to add weight every week, then every month and beyond, because any program that doesn't seek this progression is no program at all. Listen, performing random, complicated combinations of sets and reps at odd percentages of your supposed maximum ability provides the illusion of validity, but trust me, it is not going to bring you what you want. Pretending to be more capable than you are will serve to sabotage. Only the brutally simple, pure, patient escalation of total kilograms lifted will do that job.

All of this should be evident, right? But no, tiny cumulative mistakes are much harder to account for. That's because no one error seems that important.

The frog fries as he grows used to the warming oil. You could also just say that taking things for granted comes way too fucking easily to us. Meals get skipped. Hours of sleep are diverted. Eventually, feeling a little shittier year by year seems normal and acceptable. The result is that there's nothing left to build with. The barbell shifts from a tool of construction to one of destruction. It swings right through you like a demolition ball through crumbling concrete. What a consequence.

I'm tempted to mitigate this risk with a strong counteroffensive; every variable carefully reprogrammed, every macro and micronutrient tallied and balanced. But I know that this is only my overdeveloped ego yammering on to save face. The proper path is quiet diligence.

Every day is an opportunity to step in the right direction. A spare hour is all that is necessary tonight. A little block of tranquility out in the garage. Nothing needs to be overly planned. First, a few simple exercises to reinforce proper position and pump some blood into stiff regions. Then, focus on those few barbell strokes that will really make a difference. The discipline comes in knowing that the adaptation cannot be rushed. This response is going to take some time, but it will come. And apart from everything physiological, this hour reinforces what I'm after. It's a reminder of that thing I love. And what's more, it represents a tiny step in the right direction. One of many that will accumulate in time.

I never want to lose sight of my goals or the horizon again. But at the same time, staring from a distance will do nothing to get me there. I'll remember that my bucket will fill drop by drop. I'll be patient, carrying that water where it needs to go. It's this habit that will make me what I wish to become.

MILE MARKER 17

"There are only two mistakes one can make along the
road to truth; not going all the way, and not starting."
– Buddha

Every memorable road trip starts off just about the
same way. The night prior to departure is flooded with
nervous excitement. The thought of arriving at the
destination might be enough to energize. Or perhaps
it's the opportunity to break out of those daily ruts and
experience another life, another perspective for a few
days that serves as the real lure. I can say I'm personally
drawn by the latter. Regardless, we prepare like mad.
We pack ten pairs of underwear and an abundance of
snacks for a five day trip. We sync carefully constructed
music playlists to all of our touch gizmos. We peruse
that bloated itinerary at the last minute. Then, after all
is in place, we mutter a question under our breath: "Am I
forgetting anything?"

All that initial arousal gives way to a cold reality
when the alarm chimes at 4:00 a.m. "Who's fucking idea
was this anyway? ...Oh, yeah, it was mine." The decision
to get up at the crack of dawn always seems great the
night before, doesn't it? Luckily, preparation has spared
you the early morning scramble. You need only grab your
car keys, start the engine, and pull right out of that dark
driveway. It would all seem easy from there, but actually,
I've always found the hardest part to be that first leg of
the drive. The route is set, the music spins, but there is no
rhythm yet. All that initial nervous energy burns off with

the rising sun. What's left is the eight, nine, or ten hours you hope to put in that day. There are hundreds of miles out there that will have to be logged one by one. Sure, you can play the game of skipping meals and piss breaks to shave a few minutes off your time, but the mathematics of miles per hour holds the truth. This is going to take a while.

What's interesting is that no one ever grows so discouraged that they bail on their trip, do they? It's never really an option. The lure of the destination encourages patience. We simply wait for that rhythm to appear, as it always seems to do. We lose ourselves in conversation and in music. We feel the full weight of the vehicle as it climbs and descends highway hill after highway hill. We briefly catch a glimpse of those little mile markers in our peripheral vision as they fly on by. Marker 15, 16, 17, and soon the count is in the hundreds. Notwithstanding a few leg cramps and sleepy moments, the trip is over before you know it. Hopefully only a few small doses of that low grade, over-the-gas-station-counter trucker amphetamine were required. You can never underestimate the utility of a few strategically imbibed drugs, friends.

I find this little allegory incredibly insightful for two reasons. First, it seems to mirror the reality of our pursuits. Setting big goals is the easiest thing in the world to do. It's also addicting. Yes, it's a gigantic rush that's followed by that goddamn alarm at 4:00 the next morning, figuratively speaking. Crawling under that barbell, running laps, or preparing a week's worth of high-quality meals is far less exciting. But you cannot arrive at your destination without those first steps. And let's be honest here: unlike that road trip, many people quit as soon as reality sets in. They'd rather go back and just repeat the initial rush, this time with a brand new goal and the promise of magically sourced commitment. Nothing ever changes. But what's amazing is that a rhythm soon comes to the diligent. With time you are able to take your focus off that big goal that's sitting a year or so down the road. You barely even notice those two or three large sub-goals that lie between you and the future. You simply grow to love watching those markers fly by one at a time. You learn to deal with the down swings, and savor the upward momentum when it comes. Sure, some days will come more easily than others, but a step forward is a step forward.

A one-hundred-pound improvement in your squat can come by adding an average of two pounds of weight to the barbell every week for about a year, give or take. Drastically improved conditioning is cultivated by pushing harder for just a few more meters or seconds, session to session. Mobility issues and bad habits sowed over the course of years and years are not addressed by lazily touching your toes a few times before you train. Rather, it comes like anything else that's truly worth having: you must make it a priority, gnashing those tight tissues and working those positions day in and day out until the act alone becomes as ingrained as brushing your teeth or showering. You reach the destination one marker at a time.

Employ this simple strategy: with your feet planted in the future, right beside your big goal, measure the steps that take you back to the present. How many will it take? How long do you have to take them? From there, all you need in order to set your milestones is a little math. It sounds easy, but keep in mind that some steps are harder than others. At times life will piss in your bowl of Cheerios. Your schedule will fill. Commitments will distract you. The potential barriers are endless. In those times, keep your head and drive. Do whatever you must, then put your sights on the next mile marker. When progress does come easily, remember to stick to the plan.

Take the step you intended to take, and not another more. If you rush down the path too quickly, you might take a wrong turn. That's an easy mistake to avoid.

Prepare to the best of your ability, plot your course, then turn on the radio and drive.

TOO ACUTE

"Therefore, to be possess'd with double pomp,
To guard a title that was rich before,
To gild refined gold, to paint the lily,
To throw a perfume on the violet,
To smooth the ice, or add another hue
Unto the rainbow, or with taper-light
To seek the beauteous eye of heaven to garnish,
Is wasteful and ridiculous excess."
– William Shakespeare, *King John*

There's an interesting link between cheat meals and practice.

What's the purpose of a cheat meal? Well, the idea is simple. After a week or two of strict, clean, preferably Paleolithic-style eating, you might find yourself in need of a break. Or I should say, your eye *will* start to wander towards those forbidden foods sooner or later. When you walk through the grocery store, the ice cream will stare back from behind frosty freezer shelves. The smell of fresh baked bread will enter your nose and bounce around your brain like a ricocheting bullet. While you normally wouldn't entertain the idea of eating an entire sleeve of Oreo cookies, by the time Saturday night rolls around, it will seem like a great idea.

So what do you do? Should you stay resolved, beating back the impulse and sticking to the plan indefinitely? No, that's just not possible. I would say that most diets fail due to unrealistic terms. In exchange for sticking to a predetermined, deprivational and satisfaction-depleting regime, you get to feel like you're doing the right thing for a little while. I hope you noticed the implication in that last sentence.

Depriving yourself of epicurean satisfaction is silly for a few reasons. First and foremost, may I remind you that you only get one life to live. You could choose to spend your frighteningly short years taking diet advice from Jillian Michaels's frowning mouth. Or, you could appreciate some of the finer things while your pulse still permits it. Second, we have to deal with the whole efficacy side of the equation. Do strict diets work? Well, I guess they can, sure. But not indefinitely. A reasonable diet comprised mostly of high-quality meats, good fats, veggies galore, some fruit, nuts, seeds, and as little sugar as possible is now a proven path (if you don't believe me, commit to an experiment and let your blood work results convince you otherwise). In reality, this is far less about diets and buzzwords, and more of a common sense issue. Eat foods that a local farmer or artisan can provide. The approach also happens to leave one highly satisfied and well nourished. But still, that wandering eye comes back around from time to time. So, I say take that Saturday evening and do whatever the hell you want with it! Eat the pint of ice cream, the bread, and the whole damn box of Oreos! Really, do it. I might also recommend that you wash it down with some alcohol of your choosing, tequila being my personal preference.

When life is so damn short, why even entertain the thought of leaving your lily perpetually ungilded? Why not embrace a bit of vice?

An acute calorie onslaught is perfectly fine. For starters, the flood of excess carbohydrate will be mopped right up by glycogen-hungry muscle and liver tissue, assuming that you're working that barbell hard during the week. But this also comes with a very favorable hormonal and metabolic response. Yes, taking one evening to behave like a gluttonous pig will actually cause you to loose more fat weight, faster! So much for that deadly sin, eh?

Now, before you get too excited, please remember that this epic meal will also leave you feeling a bit like a tranquilized hippopotamus. Further, all that gluten might make for a scary bathroom scene the next morning, if you catch my thinly veiled intent. What better incentive to spend the next six days abiding strictly by the paleo code? To actually gain a significant amount of body fat, you would need to replace those pesky dietary and training habits throughout the week with a new habit: eating little servings of shitty food every day. Fast food here and there. Tiny tastes of dessert to pacify and scratch the urge.

These are insidious routines that actually undermine our intentions and ensure a disease ridden future. The single splurge hardly matters. Rather, please remember that you only become what you practice.

Speaking of practice, let's consider what we know. What's better, five hours of practice once a week, or thirty minutes to an hour of rehearsal once a day, just about every day? Of course, we pick the latter. We understand that five hours of anything, even play, is utterly exhausting. You cannot learn and retain complex information in a fatigued state. So, the latter route is the obvious choice. We choose a high frequency, working on skills almost daily at first, then increasing the sessions until we're completing two or three a day. The time allotment is long enough to thoroughly grind out all of the fine detail, every motion, and every cue and concept, but short enough to not encourage bad habits that can set in under fatigue. Regardless of time, the repetition factor is the critical piece of the pie, not necessarily the degree of acute stimulus or effort.

This fact also gives us a bit of reassurance and room for error. Session after session, workout after workout, we accumulate training effects. We absorb knowledge. We learn. We improve. This is not immediately lost with a change to our schedules, an illness, or a missed training session. The habit just doesn't permit that. It keeps the rhythm and effect steady. A true loss would require a newly formed habit. We would have to work hard to suck.

Our bucket continues to fill drop by drop. The daily milestones we set in place establish the steps and cadence that we require to eventually reach our goal. There are no shortcuts, no large leaps that can be made to accelerate progress. Focusing on the daily rhythm can loosen your intense focus on the long-term vision, keeping you on course, content and oblivious to the timeline. That goes a long way toward making this dream of yours a reality. But we have to also consider efficiency. Attempting to make large jumps and applying a large, acute stimulus is simply ineffective. If it *could* be done these goals would be reduced to commodities, with anyone capable of envisioning a goal finding immediate success.

Remember this lesson: habits matter. One large cheat meal, while it may sour your stomach, can never make you overweight. That takes willful daily steps. Enduring virtuosity, skill, and strength cannot be acquired during one long study and drill session. If that were the case, any bored asshole with an afternoon to kill could learn to play guitar or snatch one-and-a-half times his bodyweight. No, the stimulus that will cause the significant change, in either direction, mind you, has to be applied chronically.

You are what you practice, so what is it that you're practicing?

TINKERED

"It is not the strongest of the species that survives, nor the most intelligent, but the one most responsive to change." – Charles Darwin

Humans struggle with time and scale. As a member of the species, I feel qualified to say as much. Regardless of what we know to be true or probable, our primary concern is not for tomorrow; it's for today. This is not necessarily intentional or inevitable, but rather a strong biological disposition. We are desensitized and numbed by news stories reporting the latest spike in disease incidence or rapidly inflating budget shortfalls numbering in the millions, billions, and even trillions. How does one make sense of such figures? We cast doubt over scientific results that reveal the age of the rocks beneath our feet, the unimaginable sum of suns spinning above our heads, or the adaptations that have accumulated across scores and scores of ages to bring our flesh to its current form. Cite any number from any subject, no matter how large. It doesn't matter. Our capacity for connecting personally to those ideas was already compromised once you got past the first hundred and fifty or so. What's more, we started doubting the bird in hand as soon as we heard another tweet.

Some folks will struggle against the innate hardware and software limitations within their skulls to understand, accept, and adapt to these stunning realities, while others will retreat back underneath their warm blankets, confident that the world is in fact as simple as they wish it to be. I hope you are here to represent the former.

The reality, as vexing as it might be, is that large-scale shifts and adaptations occur one tiny motion, shift, or tweak at a time. Think about what you can see with your own eyes. Mount Everest came into existence inch by inch, as one continental plate buried itself under another. Similarly, our current form arose after a terribly long series of births, deaths, successes, catastrophes, outbreaks, and astonishingly close calls with oblivion. The odds were so terrible, yet here we are, living to evolve another day. It's astonishing to be the improbable product of one tinkered step after another. If you can realize that and yet grunt with indifference, returning to your remote control, couch, and greasy bucket of popcorn chicken, then may I ask that you reclassify yourself as another species? The rest of humanity could do without you and your bullshit.

These goals we construct, which represent the promise of our own personal and grand shifts, can only be realized by putting one foot in front of the other. Time delivers our results. But do we face limitations? We do. The journey begins with an assumption that progress will be linear. That has to be the starting point because there is no way to accurately plan for the unforeseeable, such as a change in schedule or personal circumstance, or perhaps the failure to adapt and perform up to the standard. But this is the sort of thing we must cope with from time to time. We are organic, not mechanical. We are subject to seasonal changes, temperature shifts, hormonal fluctuation, distress, eustress, and ever-changing motive. This is the human condition: a continuous state of flux in which progress can accelerate, slow or stop altogether depending upon the situation. It's not bad, good, or avoidable. It's the way it is.

So this raises the question: how can we adjust our plan appropriately as we move along? How do we learn to tinker with and navigate the flux? I will submit that there are two choices. First, you can take a random approach, manipulating known variables until progress happens to resume. This is the common choice for many who will spend year after year fiddling while making no gains in any aspect of their lives. As you might guess, planning on getting lucky is no plan at all. Rather, you might prefer the effective, systematic approach. You could learn to be more like Mr. Bayes.

Thomas Bayes was an eighteenth-century mathematician and minister from England. From what I've read he was quite a smart man, which is obvious, I know. But there must be few mouth breathers out there making a living via their mathematical and oratory skills. Bayes kept many notes on probability during his later years, which were eventually compiled and published after his death. That posthumous manuscript contained Bayes's theorem, which is essentially a mathematical means of assessing outcome probability, considering experience, then updating beliefs.

By now, you should be at least a little geeked out and curious.

If you've ever taken a course in statistics, you might recognize a common approach to experiment. You measure something, say, test scores between two different classes. Perhaps the students received different books, or maybe one class was dosed heavily with psilocybin or mescaline. In any event, you want to know if there's a measurable, repeatable difference in their test scores. You would record the results, run the numbers with something like a t-test, then based upon the difference in the average scores and individual score variability you could assess whether the difference was real or not. Well, you would be about ninety-five percent confident in any observed difference. That can be very useful. However, according to my modest statistical knowledge, you cannot stop halfway through the test if you're already confident in the outcome. And you do not repeat the test with values that have been adjusted to account for your recent experience. But this *is* the beauty of Bayes's approach. It's something we can utilize during our journey.

Let's use a strength-training example to illustrate the essential elements of the theorem. What are the odds that performing five sets of five repetitions in the deadlift will improve your ability to pick heavy things off the ground? The answer is that it's very likely, maybe a ninety percent chance or better. Here, the weight is really heavy, but not so heavy that you cannot perform a relatively large amount of work. Those twenty-five really tough repetitions make for an intense growth stimulus for both flesh and bone. And what are the odds that a healthy, well-trained individual would be well-suited for this style of training? Again, really high I would think.

With that said, there would be little reason not to give this approach a try. It's a solid bet. But let's say that four or five weeks into this program you start to struggle. The barbell begins to feel heavier and move more slowly. You might even experience a slight strain here and there, but as tough as you are, you finish the work anyway. At that point you've got enough data to determine whether the current course is sustainable. *Is it possible that I'm trying to do a little too much? Would it be more effective to perform five sets of three, two, maybe even one repetition? What else am I missing? Am I sleeping enough? Am I distracted and stressed? Should I eat more?* The tweaked variable doesn't matter. After a few rounds of experiment you might come to the realization that far less weight, moved very quickly a few times, allows you to train more effectively week after week. Sure, you started out wrong, but that calibration process brought you to the best answer anyhow. What's more, by continuing the experiment you might be surprised to find that the outcome could change in time. Observation never ends.

Oh yes, I forgot to talk about your third option. In addition to random or systematic chance, you could also choose to keep training as planned, keeping calm and carrying on, as they say. I commend your commitment, but I wouldn't be surprised to see you bottom-out, fail, or get injured. These are the consequences of a dogmatic view. But there is an upside. While the prospect of abject failure sucks, at least you would know for sure that your programming was way off! You can check off at least one option when you pick up the pieces and reboot.

The time scale by which we grow and change is incredibly short, especially when you consider temporal changes in Geology or Biology. Yet it's fascinating to realize that the mechanism of change and adaptation is similar. Drip by drip, inch by inch, we build towards our goals. We can also drift further and further away if we do not remain open to change. Missteps are highly probable, but we always have the opportunity to observe and tinker as we go. Disposition be damned.

SQUEEZING THE FISH

"Many men go fishing all of their lives without knowing that it is not the fish they are after."
– Henry David Thoreau

I wish I could call myself an outdoorsman. In another life, my wardrobe would consist mostly of flannel, I would never trim the edges of my thick beard, and I would make it a point to always keep my remote cabin stocked with freshly slaughtered salmon and venison. But alas, this is not my reality.

You could say that some folks are just more gatherer than hunter.

I have never climbed atop a frosty deer stand at dawn, covered in doe piss, compound bow ready and drawn. And while I'm sure I could obtain some proficiency with a hunting rifle in due time, I really don't have the heart to shoot anything innocent, whether it be hoofed or horned. Perhaps I've betrayed my cave man brethren that came before me? It could be a flaw of this domestication, or perhaps even

willful ignorance. I know where my meat comes from and by what bloody, brutal means it arrives on my dinner plate. But if it's all the same to you, I'd rather hand over some money at the market and skip the field dressing and butchery business. That's just a little *too* paleolithic for my taste, thank your very much.

This is admittedly something that needs to be addressed sooner rather than later. As it stands now, I'm woefully unprepared for the impending zombie apocalypse. There's little time left to develop and hone those precious killing skills!

You might say that, relatively speaking, fishing has always been a little more my style. That is, I actually have some experience here. While I remain clueless when it comes to launching a boat or repairing a broken reel, I do feel at ease out on the water. It's nice to feel the full throttle of the engine and that rush of chilled morning air as it sweeps up from the lake and across the face. There is a pleasing rhythm in baiting hooks and casting lines. But by far, the best part is coming up with your strategy.

You usually start with this general understanding of the geography, the depth and temperature of the water, the shape of the shoreline, the location of submerged trees and the like. All of this provides you hints as to where those little bastard fish could be hiding! But what this data gives you is far from a guarantee, no? As my father-in-law often says, "That's why they call it fishing, not catching." Indeed.

Of course chance plays a part in everything. You can get lucky and net something really big with little to no experience, but the probability of that outcome is really low. In the end, the best fishermen always seem to catch the most, biggest and best fish. That shouldn't surprise us. What's more impressive still is the ease with which these sportsmen handle their catch. They can unhook and release a fish in a matter of seconds with only a quick grasp and slight twist of the wrist. They feel no need to rush, yet move quickly through catch after catch. In stark contrast I imagine myself performing the same task, somewhat resembling a drunk chasing a bar of soap around a hot shower. These skills are like any other. They are the product of diligence and continual refinement. Every water ripple and nibble at the hook is a clue. Every cast of the line represents an improved shot at success. There is no such thing as luck and free lunches here. And as with any skill, the performing part looks effortless to an untrained eye that only sees the end product. A fool, attracted to chance alone, would make the assumption that it's easy.

You can try emulation, sure, but there's just no substitution for years of trial, error, and careful observation. These sorts of things cannot be rushed. And yet, we often try.

If I may stretch the illustration one sentence further, you will catch your big fish by observing one ripple at a time. The big goal remains in the distance for months and months on end, but you will close the gap cumulatively, step-by-step. That means focusing intently on adding just a few kilograms, meters, or seconds every week. I think you'll be surprised that things often go just as planned. But not always, of course. There are two likely alternative scenarios. Sometimes that next tiny step will not come easily.

And luckily for us, we don't want that. Imagine, making progress indefinitely until you bored yourself to death with your accomplishments. The horror. Nothing worth having comes easily or on time.

In these instances, there's one tried and true solution. Pause. Rest. Remind yourself of why this goal is important to you. Then, take a few steps back and resume your march. Quite often a brief respite is just what is required.

On the flip side, a second scenario is actually harder to deal with. What if you adapt quickly? What if the steps are not that challenging? Can you reach the goal more quickly by jumping a few steps ahead while you've got the chance? No, unfortunately not. Really, don't try it! Nothing enduring comes easily or quickly. Skipping forward to the good parts is nothing more than a short-term sugar high. It gives you the illusion of progress, when in reality no meaningful adaptation has occurred. You're not stronger, faster, leaner, more mobile or better in any way. You just got lucky and caught a big fish on an early cast. There's absolutely no guarantee that you'll ever repeat that outcome, tomorrow or any day thereafter. You cannot substitute this kind of short-term luck for long-term refinement.

Before you go squeezing your time lines and rushing the progress, remind yourself of something. The harder you grab at your goals, the more likely they are to slip right out of your hands like a flopping and writhing fish. With that I will make a simple suggestion. Try to keep a delicate grip.

NUMBERS AND EVERYTHING ELSE

"Courage is poorly housed that dwells in numbers; the lion never counts the herd that are about him, nor weighs how many flocks he has to scatter."
– Aaron Hill

I am a product of the 1980s. I feel lucky to have gained full sentience right around the time that MTV was rising to prominence. I spent many hot summer afternoons and evenings within the confines of my cozy, air-conditioned bedroom watching endless hours of shows like *Headbangers Ball* and *Yo! MTV Raps*. I fell in love with it. Tell me, how may grade-schoolers get the opportunity to become well-versed in bands like Black Flag or Public Enemy? Not very many. You could call it questionable parenting if you want, but I feel very fortunate. I quickly learned that song lyrics and music video imagery had a much deeper meaning and intent than what my parents or authority figures were willing to recognize. All they heard was the bad language, all they saw was the aggressive and provocative imagery.

No, I wasn't really mature enough to fully grasp all of the messages. And yes, I suppose I did get at least a little bit affected. My salty tongue, which I still proudly wield, was notorious all throughout my childhood. But I also gained exposure to core punk "philosophy" and some of the social struggles that gave birth to hip hop. By the time those teenage years rolled around, I understood that all of these issues, the attempts at control, and history were far more complicated than the bleached-out, watered down lessons I was exposed to through my parents and my school classes. There was something more to be learned, something that was hidden from plain view. It took another ten years before those lessons where put into practice, but I like to think the seed was planted in that old bedroom.

Another interesting reality of this time period was the hypocrisy around drugs. On one side we were all being inundated daily with drug war propaganda. Maybe you recall the same? Did a delegate of Mrs. Reagan's task force come to your school, handing out those little green shirts stamped with the words *Just Say No*? We were all too young and clueless to recognize the political motives at work. We just put the shirt on and posed for the pictures, serving as little more than tiny political props. "Hey, free t-shirt! This will look great paired with my Husky jeans and He-Man sword!" They said they were just trying to protect us. How hypocritical.

At the same time I was required to make my way to the principal's office each day at lunch so I could be dosed with a mood-altering prescription drug, Ritalin. I was judged to be too hyper and distracting by someone's measure, so I was chemically coaxed into behaving. This wasn't an isolated event. By some figures, ten percent or more of all kids were labeled as being *attention deficient.* That's a lot of lunch time pill trips, no?

It seemed after a million years of evolution, humanity finally became empowered to address this disease burden. Well, in reality, more than a few pharmaceutical executives got rich by stoking the fears of concerned parents. Somehow, these drugs were deemed perfectly fine to shove down the mouth of a child who was guilty of nothing more than curiosity.

I'll never be able to quantify the harm from a pharmacological perspective, but I'm also pretty sure it did not help me. My love of science and classes like art and music remained, as did my compulsion for telling inappropriate jokes and disturbing the numbing drivel coming from some of my other teachers. If you listen to the Barbell Shrugged podcast, then you've perhaps heard me digress into those childhood habits. And no, I don't take all of it lightly. To my detriment, my relatively poor math skills did not improve. Charts, illustrations, figures and rich text were easily tied to reality. The connections to every day life and what I could imagine in my mind were vivid in those scenarios. However, equations, formulas, fractions, and ratios were just too abstract. The numbers never took shape. Luckily, now I have an amazing little computer in my pocket at all times that, with the touch of an app, will calculate my tips and balance my books for me! Isn't technology grand? Call it indolent, or just inevitable displacement of the one inferior tool for another. It is what it is.

This illustrates a real challenge. We all must carefully consider the real meaning behind these paper scratches and screen pixels. Blocks of words between page margins are only important because of the ideas they carry. They mean absolutely nothing on their own, or when placed in the wrong context. The easy and lazy thing is to make a judgment after only a hasty interpretation. The rough tone of a punk rock song or rap lyric distracts many from what the artist is actually trying to communicate. Sure, it would be more effective if the content could be scrubbed down and sanitized for all audiences without losing its punch, but that's not reality. The truth is that life is not sanitary, and the message cannot be separated from the blood, guts, and grit. It's actually beautiful when you take time to appreciate it.

Much of that is true for numbers as well. Not in a mathematical sense, mind you. If I may paraphrase and expand upon Neil deGrasse Tyson's famous quote a tiny bit, the thing about science and math is that it's all true whether you believe in it or not! Yet, a number can only deeply affect and change you if it represents something truly meaningful. On its own, it's too abstract. It can trigger no emotion and no real change. Imagine reading a news story about the multi-trillion dollar national debt, the latest figures suggesting that the stars in the known universe number in the sextillions, or, more commonly, a routine headline projecting that, in the next 20 years, the majority of the nation will be obese. It's enough to raise an eyebrow and perhaps cause a gasp, but does it change anything? Does it compel you to write your congressman? Do you now stare up at the stars in dumbstruck amazement every time you step outside? Has a news article ever shaken a family out of dire dietary habits? The answer is almost always *no.* Ultimately, these are just abstract notions, for better or worse. But a first-born child's birthday? Missing figures on a paycheck? Our numerical goal scribbled down on paper before us? That's the kind of stuff that typically grabs our attention and, especially in the case of the latter, should provoke some action. At least, if we plan correctly.

Remember that a number is just a number. Increasing the weight on the barbell every week is evidence that you're growing stronger. That's a welcome sign, without doubt. But the meaning and reward begins to dilute when you simply rush after something. The focus inevitably shifts away from what's personally important, towards something far less genuine and more artificial. It's perhaps better represented by the dieter who needs the scale to display a certain number. They fail to realize that the result is meaningless if other factors like body-composition and key metabolic markers fail to improve. Or consider the lifter who has been able to add fifty pounds to their bench press, yet can only see that they don't yet measure up to the stronger athletes in the gym, or the performances they see posted to YouTube. Maybe that's the final point that we should consider. Individual numbers don't matter that much in isolation. There must be some correlation. As select numerals increase, so too should our performance, our understanding, *and* our overall well-being. Stepping ever closer to our goals should bring satisfaction! If not, then what the fuck is the point of all this?

ISOLATION

"...the monotony of a quiet life stimulates
the creative mind." – Albert Einstein

The topic of progress usually centers around how you can attain more. More strength, fitness, money, power, what have you. I've only recently come to realize that learning to do without is sometimes just as beneficial. The pod reinforced why.

Most people get a little uptight when you mention something like sensory deprivation. I can understand why. It's hard not to envision a psychological experiment, or associate the experience with an imagined solitary confinement cell at your local penitentiary. Tell people what you're thinking about trying and you'll get a predictable reply along the lines of, "You're going to do what?!"

My nerves settled as I walked through the door of the spa, although the complete novelty of the visit did have my attention at a peak. The first voice came from the receptionist behind the counter. She was fairly young, tattooed, fully dreadlocked and otherwise proudly displaying a bit of hippie crunch.

"Hey, you guys must be Scott and Chris. Welcome!"

A little warmth is always nice when you walk into a novel situation. And I might add, the waves of Peruvian flute music and aromatherapy were more than enough to wash out any traces of reservation. They had nailed the vibe they were after. I was already quite relaxed as I signed in, typing all the standard information into a handy-dandy tablet device. I love it when a business is with it, technologically speaking. I filled in my name, then address and some basic contact details. That's when I noticed the three questions down at the bottom of the form.

"Are you currently taking any prescription medications?" *No, nothing that will interfere with my capacity to float motionless and silent.*

"Do you have any injuries or disabilities that we should be aware of?" *Oh no. I'm as fit as a fiddle, if not slightly worse for wear here and there.*

"Do you agree to pay a $500 tank cleaning fee in the event of involuntary defecation? *Oh shit, really?* The receptionist anticipated my reaction, this not being her first rodeo and all. "I know, right? It *can* happen." I checked the box, reasonably confident that even in the event that I did shit the pod, this girl surely had seen worse. This tiny assumption was reassuring.

We made our way back through the little community and lounge area, passing by countless Siddhartha figurines, some tiny sand-meditation gardens and a charming little tea bar. This was our first float, so as rookies, we needed some coaching in the form of a quick video tutorial. Much of it was intuitive. *Take your time settling into a comfortable position within the tank. Start by counting your breaths one by one, breathing in deeply then exhaling slowly. Clear your mind and enjoy the silence. This time is for you! Oh, and make sure you cover all scratches with Vaseline and, for Christsakes, do not touch your face!* I'm taking liberties with the wording here, but the little animated man did rise abruptly from his reclined meditative position into more of a tortured, cowering pose. His hands clawed at bright-red animated eyes.

I muttered under my breath, "Oh yeah, the salt. Note to self...do...not...touch...eyes." That's where the *float* comes in, you see. The pod contains something like 1,200 pounds of magnesium sulfate suspended in solution. A veritable Dead Sea, if you will.

Everyone gets their own room complete with a well-stocked shower and pod. After a quick strip and rinse, it's time to float. The pod itself is large, gleaming white, and quite imposing, almost science-fiction like in appearance. The large door opens slowly, which to my eye gave the impression of a trans-galactic sleeping chamber right out of the movie *Alien*. Getting inside was almost as surreal. I stepped in carefully, quickly bending down to one knee so I could close the door behind. A blue light filled the inner space while that same flute music echoed up from submerged speakers lining the pod walls. I loosened my grip from the hydraulic door uprights and became absolutely giddy with the sensation. My body floated, weightless and wandering about in the warm water, searching for stillness. That's a feeling that's very hard to describe, mostly because it's been so long since we last experienced it back in the womb. I think that's why it felt special, as if a long dormant memory got stirred up a bit.

The water is perfect, with the temperature making it hard to judge where the fluid ends and your skin begins. Every muscle relaxes. Every sensory loop and joint reflex becomes idle. The music takes on odd tones as it makes its way to your ear. An ever-shifting light gives an ethereal feel to the enclosure. But that's only the

start. After a few moments the light and music fade into perfect black. Once you are truly still, after twenty minutes or so, there's no light, no sound, no anything.

I recognized two primary effects during this virgin float. The first was sight. I kept my eyes open the whole time, even though there was nothing to see. I don't know why exactly, but it seemed as though this caused my brain to search for something to visualize. I noticed a few tiny sparks and faint tracers form in the periphery. Next, while not very distinct, I could see purple clouds rolling through my vision from the bottom up, each one popping out from a stark black backdrop. I wouldn't call this a hallucination, but it was quite vivid and amazing. The second effect was thought. The genesis of each idea was no different from any other random thought I may have during an average day. I saw creative ideas, my schedule, challenges I've experienced, goals I have set, random sexual fantasies, and all-out crazy-ass imagery come into sharp focus. Only now there was no external influence or stimulus to derail these thoughts. Each was left to spin off into fractal patterns until an end was reached. In that way, each thought vein was fully drained by its end.

The longer you remain in the pod the more irrelevant time seems to feel. The first moments are spent shuffling and adapting as your ego becomes very much aware that you've disconnected yourself from the outside world. However, in an hour's time you forget what's outside. It's a meditative state, described to me as the stage where the brain shifts to Theta waves. I'm not trained enough in brain physiology to confirm or deny that, but I can attest to the overall dreaminess and complete sense of well-being that came on by the end. Once the music and light cues began to fade back in to signal the end of my session, I wasn't sure whether what I was now sensing was real or imagined. That's a hell of a thing. I can almost understand a defecacious outcome. By that time, it probably just makes sense.

The door opens to reveal a room that feels markedly different. A quick shower settles your perspective, and also serves to remove a crusty thin layer of salt now forming on the skin. By the time you dress and step back out into that common area, you feel a real lingering effect: a deep sense of relaxation and optimism. For a while, I didn't check my phone. I had no concern for my plans, or who might be trying to reach me. I didn't think about the remainder of the day. I just smiled as I happily paid that tattooed, dreaded young lady for the session, asking myself, "When can I do this again?" This is an experience I need to repeat and thoroughly explore,

I must admit. But the lesson applies to more than the tank. At a slightly higher viewpoint, it can apply to everything we do.

From an evolutionary perspective, our brains are not entirely equipped for contemporary stimuli. Jam-packed schedules fill our days. Mobile devices maintain a steady-state of connectivity. A rapid-fire kaleidoscope of loud sounds and bright lights pollute our senses from dawn till midnight. And yet our brains seek shade and silence. They search for subtle movements along the shoreline, a sign of food, or a potential predator. These were simple times, though not always easy. We should love and appreciate the mobile super-computers that now occupy our jeans pockets. But at the same time we must learn to turn the fucking things off occasionally! We must learn the beauty and efficacy of focusing on one thing at a time, removing undue complexity, and de-cluttering jam-packed agendas that do little more than contaminate our already swollen and inflamed senses. Yes, it feels really good to shut that world out, even if it's for a few brief moments. Remember that the next time you're blessed with a few moments of silence in the office, or in the calm moments before and after a grueling workout.

Deprivation is not an experiment. It is not a form of austerity or punishment. It's freedom, and it will allow you to see what it is you really want and need.

HAPPY

"We are enriched not by what we possess, but by what we can do without." – Immanuel Kant

There I was, splayed flat on my back across the rug of my home office. I kept my eyes closed, my breaths deep, and my limbs stretched outward towards the corners of the room. It must have been quite the scene. Picture in your mind the famous image of Leonardo da Vinci's Vitruvian man, only now bald, quite large, and far less nude. I know this isn't the typical meditation pose, but it seemed like the most comfortable position I could adopt at the time. Well, I should say, it seemed to be a far better option than sitting upright in the corner of the room for a half-hour, fighting to maintain some semblance of vertical posture with these chubby crossed legs of mine. For what it's worth, I commend Siddhartha for sitting underneath that Bodhi tree for 49 days. His posture and patience prowess earned him his enlightenment, along with a fancy new job title. While an impressive example, my new journey towards illumination was going to start lying down.

My interest in meditation was stoked some years ago after reading Matthieu Ricard's excellent book *Happiness: A Guide To Developing Life's Most Important Skill.* Ricard was a former cellular biologist who abandoned his promising career to study Buddhism in the Himalayas. Now a Buddhist monk, he's often referred to as the happiest man in the world (admittedly, I'm not sure how you could objectively determine such a thing). Why did he make that decision? Simple. He recognized at a fairly young age that, despite achieving more and more year after year, he was left deeply unsatisfied with his life. Pressing on and expecting a different outcome would have been foolish. That's an impressive decision – one that I'm sure I would not make myself.

I loved reading his work for two reasons. First, despite his primary pursuits he remains active in science and research, participating in several imaging investigations of the brain that have demonstrated significant, beneficial neurological changes in long-term meditators. That was something really impressive. Here was strong evidence that you *can* rewire your own brain to decrease stress, anger, frustration, discontent, and of course, unhappiness. I simply found that amazing! Second, Ricard describes happiness not as something that is attained by any one thing, event, or circumstance, but rather as the product of habit. It's a skill you develop on a daily basis.

I wanted that skill.

Life gets a little more complicated with each passing year. Free weekly hours dwindle in the face of ever-growing to-do lists and worries. It has gotten so hard to focus on one thing at a time without having multiple competing thoughts jumping into my contemplative pool, even during training. While this has always been a time when I could recharge and calibrate, I've recently struggled to keep the world out of my head. Despite my best of intentions, my first attempts at developing a meditation habit failed. Honestly, I never thought it would be so hard! If you don't believe me, just give it a try. Find a nice and quiet room. Now, go in and have a seat, legs crossed, arms laying neatly across your thighs. With a dead-straight spine, do nothing but focus on the rhythm and depth of your breath. As thoughts begin to intrude, block each one out as you deliberately return focus to the lungs. Ignore the electric tingling that develops in the legs after the first five or ten minutes. After fifteen minutes or so your brain will start to bounce around in your skull. Such an untrained, undisciplined mind is not much of an asset in daily life. It is not that easy to fix, but this is something anyone can achieve in time. You just can't give up once you get frustrated, as I had done in the past.

This brings me back to square one...this rug. I've finally found a position that allows me to keep more of the noise out flat on my back and spread around like loose peanut butter. But I might add I've taken the alternative approach one step further. I'm utilizing technology, not to distract, but to practice my new fangled skills more efficiently. From my right hand, my smart phone pumps stimulating music into my trusty bluetooth headphones. The task? At random intervals, the app stops the music. You must tap the screen of the phone at just about at the same time. Any delay and the phone will buzz with displeasure, which is a surprisingly effective source of feedback. The simple effect is that you begin to learn how to identify intruding thoughts, disarm them, and steady your focus. I can tell you, music never sounded so good.

I'm not really sure what enlightenment is, or whether it's actually possible. All I know is that it feels pretty fucking great when I get up off that rug, as if a warm tide has just washed right over my flesh. I know that it will take some time before those real neural adaptations take hold in my mind, but still, there seems to be a rapid benefit. Even now I find myself flagging rogue or misguided thoughts as they zip through my mind. So, I'm confident that, with time, I'll be able to shut them out completely. What's more, I'm even considering getting up off the floor and sitting in the corner for once! Yes, the habit is beginning to take hold. And yes, anybody *can* develop this skill. We can learn to take some focus off of our expectations and perceived limitations, returning it to whatever it is we actually need, whatever we're after. We can learn to do without in order to obtain more.

I cannot say for sure, but I will probably not end up as happy as Dr./Monk Ricard. However, I can at least avoid those wasted years chasing stray thoughts and rogue emotion. I can remind myself daily that happiness is actually nothing more than a choice.

WITH TIME

"Time discovers truth." – Seneca

Everything abides by a natural cycle. An inexorable order. This is no mystery. Carry a beating heart for long enough and it should be self-evident. The onset of our journey is defined by naivety. We begin by not knowing much of anything (despite what we may believe), hastily navigating towards the first shiny object within view. For a select few that shimmer will be true, virtuous, righteous, and affirming. Call it a winning lottery ticket. A personal big bang that leads to the rapid expansion and cooling of one's previously pathetically narrow perception and capabilities. Life upgraded. From this vantage point, there are no safe assumptions, sacred cows or perceived limitations. Self-doubt and reluctance never get an invite to the party. Rather, the world is one giant oyster, filled to the brim with juicy opportunities. Here, goals are carefully crafted and dreams come easily. These lucky bastards didn't face the challenges of picking the path themselves or generating their own momentum, but fortune allows for that sweet, rapid acceleration. How amazing it sounds, but I'm one of the ninety-nine percent who cannot relate. But thankfully this is not an exclusive party. It's just a matter of time and perseverance. Everyone gets their chance eventually, but only after we've squandered more than a few years, faced our fair share of fuck-ups head on, and have found the courage to hit the reboot button. The cycle closes one mistake, one tiny correction at a time.

Better late than never, I say. There's absolutely no shame in blooming late in the game. In fact, maybe this is the more beautiful path. The bigger the fight, the sweeter the reward.

Facing the reality of losses and missteps is brutally hard and quite painful. If I may borrow a cinematic metaphor here, this is why many choose to take the blue pill. Ignorance is indeed bliss, and hell, why not just polish off that pint of chocolate therapy ice cream and burn away the evening playing some video games instead? My love for ice cream aside, some of us are drawn towards taking that red pill. We look back at those missteps and misspent years out in the wilderness and cringe. Hindsight is not always kind. The common theme seems to be a heavy dose of certainty, stubbornness and dogmatism coupled with an affinity for confirmation. Quite the poisonous mix, wouldn't you say?

I churn my memories within the walls of my garage gym. If I may be honest, and a bit self-deprecating, I was never that impressive in sport. Back in the old college football days, I knew that I didn't stack up genetically with the athletes lacing cleats beside me. But that is fine, because when it came to the other average, slow, pudgy guys on the team (of which there were a few), I knew I could beat at least half of them on any given drill. That's pretty good! The same is true with my strength endeavors. I made the most of what I had, getting about as strong as my flesh would permit. And while I'm in no position to compete at this stage in the game, I dare any washed-up arthritic meathead to take me on!

I fought hard to win a small measure of wisdom. At this stage in the grand cycle, I am left humbled and appreciative of the opportunities and experiences. But there's always a price to pay. Lessons often come via defeat, accumulating shot by shot like craters scarring the surface of the moon. Sure, it would have been great to win that lottery ticket and avoid the wear, tear, and loss. Can you imagine what it would be like to be born with the optimal genetics and coached by highly competent eyes from the very start? That's an incredible gift. In that scenario there would be no oyster out of reach. I didn't have luck in the draw. And what's worse, my youthful stubbornness didn't often allow me to fully appreciate alternative perspectives or paths. That left only one jagged, hard way forward. But still, forward is better than laying static or regressing.

I'm learning to be still from time to time. After some years chasing, I found peace in the garage. There's a highly spiritual tone to workouts when it's just you and the barbell. There is no excess influence or stimuli. There are no training partners to compete with and impress (sometimes a key to success, sure, but sometimes a detriment). It's just your force against the inertia of that metal. You can call it elemental and romantic, but the topical quiet also brings all the past squandering and fuck-ups into sharp focus. "If I only knew then what I know now": that's a statement you'd rather not make. And you don't have to, at least not down the road. All you have to do is take a look from a different angle. No crater strikes necessary. The trick is in acknowledging a basic human limitation.

We are terrible when it comes noticing. Consider

this example. Let's say you just moved into a new place. Just in time, too. You needed that extra space! But there's a downside to moving on up to the east side. That thirty-something inch television that once consumed your lowly college dorm room now appears rather pathetic in your brand-new, massive living quarters. All of a sudden your perspective shifts. Now, you cannot help but notice every TV ad in your Sunday paper. Going to a friends house is no longer good times spent watching the big game. It's a chance to assess their screen to square foot ratio. That tickle builds until it must be scratched. And boy do you scratch! Two grand worth of credit card debt later and you've got your self a brand new seventy-inch monument to consumerism adorning your abode. *The Walking Dead* never looked so real, am I right? What happens next *is* evident. Within a month's time that TV is just another thing in your house that seems all too ordinary.

Now, *The Walking Dead* is just *The Walking Dead,* something you glue your eyes to in order to pass the time. And there you are, stuck with $20 dollar minimum monthly payments for the next twenty years. If only an actual zombie apocalypse could shake you from your torpor.

Does it surprise you that training, diet, and the lot are not at all different? One day we wake up and realize that we're not as strong, lean, fast or fit as we would like to be. That's fine. It fuels our goal-setting process. We need that fire under our asses to generate the momentum. But this comes with an inevitable shift in perspective, doesn't it? We begin to take notice of those who have what we are now striving for. We follow shimmering programs and fads. We search for the path that other folks have successfully taken. And sure, we may work terribly hard in the pursuit. But you cannot avoid the inevitable numbness. Pretty soon a workout is just a workout. A meal is just a meal. The rut gets dug. Assumptions get made. Weaknesses get ignored and rationalized. Before too long you realize that, despite your best intentions, you might have taken the blue pill.

Our dull eyes will not do. We need help with generating momentum in the right direction.

Yes, whether the route is easy or tough, the cycle takes us from beginning to end. From naive to experienced. Through trial and tribulation if need be. But why not take the shorter path between these points? If I could change one thing about my own history, it would be this: I would bob my head a lot more. I would change my static vantage point as often as possible to see the same goals, milestones, set-backs, weaknesses and constraints from an entirely different angle.

The new angles bring more data and new possibilities. No one likes to accept criticism, especially me in the prime of youth and brashness. What a mistake. From the more kind side of hindsight, I realize that occasional feedback and a bit of healthy criticism from qualified eyes is actually a tremendous gift. It's a chance to save some of those squandered years, or perhaps redeem them. No lottery ticket, but a damn fine consolation prize.

We reboot by listening and learning. Therefore, the most important thing you can do is join every discussion. Share your experiences, your video clips, your programming and planning often. See it all on paper. Hear it come off your own lips. Have someone else help construct your plan. Be honest, don't you always seem to slant hard towards your strengths and preferences, and far away from that hard stuff that you need the most? That's something only a fresh pair of qualified eyes can see for you. And beyond writing and talking, travel and be present so that you can put your flesh in front of those trusted eyes as often as possible.

Dear Reader, let there be no safe assumptions, sacred cows, perceived limitations, doubt, or reluctance! We cannot tolerate the notion of willful ignorance and self-delusion. Instead, we must focus on getting the right answers as soon as possible. It might take longer than expected, but still, we will have our chance. Let's not miss the opportunity.

SEARCHING FOR OBSTACLES

If you are reading this then you are alive. Let me be the first to offer congratulations! And because you are alive, it's also fair to say that you are surrounded by noise. Hundreds of feet shuffle by your door every minute. Devices buzz and clamor for your attention. Deadlines loom. Faces rapidly come in and out of view. Marketing paints you as the prey. That much sensory input can easily overwhelm. We filter, interpret and cut through all of that noise as quickly and efficiently as possible, searching for only the essential information and plotting a straight course forward. The trouble is that our hurried, tinkered, mammalian powers of perception can be flawed. This should not come as a surprise. We sometimes don't notice things which we should notice, like potential threats or hidden opportunities. Of the things we *do* notice, we often get the interpretation flat out wrong. Luckily there is absolutely nothing wrong with being flawed. Once we are aware, then we can improve.

Picture yourself in a crowded movie theatre or airport terminal. I trust you've experienced one of these two scenarios in the recent past. If not, may I ask that you please exit your utilitarian isolation hovel and join modern society? I assure you it's quite nice. We all have these things called iPads now, which are simply great for pornography!

Imagine that you are making your way down that crowded path or isle, shoulder to shoulder with the other human-cattle analogs. Your patience fades quickly. Any sense of optimism is easily washed away by your rising blood pressure and stress hormone response. That minute spent standing still feels like a half-hour to your spoiled, slack posture and attention-deprived mind. Worse still, you only seem to notice the obstructions in your path. "Why in the hell is that doorway so small?! Why would they put a pole right there? It makes no sense! Couldn't they just open up another goddamn line already?!"

Does this sound familiar? There's a very good chance it does. We're all guilty of being an asshole from time to time.

Let me first state the obvious. After we're done throwing a fit, it might be useful to consider that we might be pretty ignorant when it comes to architecture, physics, or collective behavior studies. Just maybe. After all, you would need to dedicate a decade of your life, at a minimum, to the mastery of any one of those subjects. At the very least, you could spend half an hour skimming over a Wikipedia page. But no, this also appears too complicated for the majority of mouth-breathers doing the lion's share of the complaining. A little taste of knowledge would bring with it an understanding of some basic governing laws, like fluid dynamics as an example. It's interesting to note that fluids, gases, and even people do not flow from point A to B optimally when unimpeded, When left unhampered, molecules and people will pack together too tightly. You can only increase efficiency by introducing something into the stream. In our theatre or terminal, that might be a ticket check, odd exit, pole, or perhaps a disgruntled passport agent. It doesn't matter. The effect is easily described. These items will break up the symmetry of the stream and create oscillation, which actually improves the rate of flow. Sure, it seems crowded from where you're standing, but you also have to consider the madness that's not occurring on the other side, where your angry and patience-deprived eyes cannot see.

This is why it pays to know some science, folks. It could keep you from making an ass of yourself in public.

My mind is always in search of the associations between ideas. In this case, a really cool and obvious one just leapt right off the page and embedded itself within my brain matter. That idea is this: we probably do not want to live a life that is free of obstacles. There it is, my common-sense moment of Zen.

This is almost a scary thought. What if it all worked out like we planned? What if we experienced success with every first effort? What if we got just what we wanted? Well, I cannot speak for you, but I would certainly be living a drastically different life. A worse life in many, many respects. I would be in a dead-end career. I would not have my family. I would not have this wide array of varied experiences and accumulated lessons. I simply wouldn't be me at all!

I don't want that smooth path. I consider myself very lucky that nothing has ever come quickly. I hope you feel the same.

The practical lesson is that, yes, something like a choke point at an airport seems like a gigantic, counter-intuitive pain in the ass. Stretching the illustration a bit at the edges, we might also say the same about time, money, and resource limitations. "You do not understand," you say. "I have to deal with X, Y, and Z!" I do understand. We all do, probably. I would answer with this: it's inappropriate to presume that an obstacle is always a bad thing. It's foolish to look down from a high level and assume that you know better, because you very likely do not. But that's not enough. I think we should all work harder to actually appreciate the barriers in our path. Perhaps we should even go out of our way to find them and plant them intentionally! It will slow our hurried pace, giving us pause and a chance to gather our thoughts and experiences. Maybe it's at those times we can notice what is really essential for us.

Remember, what seems important and encompassing today could be cast in a very different light tomorrow. When you slow down, take it as an opportunity to look around for awhile. I think you'll find cause for optimism.

P IS FOR PASSION

> "Most people are other people. Their thoughts are someone else's opinions, their lives a mimicry, their passions a quotation." – Oscar Wilde

It has been said that time heals all wounds. Maybe that's a bit generous. In reality, it's more accurate to say, given a few years, there's absolutely nothing that we cannot forget. That certainly covers our losses, failures and injuries, but it also includes all of our goals and aspirations. What once seemed all engrossing and critical eventually fades into something bland. No, there's nothing wrong with that. It's not a failure. Rather, it's a sign that you're changing, and likely for the better.

Can you imagine never shedding the raw ambitions of your teenage years, or in my case, even those of your twenties? I shiver and gasp at all of the alternative realities where I got exactly what I wanted. Perhaps I'll feel the same way about the present once I'm ten or twenty years down the road.

Your future, with all of its astounding opportunities and potential for struggle, can be boiled down to one basic choice. Are you happy with what you've always been? Or, is there another version of yourself that you would like to meet? The former requires that you grow comfortable and carry a warm, heavy blanket of inertia, while the latter demands that you let go.

Together, let's say a little prayer to Kālī so that we realize what it is we could become, and once changed, let's retain a little bit of fear so that we never forget what we could go back to.

What do you want to be when you grow up? How would a child answer that question? Of course you know. They will almost certainly respond with something fanciful like astronaut, dinosaur wrangler, race car driver, ninja, or maybe even Batman. Some of those things could actually happen, although the odds are not that great. I'll let you decide. We realize that the kid will almost certainly grow up to do something very normal, hum-drum, or perhaps all-out fucking boring. *They just don't know any better.* So what does that say about us, the grown-ups in the room? Do we know better? I'm not so sure.

The expectation is that you'll set a true course sometime between the ages of twenty and twenty-one. That's when you pick your university major, the thing you want to do for the next forty years or so. Tell me, how is this any less silly than studying the fine art of dinosaur wrangling? No, it's not about age and maturity. It's a matter of perspective. An open-minded, inquisitive higher primate will accumulate a very large amount of data during any one year. To keep the same world view, goals, opinions, beliefs, prejudices, and perspectives over time is impossible! That is, unless you choose ignorance as your warm blanket.

Many realize that this big hasty decision was a poor one only when they've settled into a corporate, real-world gig. That's when they realize that they really, really hate it. This is not immediate, as it takes a little time for all that excess hope and optimism to burn off. Where do you go from there? The next step is to turn your attention towards the *P* word. You know, passion.

Now it's time for the bullshit!

What's your passion? What is it that you love the most? If you didn't have to worry about money ever again, what would you choose to do with your time? It's sounds so simple and intuitive that it's hard not to immediately rack your brain searching for those answers. After all, the promise is just so much better than your present reality. But this question is again a false one. Your passion changed from becoming a child ninja to getting a bank job after graduation, then your heart compelled you towards the path of pop-fiction writer/restaurateur/ fashion blogger. But tell me, is this decision any different than the previous ones? Is it possible that you are still reaching out too far, seeking to shove yourself into the first promising mold you come across? Square peg, meet round hole.

It's not very easy to figure out all on your own, but there's an alternative. We have to decide to be true to who we are at this very moment. After all, there are plenty of people trying to mold themselves into another shape or form. But the really amazing, beautiful and truer than true truth is that there's no one that can play your role as well as you. And yeah, that role will undoubtedly change over the years. Yet we don't fret when we lose what we were. We rejoice at the opportunity to meet someone new.

Goals, passions and pursuits should change. We cannot assume that the big timeline is set in concrete. But

now we need to get past another presump
is, we cannot keep believing that the next
will make itself apparent via divine will, n.
and obvious signs, wild inspiration, or just blin.
Here, the truth is simple and hard. We have no mag.
mirror, only a series of opportunities, large and small,
that pass by every year, month, week, and day. And no,
we don't need to rely on chance. We simply have to
work for it and earn it. We have to say *yes.* That means
showing up on time and taking on every professional
challenge within reach, even if it's not exactly inside
your wheelhouse. It means holding back the ego and
listening to those who have something novel and
informed to say. It means acknowledging that there's
a certain amount of luck that's required from time to
time, sure, but that you can drastically improve the
probability of doing something amazing by jumping
on top of every opportunity that floats by, and sticking
with it long enough to realize your outcome.

Maybe your passion is not a trade, hobby, or
grand personal pursuit. Maybe it's the change itself.
You find it while in motion.

DIMINISHED RETURN

"If at first you don't succeed, try, try again. Then quit.
There's no point in being a damn fool about it."
– W.C. Fields

We train for a very good reason: growth. That motive starts with some sort of recognized limitation, right? We feel that we could be leaner, bigger, fitter, stronger, faster, or perhaps more efficient movers. These are the obvious, discrete physical traits and abilities that can be improved with progressive, focused work. In other words, this is the stuff that can be easily measured across days, weeks, months, and years. But we often forget that there are mental factors at play as well. There is no fault in admitting that we are all quite naive, especially at the beginning. We start raw, innocent, and ignorant when it comes to assessing our true capabilities, whatever they may be. If there is a limitation to address it's this: we are quick to answer "Why me?" instead of "Why not?"

It's not just the flesh that is sharpened by the barbell. It's also the mind. In our virgin state, we are truly untrained from our tip-top to the bottom of our feet.

Here we find ourselves at the beginning, with the ink of our goals and milestones still wet on the page. What can we reasonably expect? Our immediate advantage is that focus and hard work will deliver real results, quickly. Consider this the surest investment you will ever make. Your deprived or underutilized physiology will respond rapidly. The metabolic fire will build from a tiny ember to a roaring blaze. Muscle tissue will rapidly adapt to the mechanical stress and strain, improving both in terms of quantity and quality. And most importantly, your beautiful and amazingly plastic nervous system will anticipate, regulate and capitalize on these improved capabilities.

I know your physical form might appear a bit boring and average in the mirror as you brush your teeth tonight, but consider this reality. You're the owner of a machine which is the product of millions of years of experiment, struggle, and preservation against all odds. Do try to act like it.

This boom phase is accompanied by a comparable upgrade in perspective. Call it the first great personal shift. You begin to realize that, yes, you *are* capable of much more than you once believed. Goals are no longer abstract notions, wishes or lottery prizes. Rather, they are real and attainable, much more like skills that are the expected outcome of practice and diligence. I don't know about you, but just reading that last sentence gives me a sense of freedom. The promise is so enticing. Yes, you can do just about anything you deem important and worthwhile in this life. No, you are not bound to any script or pre-determined genetic fate.

Revel in the surge of confidence as the milestones and goals fall one by one. Lose yourself in that progress. Hell, you might even be tempted to buy yourself a wallet boldly embroidered with the moniker "Bad Motherfucker." Go ahead, you've earned it! These are good times, so enjoy them.

But there is one thing I would like for you to consider.

u grow forever? Will each vanquished goal
bring as much satisfaction as the one that
Could it be that our bodies are similar
capitalist markets, where expansion can be
maintained indefinitely and no idea or entity is ever too
big to bust? Is it appropriate to assume that our bodies
and minds grow refined in the same way, intimately
linked and bound to the same constant and upward
trajectory? The answer begins to get obvious as you ask
the questions.

No.

History and recent experience have proven that
markets are highly subject to ebb and flow. Rapid growth
is often followed by catastrophic collapse. While we can
place modest bets that yield a decent return and carry
reduced risk, we are never immune. As sure as the sun
rises and sets within our view, gains will inevitably begin
to diminish with time. Our best bet is anticipation.

This shouldn't be a surprise. Think about it. If
continual progress were actually possible, world records
would be as common as sporting events themselves. The
extraordinary would be redefined as routine, possibly
even boring (Oh, to be boring...The worst of all sins!).
But no, these events are quite rare because it takes a
special human with a special mix of genetics, skill, luck,
perseverance, and often pharmaceutical intervention to
navigate through the tougher, higher levels of this game.
But this is not to suggest that we quit once the going
grows tough. On the contrary, we learn more once our
physical progress begins to slow. This is when training
becomes more of a chess match than a simple matter
of exertion. That combination of sets, reps and load
that used to work no longer does. So, we introduce new

methods and manipulate variables. We progra[...]
movements and new progressions. We learn t[...]
more measured goals with precise and finely t[...]
milestones, as we have to fight for every pound, mete[...],
second, and additional round. And a fight it is. At this
point there's not much left for your body to offer. Yet
it's common to keep pushing, with that continual
search for more resource, time and passion to place
upon the altar.

I hope you give your journey everything you've
got. Set your course and see to it that your goals
become reality. If you can repeat that process several
times, then I commend you. That's something I have
only rarely achieved. It's special. But understand
this continual pursuit comes with a price. Your life
will grow imbalanced with time. You will eventually
experience injury, whether minor or severe. Worse
still, you might wake up and realize that you're just
not happy.

This next statement appears every twenty
thousand words or so (I've become so fond of it that
I've considered making it a personal governing law).
*The moment your pursuit begins taking away more
than it gives, be prepared to quit.* That's something
worth abiding by. Learn when to move on to the next
challenge.

No matter how good you become at something,
you will still suck terribly at a thousand different
things! I know this sounds derogatory, but you should
actually consider it a beautiful reassurance. If you
find yourself in a rut down the road (and you will,
eventually), remember that there are countless new

challenges for you to take on. While you might become a master of one domain, you are untrained from top to bottom in a host of different skills and movements. Just consider the infinite possibilities for new investment and fresh booms. Now is the time to gain experience. Now is the time for your next great shift. For me that's the true beauty of training. Realize that your goals can be made real. Be willing to step away when you've had enough. And then, find the courage to start all over again.

That's progress.

UNBOUND

After a decade or so I stopped noticing the ficus
tree in the corner of the living room. It had become
no different than any other fixture, switch or aging
decorative accent in my parents' home. While it must
of stood around four or five feet tall there in its pot,
that didn't stop it from fading completely into the off-
white backdrop. I was just too used to its presence.
So go all the boring little details that our brains deem
inconsequential.

For better or worse, we tend to only see
that which is novel, unique, exciting or potentially
dangerous, none of which applies to household flora.

My father planted the sapling around the time
I was born, if not well before. I can imagine those
little roots sprouting quickly, racing towards the
boundaries of that same pot in search of opportunity,
or perhaps the presence of competing neighbors.
I'm not aware of the exact mechanism, but with
every inch of perimeter mapped that tree must have
known ahead of time that its fate was more aligned
with the bonsai than red wood. I find that a bit sad.
These trees can grow upwards of a hundred feet tall
in their natural habitat. But no, regardless of genetic
pedigree, there would likely be no escape from the
confines of that pot! Sadder still, have you ever seen
a long potted plant removed from its cage? Countless
layers of bound and tangled roots provide evidence of
incessant searching for even a tiny crack from which
to branch out and break away.

That alone is a lesson. If a humble houseplant can persist this long in pursuit of its reward, then why can't you?

Call it broken-down, fully domesticated, constrained, removed from nature, and withheld from its true potential. This storyline would be little more than an interesting observation if it weren't for the fact that we all have more in common with this situation than we would like to admit.

Yes indeed. Here we are, sitting comfortably in our tiny pots. And may I say, mine feels extra tight.

My love of sport and training is now a bit faded and worn, but this is a passion that is sewn into my very being. Any attempt at walking away from it would be about as foolish as trying to run away from my own shadow. Still, this affair began as something else entirely. If I'm to be honest, the only reason I ever pursued little league soccer, baseball, karate, football, powerlifting, strongman, or any other sport is that, deep down in my core, I doubted I could amount to much without it. I was a chubby, overly self-aware, genetically average kid who wanted desperately to show the world that he was different in some meaningful way (this is perhaps still the core motive). This was not is not a failure. It's not something that I find embarrassing. This was simply a chance at breaking away. As limited and average as my genetics may be, there was never anything stopping me from taking a shot, aside from the fears and self-doubts I harbored of course. Acclaim is never probable, but we can all get in the game and improve.

Let's consider the alternative, just in case we've made one too many assumptions here. Could it be that the pitiful ficus actually had it lucky? After all, we are the poor souls that are often left to serve sentences with more than one pot at a time! Oh, the horror.

I no longer wrestle with my physical limitations. Those battles are largely over now, thank god. But new, ever-evolving struggles seem to have emerged with time. There's a few that come to mind immediately. The fight to squeeze more time from each day, so that I can spend more on the important stuff. My frequent loss of perspective when it comes to recognizing how far I've come or having confidence in where I'm going. Or, worse still, and the most painful one of the bunch: failure to fully believe in and harness my own voice, the only thing that's truly unique and mine!

That doubt stands between me and everything in this world that I could positively effect, or that I could be affected by. But fortunately, my roots continue to search high and low for that next tiny crack, the next opportunity. And therein lies the silver lining, as this is something well within our control. The primary limitations we face are virtual, having been manufactured by the chunk of fatty tissue suspended between our ears.

I don't mind sharing my baggage, mostly because I know there's nothing unique about my story. There are countless others who share similar, or far more severe struggles. In fact, absolutely everyone who gives even two shits about their lives shares in this. We bury ourselves in our history and often grant it the authority to distract us from our future. This is a lie and a goddamn shame, and we should stand up and shout about it.

I've come to believe in two crucial lessons. First, you are not bound forever to who you were. You are free to abandon insecurities, past mistakes, failed plans of all sorts and poisonous dogma, all of which serve to keep you chained, head down. Yes, there are certain conditions, such as your genetics or the predisposition of your parents, that cannot be reset. No amount of action can completely displace those influences. But this doesn't prohibit you from taking a step right now and fighting for what you want, does it? Of course not.

It's never easy, but there is nothing stopping you.

The second powerful lesson is that you are now free to step outside the pot. Try this. Just as you would sit down and write a list of goals and milestones, write a list of everything that seems to be standing in your way right now. It could be limited strength, excess bodyweight, lack of free time, fear, assumptions, laziness, anxiety, injury, distraction, self-doubt, whatever. Then, ask yourself, "Are these limitations real or imagined? Or, could it be that I'm the only one holding back here?" I'm as human as you, so I can state confidently that the answer to most of your questions will be the latter. Almost all of the challenges we face can be pushed aside utilizing a bit of bravery and diligence. And let's not make any excuses for the real limitations that remain, but rather, let's adapt. We can always adapt. We have to adapt. With that we *will* become more, so long as we keep believing that it's actually possible.

Here's our assurance, something to keep handy and remind yourself of daily: *regardless of what I face and feel each day, I know that I have the freedom to make my own decisions. I can face my mistakes head on. I can learn.*

I can change. And no matter what, I will not allow myself to fade into the background or be distracted by imagined limitations. With forged confidence and ready hands I know that I will grow to be a hundred feet tall.

WE'RE ALL MAD AROUND HERE

The trouble with planning is that the process is both essential and useless. Bizarre, I know. We cannot expect to get much, if anything out of this life by standing still, brim high with inertia and the expectation that all things will roll downhill toward our feet. Rather, we must draw a line, any line, and project outwards towards the chosen reward. We plan to get that thing we most want right now. From this place, we can estimate how long the journey will last, how often we must take our steps, and how quick our pace should be. Execute the plan and a positive outcome is all but guaranteed. Yeah, but by now you know that there's twist, don't you? Of course you do.

While you will have your reward, it might not be what you had in mind at the beginning. And rightly so! It's silly to expect to be unchanged after a few years of diligence. That goal *will* warp, mutate, and grow with you as the milestones are checked, the unexpected obstacles are cleared and all the hard lessons are learned. In truth, we don't get what we initially wanted in the end. Well, we rarely do. Despite our best plans, safeguards and attempts at controlling our fate, the journey does take *us* in the end. But I do not find that troubling. It's really quite beautiful. You can only know your true destination once you've arrived somewhere else first. Your plan, inherently flawed yet well intentioned, is what makes that little revelation possible. Your new vantage point allows you to see what was previously out of view.

That's a little more than some silver lining. It's actually the real reward.

I want to leave you with the most important nugget of wisdom I can share. You must go out and get the information you need. You must surround yourself with truly great people who will share their valuable experience and knowledge with you. You should read all you can, and watch all that you can if it offers even a tiny grain of insight. And yes, we all need some kind of model to work from. But know that none of that will amount to much if you do not learn to look for yourself and set your own course.

Here's the thing about teachers, coaches and boisterous media personalities. They are not you. Ultimately they cannot hope to understand your body the way you do. Its history and limitations. Its capabilities. And what's more, no one can offer you happiness and contentment. As the cliché goes, that's something that must come from within.

Here's the other thing about teachers, coaches and boisterous media personalities. They can let you down. People screw up. They say silly shit. They sometimes give bad advice. And there's a very simple explanation for that: no one can meet your expectations indefinitely. Some bit of wisdom will fail to resonate. The luster will rub off. Some act or decision will only serve to disillusion you. This is all as sure as sunrise.

I'd like for you to forget about your expectations and plans for just a moment. Let go of your worry and fear that you might fail. Instead, remember that the right habits, perspective and attitude will ensure that this journey will change your life for the better, most likely in meaningful, fantastic, and liberating ways. Sure, you might make a few missteps. You might struggle against quite a few obstacles. But in the long run, and with hindsight, those instances will mean very little. In contrast, what matters most is what you become day by day through habit and purpose.

For years, I rarely read any books. I'd say only on those occasions when a grade could not be earned otherwise. And I never did it for pleasure. But all that has changed in the last six or seven years, thankfully. Now, thanks to a slowly formed habit, I really love to read. Although I do still struggle with longer stuff. I much prefer short, lean, mean, and punchy books that are more tequila shot than light domestic lager, so to speak. And after becoming a parent, I would say that includes good children's books as well (perhaps minus the *mean* bit).

I was recently reading through Lewis Carroll's *Alice's Adventures in Wonderland* again, maybe for the first time in fifteen years. You should do the same. The book is simply lovely (and free copies are available online). And no, as you might guess this work shouldn't be classified simply as a children's book; it's more about the enduring lessons. The vivid imagery.

There's one passage in particular that I find engrossing. Alice is walking through the woods, confused and unsure as to which path she should take. At that moment, she meets the famous Cheshire Cat, who is sitting contentedly in a tree. Somewhat nervously, Alice asks this highly unusual animal for some advice on which direction she might take.

"Would you tell me, please, which way I ought to go from here?"

"That depends a good deal on where you want to get to," the Cat replies.

"I don't much care where," says Alice.

"Well," the cat answers perfectly, "Then it doesn't matter which way you go."

It doesn't really matter which destination you pick, or the steps you take. What matters most is that you make your decision and then put a plan into place. With that, and a perspective that allows you to adapt and evolve along your journey, you are sure to arrive at higher ground. No, it might not take you to where you initially wanted to go, but I promise, you will find yourself somewhere interesting.

Original Cover Art

WAY PAST STRONG

Original Cover Art

WAY PAST STRONG:
TALES OF STRENGTH, PHILOSOPHY, LIFE, FAMILY, SCIENCE, AND VICE

Let's remind ourselves of one of the most important lessons – don't take things so seriously! Loosen up and enjoy the ride.

That's when the magic starts.

BEFORE WE BEGIN

Words are amazing. They are beautiful. They give meaning. But they are just words.

This book will stir your brain and slap your ass. However, it's not a replacement for qualified, hands-on guidance.

Get some coaching.

No matter where you are in your journey, you need to work with kind, smart, capable human beings in order to reach your potential. Seek them out, invest wisely, and be prepared to work hard.

These are actions that will change your life forever.

OVERTURE

"Music is a higher revelation than all wisdom and philosophy." – Ludwig van Beethoven

Our strength journey begins with a unique analogy. Let's imagine the set and setting.

Picture yourself as an aspiring magician working a twelve-year-old kid's birthday party because, hell, you need the money. By all accounts this should be easy money. There's just not much work and fuss between you and that rent check, right? Maybe so. Still, you are eager to please. As the crimson cheeked mini-caveman brutes settle into place, hands carefully cradling bowls of freshly baked chocolate pound cake and salted caramel ice cream, you take the stage ready for your first trick!

Full disclosure: I should make it clear that this exact cake and ice cream combination is what I want for my own birthday. If you truly love me, you will bring this to me. That is all.

The question is, what should your first trick be? If I may, perhaps starting with a warm-up is wise? Just something simple to get the crowd into the mood and loose. In fairness, no one trusts a magician, not even these ignorant little prepubescent cavemen.

Open with an easy card trick, or maybe fake a sneeze, then go on and dramatically pull about ten feet of handkerchief from your nose. Next, do absolutely anything else while making a series of synchronized fart noises.

That's guaranteed to kill!

Some may find this approach predictable, routine, and a little boring. Well, alternatively, I suppose you could start the show with a bang! Perhaps you could escort a stunning brunette women out onto the stage, every contour of her body wrapped perfectly in a bright crimson cocktail dress. After a brief moment spent melting the desperate and lathered minds of these poor little creatures, lock the woman into a cabinet and proceed to slice straight through its center with that hot chainsaw sitting, for the moment, just out of view at the side of the stage.

We both know that the blood pouring onto your black shoes is just corn syrup mixed with a few squirts of tomato-red food coloring, but these poor kids sure do not!

Standing proudly before stunned faces and agape jaws, you smile and bow, only then realizing that this gig pays by the half hour. "Shit, what am I going to do now?" Well, I know what you can't do. A rabbit cannot be pulled out of a hat! You'll have to go full-blown David Copperfield to earn your coin today, and let's be honest, you do know what it takes to go full-Copperfield, do you? No, that skill takes decades to master.

In hindsight, you should have just started out with that farting handkerchief gag.

I often tell some version of this story when I'm asked training questions. That's because the easiest mistake to make is to fall for the lure of complexity and novelty. I doubt any human being in history has ever happily forfeited the enticing and exciting option for something elementary, intuitive, and potentially boring, regardless of efficacy. No, the jangling and sparkling lure quickly draws your attention like a moth to a flame. It makes you compare yourself, your training, and your capabilities to others. It makes certain promises, all of which have been heard before. "Why aren't you further along by now? You should try something different, something better, something quicker! Why not just get out your chainsaw?"

There's nothing sillier than needlessly assigning complexity to something as personal and organic as training. I suppose cherry-picking the sweeter parts of every program you stumble across is no better. Your plan should not equate to a common trip to the grocery store, where the shopping list can change at any moment based upon the growl in your stomach, or the presence of a cleverly crafted display at the end of the isle.

Your planning should not be subject to whims, fancy, or passing fads.

Maybe what we need is a better analogy.

The whole magician thing reminds us that we can't just go straight to the finale. Rather, if we want to put on a good show, then we have to start with the very first act and go from there. This is how we earn the audience's trust. This is how we build a relationship. This is how you hook them for the actual finale. But this little analogy doesn't teach us much about what happens in the middle.

Just how should we work towards that round of applause? How do we get what we're after? How do we become that stronger version of ourselves?

Music might be the better analogy. A well written training program should look a lot like a well written song. For the musician, songs are not written irrespective of history. Influence flows from every up and down moment, every heartache, every failure, and every moment of bliss. For the listener, the music begins right here. Think of all of the preceding steps that have shaped your hearing and perspective. The artist had their moment of inspiration and insight, but this moment is yours. Now, what matters is your ups and downs, heartaches, failures and moments of bliss.

I'm not a musician, but I've read a thing or two over the years about writing good music. It seems that the piano is one of the best tools for a song-writer. Simple, essential chords can make it easy to develop the basic melody as the lyrics sort themselves out. Here, barriers are removed. That alone is enough to take us from nothing to something – A beautiful expression of our damage, limitations and aspirations. Once we understand what the song should sound like, you start to think about what it could sound like. The music can easily be scaled up to include more instruments and complexity. With time we can also alter the arrangement to highlight a different take on the song, a different meaning and experience for both you and the audience.

My suggestion is to play the piano first.

Your journey to become stronger begins with a few essential habits and behaviors. Sure, knowing the right exercise to use, and when and how to use it is very important. However, we need to drill down towards something even more essential and fundamental. Something vital. Tell me, what inspires all of the great songs? Did the musicians simply grow interested in the latest trends and tools? No, I don't think so. While inspiration comes in many forms, isn't it true that music begins with something personal? Perhaps it's a story that must be told, or an ache or joy that needs to be expressed? Yes, that is the source. Everything else is just a tool. That is how we should look at training.

First, find out just what your melody and lyric should be! What's the ache? What brings the joy? Carefully define what the goal is, and often forgotten, what is not the goal!

Build the program on the tenets of balance, understanding, fulfillment and reflection.

The song-writer has their pen, paper, piano, and a story that must get out into the world. You have this barbell, some chalk, ready flesh, and a brand new journey to get underway.

Are you ready to begin?

Strength begins where you are,
not where you were, or where you wish to be.

The further you reach out at once, the more likely you are to
fall. So don't focus too much on what's far off in the distance.

Instead, get comfortable right here. If you're a beginner, add
weight weekly and in small bits. Master simple movements and
stick with them for at least a month at a time. Be patient.

Once trained, start adding weight and changing the movement
every other week. Once you become advanced, add weight
once a month, but change the movement weekly. This will
ensure that you recover quickly and keep making progress.

Be honest with yourself. Be patient.
Start your journey the right way.

LEARNING TO FLOW

Philosophy for the barbell and everything else

"Life is a series of natural and spontaneous changes.
Don't resist them – that only creates sorrow.
Let reality be reality. Let things flow naturally forward
in whatever way they like." – Lao Tzu

FLOAT ON

"By letting it go it all gets done. The world is won by those who let it go. But when you try and try, the world is beyond the winning." – Lao Tzu

I'm different now than I was before. That's true from multiple angles. First, there's the literal one. The atoms that make up my current form differ from those of my early childhood, teenage years, and my roaring twenties. This amazingly complex assemblage of water, proteins, minerals and cohabiting microorganisms I call my flesh has been completely turned over and recycled many times over. Yet somehow I retain these emotional imprints and crystal clear memories of all the growing pains, embarrassing failures, and countless missed opportunities from the past.

That realization, that truth, is more amazing than any fictional tale I've ever heard.

The same is true of you, and you should find that breathtaking. If not, you might be the kind of person that watches far too much reality television and listens to far too much terrestrial radio. You poor son of a bitch... Change while you can!

Do you want your mind blown right now? Consider the reality of your life and physical being. While the myth is certainly more dramatic and brilliant in its imagery, believe me, you are quite literally a Phoenix. Yes, the fictional bird. You have been burned down time and time again, only to rise from your ashes renewed, wiser, and ready for the next round. Maybe the only signs from your past are a few well-placed scars. Call them vestigial reminders of the past.

This is an incredible realization – a stunning union between fiction and your reality.

Trippy allegories aside, and despite this extraordinary renewal process, in many ways, I am the same as I always was. I don't feel any older. I still laugh at the same inappropriate jokes. I remain susceptible to some of the old traps and snares that caught my former self off-guard. Yet this new form comes with countless intangible modifications that I'm slowly discovering. Maybe the best example is how I now choose to spend my spare time.

There's nothing wrong with passing hours watching a great documentary, tinkering with some crafts, shooting guns, or whatever else tickles your fancy. However, I find my renewal more and more by sitting still, alone. Inside the walls of my office, I have the opportunity to crawl deep inside of my own head. Without all the stimuli and intrusion, I can listen carefully for the Muse's call. That energy subtly reaches out and pokes me. "Hey, wouldn't it be cool to do something different."

I've learned you must say yes to that question.

The voice was always there, but I was far too busy scurrying around in desperate search of explanations, open doors, ideas, and opportunities. Maybe there is a hangover associated with those old, former incarnations. It's the embarrassment and headache you feel when you first realized all would become obvious to you if you just took the time to sit down and shut up for once!

Lao Tzu sounds especially wise in hindsight. Don't resist the natural and spontaneous qualities of life. Let reality be reality. Let things flow naturally forward in whatever way they like. And here I am, sitting still in my leather office chair. It's very comfortable. I am at ease. My ears are finely tuned in search of that little voice. It will come. So, I wait for the call. But while I'm waiting – while everything is really quiet and still, one little emotion grabs my attention. It reminds me of how cool this all is. It reminds me of those times when I've burned myself down, only to reemerge as something else. I recall the pains, failures and misses, which all seem so innocent and necessary in hindsight. I'm amazed that it all played out perfectly because here I am in this perfect chair while my perfect little family plays and laughs in the next room. I just couldn't have planned this all out on my own.

There is a flow to life. It's big, powerful, and inexorable. Whether you like it or not, you're coming along. You've been handed a ticket and strapped tight into your seat. Keep your hands and feet close, because while the ride will start smooth, let's not ignore the rough tracks ahead. Sure, you're worried about missing your stop amongst the bustle and noise, but you don't have to be. The little voice will tell you when.

From where I sit now, all I can really do is trust the little spark in my ear and project my plan outward. I can see the next few moves in my career, in my training, in everything I would like to make real in this world. What's more, from where I sit I can try and predict the steps beyond. I can estimate where my path will lead based upon my experience, these early trends, and that trust in the initial spark. I would consider this step both essential and totally worthless at the same time. Think of your retirement accounts. It's silly not to save, but how the hell can you predict the conditions of yourself and this world some thirty years into the future? You cannot, hence the frustrating paradox that is life.

Look for the spark. It will compel you to act. And act you must. It starts by answering, "Why not?" You pull out your map. You set the goals – to start a business, to lose thirty pounds, to add that load to your bench press maximum. It could be anything. But the action taken is equivalent to packing up your boat with everything you'll need and launching into those rough waters. This is the hard part, the scary part. This is what the Muse was begging you to do. "Jump in!"

Reality will be reality, but now that you've acted there's nothing to worry about. The path will be revealed as you float on. I think Hunter S. Thompson wrapped perfect words around the idea in *Fear and Loathing in Las Vegas*: "Buy the ticket, take the ride. If it occasionally gets a little heavier than what you had in mind, well, maybe chalk it up to forced conscious expansion. Tune in, freak out, get beaten."

Let go. Listen. Learn. Hold on really fucking tight. And please, try to enjoy the ride. You might as well.

THROWING OFF THE BLANKET

"Sacred cows make the best hamburger."
– Mark Twain

I'm very lucky. I've had the chance to travel fairly frequently over these past few years. It's a privilege I do not take lightly. The renewing motion has really served to raise my awareness, empowering me, and allowing me to bloom as an individual. It has also been a fucking great time!

How about an example?

I once thought I knew what a proper pint of beer should taste like. I thought I understood what the typical pub experience had to offer. But that was before I drank those steins of wheat ale down in this underground, medieval, candelabra-illuminated tavern in Antwerp, Belgium. The beer was amazing, but I'm sure the set and setting had at least something to do with it. Regardless, the moment was perfectly sublime and perspective-shifting.

These are the moments that change your life, if only in small ways. They are more than worth the ticket price.

While travel has been an essential experience for me, so much remains to be seen. Above all other trips, I desperately want to go on a pilgrimage and explore my interest in eastern philosophy and spirituality. I'm not quite sure just where, but the trip will probably include more than a few gorgeous Zen gardens, some incense-heavy Buddhist temples, and if at all possible, a full and challenging tour through India. I know this is a bit of a clichéd remnant of a bygone flower-power movement. But still, I consider that journey to be a potentially transformative trip that's worth exploring.

Still, I have my limits. I will not be wearing patchouli scented sandals over hemp socks any time soon!

As much as I would like to embark on that pilgrimage right now, I'm in no rush This is the sort of thing you undertake when you're ready. You need to really warm-up to the idea of having your carefully constructed worldview picked up and tossed right on its head.

The goal is complete immersion into a culture, philosophy, and reality that is the polar opposite of my own. It will be scary at times and uncomfortable at all other hours. Imagine, sitting intently with legs crossed in an austere Zen temple for a month or so, fully disconnected from the outside world, continually slicing away with sharp meditative knives. I can see myself in transit now, a temporary prisoner to a long sequence of over-crowded, hot-box, seemingly never-ending transcontinental bus rides. Or more challenging still, I can only imagine my reaction to India. I've always heard that it's the kind of place that scrapes away at you, keeping you in a constant state of discomfort. Yet, you feel drawn back time and again for years to come. That's something I must feel for myself. I want to observe and connect with the poverty that, to date, I've only seen within the pages of *National Geographic* magazine. I want to stand flabbergasted at the site of countless sacred beasts casually wading their way through already overflowing city streets. And I want to have my very sense of self, life, propriety, and spirituality ripped right out by the root after witnessing the infamous Ganges river burial and cremation ceremonies.

I don't think human moments can get any heavier than that.

No matter your perspective on life, love, work, death, and what may come afterward, I can guarantee that it will radically change after you've seen countless corpses, in various stages of reintegration, startlingly illuminated by a brilliant Indian sunset. This might be my final stage of development where, amongst the shadows of actual sacred cows, I can have my few remaining Western assumptions and beliefs burned right away forever. But no, for now I have plenty of rogue weeds still within reach that need to be ripped out first.

You are flowing forward towards some future, some possibility. At least I hope you are. It might be that you're stuck in a bad cycle, in this whirlpool of shit habits and assumptions. You could be serving as your own anchor, pinned down and motionless. In those times you have to be willing to drop life as is and shed your cocoon, leaving the old version of yourself behind. It's scary, it's hard, and it's essential.

Your cycle could be anything. A lingering relationship. A long-term struggle with weight and self-image. Maybe you're just a run of the mill asshole that doesn't have a very good handle on their emotions. For me, it's the search for what is right and correct. The right career path. The best training approach. A perfectly refined personal philosophy and set of beliefs.

I could continue to look and look forever, or, I could remember that so many of my past assessments were far, far off the mark. Although I felt precise and confident at the time, I was wrong! That experience informs me that, even if I could hold something perfect and shiny within my hands now, it would surely dull in time.

Here's the thing about feeling right or wrong – your definitions inevitably shift as you age, grow and learn. But the world all around is largely the same. It hasn't changed, you've changed! You've got a different history now. A new set of scars. You've seen new things. As Marcus Aurelius reminds us, "Everything we hear is an opinion, not a fact. Everything we see is a perspective, not the truth."

In fact, that's probably the root of the issue there. In a scary world of endless possibilities, we stand safe and sound here on our little foundations. Therefore, it makes perfect sense that we would freak the fuck out whenever an action, a question, or a challenge caused that foundation to shake, shimmy, or crack. Shit, the very idea that this could happen is enough to scare us into happily constructing our own dams! Anything to stop the flow and feel secure. But here's the thing – any true foundation is firm in the face of honest questions and experiences. If not, then you never had a real foundation to being with. Ask the questions.

What's there to fear? All you stand to lose is your blanket. Speaking of which, do you know why we all love to sleep while covered, either by sheet, quilt, or even the ridiculously small, steel wool-like airline blanket? Well, it has to do with our time in the womb. We were assembled under pressure from the surrounding amniotic fluid. For that reason, we retain an intimate ability to sense pressure, such as when we are covered with a warm, cozy blanket. There's nothing more soothing than that.

Travel, turmoil and age have proven just how delicate my version of the truth can be. So, I've done my best to quit chasing it. I'd rather focus on this empowering, inspiring sensation. Removing my blanket might have left me feeling a little cold and exposed initially, but now all I feel are these endless degrees of freedom.

I can see, do, and flow as I please, as long as I'm never afraid to let go. Isn't that possibility amazing?

TIME AND MOTION

I pride myself on the careful preservation of a forward lean. That's something I can hold on to, no matter what swirls around me. It's a choice that remains well within my control.

While I might be mistaken, tardy, off-track, and woefully wayward more often than I would like to admit, that hardly matters at all in the long run. What does matter is that I've finally learned to trust myself and my intuition. I'm learning to let go of the need to label everything as right or wrong. That's a tremendous fallacy that can cost you years.

Instead, I'm cultivating a new default setting. If I can just stay in a position to catch the next wave, remaining open to all sorts of unforeseen possibilities, then I know a better path will unfold ahead of my steps. Of course, some of these steps are easier to take than others, but I will put my feet out there anyway, keeping the faith.

This attitude might be the key to everything – it provides the energy we need to grow smarter, stronger, and more empathetic. We can create and contribute more, regardless of our given circumstance or mood. We can begin to control the impulses that drag us off course. Still, the lean does come with a cost. This path can be frustrating as hell!

The vexation usually floods into my world in one of two ways. First, I've noticed that all sorts of amazing experiences and beautiful, captivating ideas start accumulating once you make yourself open to all manner of possibilities. Who wouldn't want to share that knowledge as often as they can?

My intent is simple and honest. I want others to see, hear and feel these experiences. But it doesn't always work that way. You don't always get back what you give. The emotion we express often makes best sense when it is set against a backdrop of our history. To paraphrase a Confucius quote, it seems that everything has its beauty, but not everyone is prepared to see it or appreciate it the way you do. I'm learning that this is perfectly fine and that it's OK to save some things for later.

The bigger issue seems to be patience. Again, I'm getting better with time, but no one likes to wait around for what they really want, do they? Here we stand, feet firm, hands open, and ready to grab those opportunities... So send them! We've diligently put in time and work. We've taken the steps, right? So where's the reward?

Those words are more than enough to make me feel a bit spoiled right now. I can see clear patterns of behavior as I look back at my own history with honest eyes. I can see all these occasions where I found myself needing to express a measure of patience. I thought I was ready, that something was owed to me. But I hadn't really earned anything. I hadn't yet realized that years of hard work were actually just the price you had to pay to buy into the game. It was the habit that gave you a chance to be successful.

Entitlement is not part of the deal.

I'm sure it's been done, but I don't see how anyone can do anything great without treating hard work as if it were breathing, an essential personal practice that enables everything else. Yes, it would be great to accelerate the pace of our development, but in the end you'll move on when you're ready. You'll take advantage of great opportunities when you're ready. Like a snake shedding its skin, this can only happen when the time is right after some real growth and investment occurs.

No one can say how long this takes, but there are clear stages of progression which are pretty easy to recognize. At first we are all greenhorns, right? We don't know what the hell we are doing, our skill is low, and we are inherently ignorant. This all sounds bad, sure. No one wants to brag about being a beginner, but perhaps they should.

Here's something to consider – there's nothing more rewarding than moving away from a state of physical and mental ignorance towards a new state of awareness. This is a time of rapid, revealing progress that can have an intoxicating effect. Why not enjoy that for as long as possible?

Step for long enough and you'll start to get a real, elegant understanding of your skills, your mind, and the world all around. Call it a state of mastery, if only because it sounds really cool!

We've identified the assumption that being a novice is somehow a bad thing, so let's also consider the assumptions that come with this chase of mastery and reward. It's completely natural to want to get to where you're going already. We want the payoff, the punch line. But we're wrong in believing that this is the end. While it's nice to have arrived, it can also be boring as hell and less rewarding than you would have guessed. Trust me, I've felt this a few times. This is only the entry point to the last stage, which is all about teaching and giving back.

I told you earlier that sharing experiences and ideas with others can be very frustrating. That's true, but as with anything we must look past our first impressions. We need to dig down into the experience, beneath the frustration. Teaching can be one of the most amazing things you'll ever do. Even if your achievements seem modest, there are plenty of people out there that would benefit from hearing about your journey. And trust me, helping someone else develop and move along will feel just as good, if not better, than anything you ever personally accomplished. That's a beautiful thing.

I find that one of the most amazing things about teaching is how it reinforces and expands my own knowledge. It gives me an appreciation for elegant, powerful concepts. The simple things I often forget about. The act alone encourages me to identify new skills that I need to develop, or existing weaknesses that I need to correct. This is like being a greenhorn all again, only this time with an incredible amount of experience that allows you to complete the cycle more efficiently, and with greater effect.

That's the real lesson here. Do not rush towards your perceived finish line. That is an illusion. Rather, remember that there's absolutely nothing wrong with being where you are right now. Learn to lean forward and stick your feet out. That practice will ensure you are where you need to be when the time is right. And yes, have faith that the better path will unfold before you when the time is right, as frustrating as the wait might be!

You're not here to chase after things. You're here for the motion.

Define Your Journey.

We don't need buzzwords, convoluted ideas, mathematical theory or guru jargon to get really strong and happy. All we need are a few answers.

What is it you really want?

What is it you do not want?

How long do you think this journey will take?

Based on your experience in work and life, is that timeline reasonable or not? If there is any doubt, you have your answer.

Remember, every initial answer is a bad one. Drill deeper. Take your time.

How many bad answers can you identify?

TRAINING BY ANY OTHER NAME

"Nature uses only the longest threads to weave her patterns so that each small piece of her fabric reveals the organization of the entire tapestry."
– Richard P. Feynman

Even the most present and mindful among us can find some cause for boredom on a rainy Tuesday afternoon. But I have just the remedy for just this sort of thing. In those gray moments, simply pump some Postal Service through your noise-canceling headphones, imbibe a bit, then consider how everything you can see, everything you do, everything you want to be is tightly bound and inseparable.

This is not guru mumbo-jumbo speak, friends. That happens to be true.

There are long threads that weave in and out of every element and detail of this reality. I have a modest amount of brain matter, so I'll just share the best example I can think of.

You might have heard of the Fibonacci sequence, or as it has also been called, the golden or divine ratio. This is an idea developed by a 12th century Italian Mathematician named, surprise surprise, Fibonacci. Really, those are all fancy names for a rather simple and elegant concept. But the true implications and manifestation of this idea are altogether different.

Start with the numbers 0 and 1, then add them together to get 1. Now, add 1 and 1 together and you get 2. Next add 1 and 2 to make 3, then 2 and 3 to make 5. This pattern of adding the previous two numbers together to form the third repeats indefinitely – 8, 13, 21, 34, etc., for as long as you can count. The result is this clear, ascending spiral pattern. That fact alone is quite interesting, but not all that inspiring. However, that changes when you consider how deep this particular thread goes.

This sequence seems to form a big chunk of the basic design code of the natural world. The arrangement of leaves around a stalk of a plant, the placement of seeds within a sunflower blossom, or perhaps most well known of all examples, the beautiful ascending internal structure of a chambered nautilus shell. All exhibit the pattern. We might also extend the definition of the natural world to the stuff that we create, like music. A particularly fascinating example is the song "Lateralus" by Tool, where the time signatures and lyrical structure bear this same repeating pattern. As if writing music wasn't complex enough.

Regardless of your current state of consciousness, somewhat altered or otherwise dull, this realization should be more than enough to stir that rusty sense of wonder you've been carrying around in your back pocket. If not, just plug your brain back into your television and resume the slow poisonous drip of reality TV programming.

As interesting as all of this Fibonacci sequence stuff may be, it's still too abstract when weighed against your daily aspirations, efforts and struggles. Yes, it might seem that way. But remember, these threads go through everything. Consider training. If I had to define that word simply, I would say that it is just exercise with a specific aim. This is effort that accumulates with effect and direction.

At some point we all recognize that we're not quite as fit as we could be, so we draft a plan to grow stronger, leaner, more capable, whatever. That's a good thing, right? To aspire to be something greater than what you currently are? To grow? To change for the better? Yes, but there's just one hugely inconvenient truth we have to work around first. Growth, change, and aspiration are actually worth very little if the target of your aim is nothing but an illusion.

Let's tie some threads together, shall we?

The curious thing about any illusion is that it's much easier to see once you're on the other side of it. This is not unlike watching a magic show from backstage. Once you can see behind the curtain, you know how the trick is done. In that sense, grade school and higher education might be the most impressive examples of sleight of hand I've ever experienced! What's the set-up?

The premise that we all operate under is that school has a very clear, definite direction. For those that do the work and pay the ever-inflating extortion/ tuition bills, there is the promise of emerging from these studies well educated, otherwise prepared and highly employable, right? Right. But you and I both know where this conversation is going.

The reason so many people struggle to find their path and passion after becoming educated is that, in truth, a degree is really nothing more than a ticket to get on the train. It's the starting point of your development and journey, not a coronation ceremony. It's not a key to any of your locked doors, but rather, it's more like a map to the hardware store. From there you have to learn to build your own door, your new opportunity, your new life. You have to throw away your old keys and fucking earn whatever it is that you crave in this incarnation. The truth waiting for you behind the curtain is that things are not always as they seem. You can bleed out during the peak of your youth chasing diplomas, and that's fine, but it doesn't guarantee that you'll be ahead of anyone else once this race you're imagining ends. It doesn't mean you're closer to figuring out what to do with your life.

The outside world can take some getting used to. Anyone who's ever burned a few years at a job they hate will know the feeling.

These goals of ours really do shimmer like gold, but remember that nothing is ever really what it seems. They can leave feeling a bit half-full. That's because no one person or institution can ignite a passion in you that's not already there. No one can reveal your unique path through their teachings. How could they?

I cannot pretend that this is an easy thing to figure out. After all, I've spent the last decade of my life digging around in the rubble of my failures, looking for answers to all those big questions that we all carry around. It took a bit longer than I had hoped, but I found a few of them. They're the threads that connect all of my experiences. I think of all the work, love, friendships, my training, my creativity, the revelry, turmoil, fear and pain. With all that, there's a distinct and consistent pattern, one that's obvious and liberating.

A rose by any other name smells just as sweet. Or, I might say that what's true in education, work, love and life is true in training, as well. Do not anchor yourself to past accomplishments and failures. Rather, simply learn and utilize the lessons wherever you can, as often as you can. The goal – your future – may indeed be shining bright like the sun, but be careful staring. You might go a bit blind. A better approach is to follow the energy. What interests you right now? What excites you? What do you want to study? What activity, task or exercise always brings more thrill than fatigue? What teachings and experiences can you use to throw a light on the world?

If you know the answer to even a few of those questions, then you've got the only key you really need. Get to work and earn your future. Use these threads to find your path forward, follow them as far as you can. The result will arrange itself.

ALL THAT DEPTH

"As a single footstep will not make a path on the earth, so a single thought will not make a pathway in the mind. To make a deep physical path, we walk again and again. To make a deep mental path, we must think over and over the kind of thoughts we wish to dominate our lives."
– Henry David Thoreau

Do you remember the early 90s movie *White Men Can't Jump*?

The question is a rhetorical one. I'm going to talk about the flick whether you like it or not. But I promise, there is a point to it all. In the meantime, if you haven't seen the movie before, please, add it to your Netflix queue. It's worth it for the following scene alone.

The main characters are all driving along a typical, urban Los Angeles street, celebrating a successful basketball hustle down at the public beach courts. After some pithy dialogue exchange, Billy pops a cassette tape into the dashboard stereo (remember those things?). After a few clicks, Jimi Hendrix's seminal "Purple Haze" spills out in waves from the convertible's speakers.

Sidney asks who the musician is.

Billy responds that it's Hendrix, perhaps confused, oblivious to the fact that the question was just a baiting maneuver for the sake of making a point.

Sidney asks why he's playing it.

He bites back with a bit of edge, saying that he likes to listen to it.

That's to be expected. One thing I've learned in

this life is not to apologize for the music you like. Fuck man, it might very well be that you simply cannot feel alive in the morning without cranking Katy Perry's "Firework" full stop from your Marten Coltrane Supreme home theatre set-up. I get it, but friend, please, just don't do it while your friends are around.

These sorts of things should remain private and intimate.

Billy says that this is Sidney's problem: he listens to music rather than hearing it. After a long back and forth, the intended wisdom of the scene emerges. The point, of course, is a reasonable one. According to my interpretation of Wesley Snipes' Oscar-caliber performance (*cough), the act of listening is very much like flying over a city, superficially surveying from a great height. Sure, you've seen it all, but can you say you've been there? No. While you've very likely got a good understanding of all the vital statistics of the city – its scope, population density, potential areas of development, whatever – you still know nothing of the pulse, culture, and strife of the place. In other words, you have no idea what really defines the city and gives it a pulse. You're just floating above all of the interesting bits.

That's what you're after, of course.

I've learned this particular lesson many times over with music, most recently with the band Tool. I know, I know, it feels like 1996 all over again. But this angle informs my perspective on the Jimi issue. It's one thing to play Ænima while burning through aimless mid-90s high school afternoons, but it's quite another to enjoy "Third Eye" at the age of 32, with a high-dollar headset sealed around your dome, forcibly expanding your mind, and an actual appreciation of the subject matter. Yeah, this is hearing.

You should pursue that heightened experience always and with everything.

Don't just pass over something that captures your attention, even if that pass is highly thorough and analytical. Remember, the knowledge alone will not be of much use to you. I would never ask a city planner to take me out for a good time, regardless of the mounds of data they might have stuffed down their pants. No, give me raw. Give me strife. Give me the social, economic and cultural struggles that give birth to awesome blues music and midnight pastor tacos from a street corner truck.

Here's my advice to you. Sit down and stare at this thing you love. This thing you dream of mastering. Feel it. Read all the liner notes. Understand every thread of it. Then, let it aggravate, provoke, and inspire you! Let it cause you some pain. Get mad over it. Cry over it from time to time. Friction and pain are a good thing, just maybe not acutely. It will accumulate. It will give rise to great things. Just keep the heat on. Let this distillation happen.

In time, all of the subtle and profound associations between your struggle, experience and the thing you're chasing will start to appear. Yeah, it just takes a little time. In other words, give yourself a chance to accumulate some actual wisdom. Give yourself a chance to hear.

Let's be honest. Is every little whimsical detail of your life worthy of this level of inspection and commitment? No! It can probably only happen a few times if you're doing it right. But the exercise still works on a somewhat superficial level.

Just remember to take your time when your interest is snagged. Develop the skill. Take the time to slow down and inspect even one tiny thing or question a day. When you feel the urge to move along, devote a few more minutes to the exercise. Consider how you would view the thing if you were someone else. Consider the good and the bad. Turn the thing over. Smell it. Give it a whack and see what it sounds like.

As the skill develops, you'll be more and more prepared for the deep dive that could potentially change everything. But please, don't assume you're ready for that moment right now.

Learn to notice detail and make fine distinctions in any given situation. Don't be another attention-deprived mouth-breather with no appreciation for the art in this life and its subtle messages.

No more listening. Let's do this the right way, or not at all.

BEAUTIFUL FAILURE

"The best laid schemes o' mice and men
often go awry." – Robert Burns

"Then why the hell are you so surprised, upset,
and distracted then?" – Me, just now

I don't know what I expected to hear exactly, but I certainly hoped for something a little more optimistic. "I'm sorry, Mr. Moore," the program Chairman stated, looking somewhat confused. "Tell me again, why is it that you feel qualified for a position within this department?"

Even now the memory of this conversation feels a bit painful and embarrassing.

I had plenty of reasons to be optimistic before this meeting. After all, I was a prospective PhD student with great grades and loads of experience, emerging from a tremendous master's program with something like eight published academic papers and over fifty presentations under my belt. And of course, I made sure to talk about my sporting career, particularly my fancied powerlifting prowess.

The pitch was very clear. Not only was I smart and capable, I was dedicated enough to establish and go after these demanding physical goals. If nothing else, this should have been enough to at least guarantee an engaging discussion. I was wrong. So wrong, in fact, that this terse rejection left me sitting stunned and silent in that office chair.

CHRIS MOORE — BARBELL BUDDHA

There is a chance I might have seemed interesting to someone, sure, but the department chair held another perspective entirely. In retrospect, it's likely that he saw me as brash and overly confident. Here was this gigantic, three-hundred-and-seventy-pound man panting nervously before him, slowly sweating through that recently financed, ill-fitting, unflattering Men's Warehouse suit. I was very accomplished for someone my age, but he was right in his assessment. That's the honest truth. I hadn't done all of the prerequisite work. I really didn't understand what it would mean for me if I did get accepted into this program. I simply saw this place as the inevitable next step in my journey towards my preordained destination. This all explains my current embarrassment. I really was overflowing with assumption and delusion. I was a bit blind.

I had worked really hard for this opportunity. Some four years of my life leading up to this moment have been tossed into the fire that was my undergraduate and graduate laboratory. I did everything that had been asked of me and more, and still, I was met with this sort of crushing resistance.

I tell this story knowing that you have likely experienced something similar. Your moment might have come within the context of a job, a relationship, a sport, a personal goal, whatever. The specifics of the failure do not matter nearly as much as that very real sense of acute pain and desperation.

Let's get the tough bit out of the way first, shall we? It's OK to feel crushed when things blow up, when you fail, when the skies start shattering and coming down. If you don't feel shaken at a time like this, then something is terribly wrong! There's no user manual to teach you about this stuff, but this comes with being human. That's what it is, but I would also like to share the less than obvious bit with you. We're in the habit of interpreting failure, loss and rejection as being inherently terrible. This is mostly wrong.

We try our best to avoid the pain. I don't know of anyone that likes to experience breakdowns in the plan. We would much rather do whatever is comfortable, lends itself to success, and delivers a relatively stable and predictable future. Shit, our entire educational system bears that design. But this is a very dangerous fallacy, and an assumption we can do without.

Here's a fascinating twist. Those that stay on the obvious, easy path get just what they bargained for – a safe, comfortable, predetermined life that is overrun with assumption and self-imposed limitations. I don't know about you, but with that as an alternative, I will gladly take the cleansing flashes of fire.

Loud, crystal-clear and painful awareness is your friend during times of failure and rejection. At this point you can ask yourself some very important, pressing questions. First, are you a victim in this scenario? Or are you just wrong? Don't take this personally! It's likely that you woke up on the wrong fucking path, pressing ahead, hoping (perhaps naively) that circumstances would resolve all on their own. Do you really want to stay on this trajectory for the remainder of your life, or is it far better that you were kicked off now? Remember, you'll have no memory of this pain once you look back from a much wiser vantage point later on down the road.

Of course, you'd rather not feel that pain.

Take a few moments to look at where you were heading, carefully separating that reality from all of this imagined, self-imposed pain and disappointment. Instead of sitting around licking your wounds, as if someone just pissed in your bowl of Cheerios, do try and recognize that this change in circumstance has reopened infinite possibilities and opportunities for you. Sure, you got your freedom after you were shot over the prison walls via cannon shot, but now you are free!

Nothing is as it seems, not even the bad stuff like failure. Pick out those shards and build something new.

TATTOOED

"Wear your heart on your skin in this life."
– Sylvia Plath

I didn't have any better ideas, so I decided to break the news over a nice hibachi lunch. "So, Mom, I have something I need to tell you."

I noticed her expression shift as I completed that sentence as if a high-pressure front was rapidly settling in right behind her eyes. Wait, does she think I'm about to come out of the closet? I pressed on, reaching over to draw up my right sleeve. "Well, check it out…I got a tattoo!" I flashed her the bright blue sugar skull and red roses that now occupied most of the visible flesh.

"Oh, thank God!" she replied, immediately. "I thought you were gonna tell me you got yourself pierced!"

I paused for a moment, lost for words. Her comment begged the question, What exactly does she think I got pierced?

She went on, concluding, "…I think it's beautiful, Chris, really." We were both relieved.

My motive for that tattoo was simple. At the time I felt trapped in the gravity of both my past and future. You might know the feeling. It's sort of like waiting for that airport shuttle ride while you hold a heavy bag filled with old clothes that don't fit anymore. I hadn't yet realized that the opportunity, creative energy, and impulse I was searching for were all things I was going to have to cultivate, bit by bit, on a daily basis. It was something I had to earn, not something I would stumble upon.

I had no clue what to do, so I got that tattoo instead. If nothing else, it would always be there to remind me that life is finite, and that when in doubt, I should always place my focus on something I really love.

That will always be the best decision.

The addiction took hold soon thereafter. In less than a year, I added a large dragon to my chest and back, and had filled the remainder of my upper arm with an impactful song title and loads of shading. Even then, after just few months, all that ink began to look small as it reflected back from my bathroom mirror every morning. So, I decided to let the ink run down my forearm and up the next.

This is the coolest sort of slippery slope you can step on.

First there's the Hannya mask and lotus for my wife. Next came a dragon Koi to symbolize a personal and physical transformation, a snake and peony flowers for good fortune, and best of all, the name of my first born son, Max, inscribed boldly underneath my left elbow. Traditional Japanese style wind bars, clouds and waves swirl and crash around each piece, all representing the common turbulence of daily life. Taken together, my ink tells the story of a fantastic future that unfolded before me, right on time.

I never needed to worry. I worked hard, and cared a lot, so things began to work themselves out. That's a pattern that continues to even today, surprise, surprise. I suppose this was my first real lesson in Taoism. As the master Lao Tzu once said, "By letting go, it all gets done." Yes, but sometimes it just takes time to let go.

My latest piece is a lotus design under my left bicep. The flower itself has eight black outer petals, in total representing the eight noble truths of Buddhism – the balanced pursuit of the right understanding, speech, livelihood, concentration, mindfulness, effort, action, and intention. Only the inside will be colored, which is sort of symbolic of the second metamorphosis currently underway.

Ready or not, I'm rapidly growing into some new form. And let me tell you, letting go and giving in is still a terribly difficult thing to do. The future is just as unknown and scary as it's ever been. But there is a difference, this time. Now I see that I don't have to wait around. I can keep my boots light and my baggage empty. I want to remember that everything in my life will have this natural tendency to work itself out, if only I will keep putting my energy where it matters...Squarely on the cultivation...On the love.

All of the symbology is great and beautiful, but is that the only reason for getting so many fucking tattoos? Does it really explain the addiction, or the tickle to push further? No, the pain itself is just as meaningful.

I doubt many people enjoy the sensation of the needle jamming ink deep down into their dermis, but everyone surely is proud of what they have endured once they get up from the chair and look at their art in the mirror for the first time. See, that is its own reward. It's something to be proud of, and something worth showing off.

I've got lots of bare skin still waiting to be covered, but that won't last for long. I'm already planning on filling up the open space that remains on my left shoulder. It shouldn't be too hard to extend the story that far. After all, I'll be a father for the second time soon. That's only the latest example of how this once frustrating and seemingly boring life is now blooming wide and bright right before my astonished eyes, notwithstanding my worry.

Whatever else the future may hold, I'll probably continue to wear my heart on my skin, adding annually to the ink tally. That's because the lesson remains so useful and amazing. Here I begin, with a particular vision of the future in mind. But that means little if I'm not willing to suffer a bit in the chair to realize it. That's a small price to pay for such a rich life in return.

Whenever you find yourself caught in that gravity, waiting, worrying, just remind yourself that all will unfold in time. All you have to do is cultivate. All you need to remember is that your story will take shape one needle stroke at a time. Sure it might hurt a bit, but you're not going to let a little needle scare you that easily, are you?

THE TAO OF RICH

"Let a joy keep you. Reach out your hands and take it when it runs by." – Carl Sandburg

I had never pictured myself in such an unflattering situation.

There I was, shirtless, staring down and mean-mugging another shirtless man. The situation itself wasn't all that unusual. After all, I've been in a few fights in my time. Whether they've occurred on the street, or on a playing field, apparel is usually one of the first casualties. I should also add that this wasn't really a fight at all. I was in front of a video camera filming a spoof intro for a TV show. So, no, this wasn't much of a fight-or-flight moment.

I should also add that the other shirtless man wasn't just your average dude. He happened to be, quite literally, the fittest man in the world, Rich Froning, defending CrossFit Games champion.

If I could go back in time and share this bit of news with my teenage chubby self, he would be absolutely mortified by my actions and poor decision making. I can easily imagine a fiery response along the lines of, "You did what? But, why? He's got a six-pack!? Great." To which my current form would respond, "Young Chris, trust me, people are going to love this!"

We arrived at Rich's garage gym at about ten o'clock or so in the morning. His hometown, Cookeville, is about four and a half hours east of Memphis. You could feel the whole garage buzzing and humming with motion upon approach. Walking inside, there was Rich, hustling through what might have already been his second tough training session of the day.

The workout was a combination of push presses and fast meters on the standing ski-erg machine. I must have seen him go five or six rounds without a break, but there's no telling how much work was done before we arrived. He welcomed us between ski strokes. "Hey, 'sup guys? Come on in."

What was far more memorable than that WOD was his recovery from it. I turned away from a huffing, completely sweat drenched Rich to chat briefly with one of the other guys training that day. We couldn't have shared more than a few lines, really. Just as I turn back around a few minutes later, I notice a completely calm, dry, at-ease Rich casually walking across the gym, stacking plates and cleaning up his mess. In just a few minutes, he seemed to have completely recovered. This incredible capacity is what allows the guy to then go for a quick run, which could easily be a few miles, then he completes a few more workouts after that! The schedule seemed punishing.

That actually was the topic of one of my questions to Rich later on in our interview.

"Do you ever get tired of training? It's not even noon, and you've probably surpassed what most people do in an entire day, a few times over even."

"Oh, it's definitely tough. I just don't think people realize what kind of challenge it is."

"Oh yeah? What do folks say?"

"Well, there are a lot of people who think they would be great too if all they had to do during the day was train. But they don't realize that I'm out here all day, from eight or nine in the morning, all the way to five or six o'clock at night. It's not easy. It's a full-time job."

Hey, I will be completely honest. Having never met Rich prior, I was guilty of some assumptions. First, the line about training full-time has crossed my mind a time or two. But I will say, that's completely out of jealousy.

There it is, I'm a jealous man.

Second, I might have been a bit skeptical of his good guy persona. It's hard not to do so when someone has had so much success so quickly. But I must say I was completely impressed with Rich's presence and his attitude towards the people in the room. It was evident that he had a very clear vision of where he needed to go, and what he needed to do to get there.

He knew when his work would increase, and when it should decrease. He understood exactly what he needed to lift. Still, he trains as he wishes. He lifts when he wants to. He runs and swims when he wants to. And more impressively, he seems to remain completely present in the moment – confident, focused, yet at peace and seemingly unaffected by his success. He didn't feel the need to reach out for anything. With time, incredible talent, and untold hours of brutal training under his belt, he was now in a position to take things at will as they ran toward him.

My assumptions remind me of a very old Indian proverb about a few blind men who were sent to examine an elephant, all to the King's amusement. One man grabbed the tusks, one each took the trunk and tail, and the last guy rubbed his hands against the animal's side. The men were then asked by the King, "Well then, what sort of animal is an elephant?"

The men replied that the elephant was, "Like a plow, or a granary, or a brush, or perhaps a mortar." The men then did as men do when they can't let themselves agree on anything...they fight over silly shit that doesn't really matter. But I can at least understand the assumptions they were making after experiencing just one side of the elephant. It's the kind of thing you believe after looking at a person only through a few dozen sponsorship and endorsement filters. You're just not seeing the whole picture. You'll never quite appreciate it fully.

We're all guilty of this shit. Many are struggling right where they stand. What do you do when you have some weight to lose, or some strength to gain? Well, you look towards someone whose got what you want. You seek to do as they do. You naturally start to reach out for it before you've really earned anything. It's easy to go too far and rush your development in order to take your premature shot. But what you don't realize is that this is the all too common decision that's jeopardizing your success. Yeah, we must make better decisions.

Listen, you can fight all you want, but nothing's ever going to run towards you until you unclench the fists and let go of that urge. You have to be OK with what you are, where you stand. In the face of everything that's challenging you, judging you, holding you back, or whispering in your ear about how you're really not good enough. You have to remain as you are. You have to remain appreciative of how far you've come in order to get to where you'd like to go.

I won't bullshit you. Even if you do manage to remain present and patient as your capabilities improve, there's no guarantee that you will ever be half as fit as the champ. But fortunately, for all of us, that's of little consequence. You'll still be aware, happy, balanced, and more successful. That's not a bad deal.

Take this with you – do your very best to maintain balance in life. You should have well defined aspirations, but you shouldn't try and grab what's not yet within your reach. You are fine right here. Start walking. When the time is right things will begin to flow toward you, usually just before they start running. Don't entertain the idea of quitting while you're so close! Grind, grind away. Put in the work and be happy about it. When things get tough, remember that there's nothing wrong with being uncomfortable for a while, doubtful and a bit scared at times. You just have to believe in what you're doing and the direction you're heading.

Maybe you first have to be willing to grab every part of the elephant, so to speak, before you can move along. Take the time.

In the end, the highlight of the day came as Rich and I were wrapping up that intro video shoot. Just at the peak of the scene we each dramatically raised a giant butterscotch glazed donut and took a giant bite, not unlike something you would see in a professional wrestling match. We finished our pastry, chasing it down with a carton of whole milk. And there it is – the champ, less than a week away from defending his title, taking the time to stop and enjoy a well-deserved donut after yet another workout. That's Ying and Yang in action. Just my kind of Tao.

FAT BOY YOGI

"Nothing is more dangerous than a dogmatic worldview – nothing more constraining, more blinding to innovation, more destructive of openness to novelty." – Stephen Jay Gould

The older I grow – the more worn and relatively wise I become – the more I see how everything is tied together. It just seems obvious. If you find a particular pattern or phenomenon in one area of your life, you're bound to discover the same thing on a seemingly unrelated occasion, somewhere else.

Everything has a cadence and shared, fundamental building blocks, so how could we expect otherwise?

One of the curious examples I can think of right now might be the similarities between mixed martial arts and CrossFit. MMA started out as a macho test to see which fighting style was superior. For anyone with an interest in this sort of thing, this was the most natural, obvious question that anyone could ask. But it was also a false question.

While it's true that there were clearly favorable styles (Brazilian Jujitsu perhaps being the most well known), this was only true in the early, artificially segregated days of the sport. The cross-breeding started to happen quickly as fighters began to incorporate elements from all sorts of other practices into their own training. Inevitably, to be great in MMA would mean being highly aware and competent in all of these key disciplines.

CrossFit is no different.

I'm intimately aware of the stark, partitioned history of the fitness community as a whole. For the longest time, it's been comprised of these highly niche factions of powerlifters, weightlifters, strongmen, bodybuilders, fitness models, and fringe groups that seem to love kettlebells, or bending nails and shit with their hands. Each of those things has great qualities, but each group has always reveled in talking shit about the others. Imagine a big circle of meatheads, where everyone calls the person to their left a freak. From my perspective, I'd never seen so many black kettles and pots. The question was always there, and was no less natural and obvious. If you want to be your best, which path do you take?

Here we go again, searching hard to find answers to a false question.

We know what the ideal fighter looks like now, and while there's some experimentation to be done yet, we're starting to see an ideal model of "fitness" emerge from the CrossFit community. It's really quite surreal how similar this evolution has been. CrossFit's early days were no less odd, clumsy or embarrassing as seeing a sumo wrestler engage a one-hundred and seventy pound BJJ practitioner. Consider that both have been labeled as dangerous and unnecessary. But despite all of the growing pains, that inherent pattern prevails. Clumsy, raw, early attempts at merging art forms have been replaced by a simple, inexorable process. Things have been cooked down and distilled into something far better. And of course, let's not pretend that money and attention do not matter. Where there are booms, an influx of resources only serves to accelerate the experimentation. The result for fitness? ...Well, it has already happened. The current three-time champion of CrossFit is highly aware and competent. The segregation is ending before our eyes. Soon, to be great will mean exhibiting strength and power that is actually comparable to that of a competitive weightlifter. You'll need the speed of a good, competitive sprinter, the body awareness of a qualified gymnast, and the endurance of a successful tri-athlete.

The very concept of a "Jack of all trades, master of none" might be proven false! Such is a reality where athletes complete a high level triathlon, change their shoes, then lift double their body weight overhead with little rest. This sort of thing is happening now. Yes, you should be careful whom you call a freak now-a-days. You should be excited by that! It's about time all of these old crumbling silos fell. CrossFit is not the only path forward, that much is obvious. However, the dominos have been falling for years now. The cross-breeding is already a few generations on. We've seen the future, and to paraphrase Mr. Darwin, only those factions willing to adapt and learn will continue to thrive. For everyone else, they'll have to be happy wearing their Speedos on a slowly shrinking stage.

There are plenty of people who will warmly agree with me while the rest prepare to return fire and take me back down a notch. I understand, but before you do whatever it is you're going to do, let me say that I do not personally pursue CrossFit at all. I've merely dabbled and experimented with it so that

I can understand it. Further, I believe you shouldn't try to inform or criticize anyone until you've actually stood with them...until you see what they see, and have been up and down a few times with them. It's OK to be aggressive and critical, but only if it's the constructive variety. You have to understand and empathize; otherwise you're just looking to your left, calling people names. The world has plenty of that shit already. We should choose to do something better.

No, I'm not a CrossFitter, but I'm a student of the sport. I've been heavily influenced and affected by its culture. And while it's not the motive for what I do, or where I go from here, it has significantly altered my trajectory. It has shown me an alternative path, where it's more than possible to mix art forms successfully. Or just as meaningful, it has proven that you can at least explore these art forms without actually compromising anything in the process. That's really just as good to know.

If a brand new experience and all of its lessons are available, complete with great benefit or at least minimal cost, then how can you say no? That's what I've learned as a student. That's the spirit I deployed yesterday morning during my first ever yoga session...yes, you heard me correctly. And it was every bit as interesting as you might imagine.

The truth is that, despite my interest in eastern philosophy and spiritual practice, I still harbor a deeply embedded bias. As a lifter, I tend to think of heavy lifting as sitting at the center of training practice. You can do all sorts of other things, but you better not skip the heavy part! Even now I believe that to be true, but just as in MMA, the lifting can only be at its best if it's supplemented with other key disciplines.

If I'm honest, then I will admit that I've always considered yoga to be the Karate of the training methods. Sure, it has some cool kicks and neat ideas, but just don't try and take on anybody who knows Muay Thai, Wrestling, Boxing, or BJJ. But here's the great thing about Karate. When it is understood and applied by a master of one of those other disciplines, then the result is something truly unpredictable, versatile, and quite dangerous. It could be that yoga is similar in that respect. It might not be a replacement for the barbell, but it might be just the sort of activity that amplifies its effects.

I walked through the studio doors having no idea of what to expect, as with any truly novel activity. But I immediately felt at complete ease. It wasn't familiarity. Aside from my wife, who joined me, I had never seen any of these other faces before in my life. People smiled, they handed me a mat, stretching blocks and a strap. Reflecting on it, I was just feeling the good vibes. It was undeniable.

The easy explanation is that the very notion of walking through these doors must be seen as ridiculous to someone who's stressed, uptight, and generally close-minded. That energy was absent here and I loved it.

I spread out my mat, and took a seat on the clean wooden studio floor. Before I really noticed anyone approaching, I heard an introduction. "Hi there. First time, right?" the instructor asked. "Oh, yeah. Our very first. I'm not quite sure how this will go, but I'm excited to be here." I replied. "Oh, great. It might be a little tough at times, especially for you.

But you'll do great. Nice to meet you both." She was right. I'm about as lean as I've ever been, but still, I weigh in at around 134 kilograms. I knew some of the positions would be incredibly challenging. Gravity and I have never been on great terms, you see. And let me be clear, I took no offense. The comment came off as quite warm. In that instant, I didn't see her as anything other than a kind instructor. But maybe that was all by design. Perhaps I was a victim of the compliment sandwich, where you sneak your shit-talking in between two kind statements to mask and distract the mark. Come to think of it, maybe that's exactly what happened! I do remember something kind before the joke. "Hey, look at you. Most men your size can't cross their legs like that!"

Indeed.

In the end, the experience was a little bit of everything. I really enjoyed the deliberate pace. The spiritual undertone. The subtle and well-timed instructional cues that keep your focus on your posture, and how your body feels. But there was plenty of challenge. Some of the poses were well outside of my comfort zone. For every achievable position and balance point in the warrior stance, there were the mirrored moments where I was really struggling. After fifteen minutes or so of downward dog, my shoulders and arms were fucking trembling under the load of my upper body. I was immediately aware of how specific preparedness is, and how seemingly out of touch with my body I was at times. But the value was apparent. If I could gain awareness and competency at this, just what sorts of new physical possibilities could open up? How much better off would I be?

The most insightful moment came during a bridging exercise. I lay down flat on my back, positioning a small block right underneath my tailbone. This effectively wedged my hips high into the air, which I enjoyed. I was doing fine as I began to raise and lower my legs, alternating left to right. At that time, the instructor made her challenge. Well, that's how I heard it at least. "Now, if you are comfortable, you can try and raise both of your legs up simultaneously, But please, be careful and know that you don't have to try if you'd rather not." I felt like trying. Slowly, I drew up my left leg toward my right, precariously placing the bulk of my carcass across the surface of this tiny composite block, likely constructed of recycled paper, and the many discarded flower power dreams of baby boomers past. I shook like mad to hold that position, and was quite proud. That's when the instructor noticed the scene and came back around.

I smiled a bit with the exertion, expecting acknowledgement for my achievement. Wow, Chris, nice job! I've never seen a big guy like you pull off a pose like that so soon! Well done. Instead, she administered the cold truth, which I needed to hear. "Relax, Dear. Put your feet down. Breath. What you're doing...this isn't yoga." This lesson alone was more than worth the class fee. There I was, cocky, segregated in my thinking, completely ignorant to what this art form had to teach me. And right there, I could feel my body resisting and fighting. It wasn't just about being stiff. I'm not inflexible. Rather, it was more about trust. About letting go of whatever it was

I was clinging to. I couldn't have been more excited to make that discovery. It's something I can change.

The best part was saved for last. After an hour of mobilization, strengthening, and fighting for proper position, the instructor signaled that it was time for Shavasana. In other words, this is a time for relaxation, meditation, and assimilation of what's been learned. You lie right back down flat on your back in corpse pose, all muscles essentially shut down and free from the burden of gravity. The traditional Indian style music had been playing for the entire duration of class, but I noticed the volume pick up just a bit. A little trick to enhance the moment I would guess. Next, a warm towel was draped softly over my eyes, followed by a gentle neck rub with rousing eucalyptus oil. Outside of my experience in the isolation float tank earlier this year, this was just about as relaxed and peaceful as I have ever been. I was highly focused and mindful. Yes, meditation at its finest.

Every art form has its place, as every form of training has its part to play in your development. For me, the yoga experience showed me a novel way to tackle my mobility issues. I can carve a few hours out of my week to devote to this progressive, intense practice, and will be all the better for it. For me, that's so superior to simply spending a few minutes rolling around on the floor before a workout. The experiences just cannot be compared. And let me not forget, it will be nice to learn this new art form, to meet a new community, and sure, to get to know this heavy carcass of mine on another level. I think I am a fan.

Maybe the broader lesson is as obvious as any other. As soon as you're prepared to disregard some practice, approach or art form as being below you – if you harbor that belief on any level – then you're very likely excluding something that could add beauty and value to your life. Don't make that mistake. Trust me, the barbell will not mind. She'll be right there for you once class is over.

Count the steps.

Every journey begins with one act. One move.
So, what's the next step you can take?

Think of your goal as being a big bucket. Sure, there's a long way to go from here. But it won't seem that way if you focus on those single drops.

If you wish to lift fifty more pounds, then start by trying for five. That's your next big step.

If the journey seems slower than you first imagined, don't worry. This is normal. Just return your focus to those steps.

Remember, the bucket fills drop by drop.
The barbell... pound by pound.

TOO COMPLICATED

"Making the simple complicated is commonplace.
Making the complicated simple, awesomely simple,
that's creativity." – Charles Mingus

Making the most of the moment is a lot harder than
it seems. Sometimes you skip down life's path, and
sometimes you find yourself dragging along your
history as if it were a dead body. The difference is that,
in one scenario, you are looking out optimistically
towards the future while the other is all about looking
back with a scared and shitty attitude. There's no
question we would rather be skipping. But therein
lies the problem. Here we are in this moment, eagerly
pushing ahead, willing to do whatever it takes to get
what we want, and what's the risk?

One of two things can happen. First, we might
fail to act, either through fear or indifference. Second,
we might try too hard, attempting to force fate and
over-analyze all the variables. I am far more familiar
with the latter. Really, I'm just terribly impatient.
We're all impatient. The default view seems to be
– why wait for what can be taken now or earned
through force of will?

I get it. Waiting sometimes feels as though
we're allowing ourselves to be static. There's so much
out there to learn and understand. And that is true.
But the simple fact is that force of will, over-planning
and over-thinking can also be very destructive.

At some point, you must recognize the hubris

in your motives and just take it down a notch, which reminds me of a story.

Some years ago I took a training vacation up to Ohio to spend a week lifting with the best strength athletes around. For all my flaws of youth, at least I understood from the beginning just how important it was to surround yourself with amazing people. I knew that immersion into a top-shelf training environment would flood my mind with a surplus of energy and new ideas.

To be a great lifter, I needed to learn how to act the part.

But perhaps it was a small coaching pearl of wisdom that made this trip really worthwhile. The coach I was visiting and learning from took some time from our training to bullshit and talk shop with some other visiting strength coaches, both of which worked for a local professional American Football team.

I could hear chunks of the conversation bubbling up over the sound of the blaring metal music, clanging metal weights, and the belly grunts of the Neanderthal-like powerlifter savages.

The visitors were tossing some big ideas by this coach. They wanted to try some really complex loading schemes on their athletes. They talked about some convoluted exercises they thought would improve the training effect. You name the buzzword, they used it.

The coach carefully entertained each one of these ideas, often nodding along as if in agreement.

"So, what do you think, Coach? Any other ideas?" the visitors asked. "What do I think?" he replied. "Well, I think you guys think too damn much!"

The fancy ideas were not terrible, or unfounded, or flawed. They were just too much tool for the job at hand. You shouldn't need a degree in theoretical mathematics to get stronger. No, what these guys were actually looking for was a way to differentiate themselves from all the other coaches out there in the wild. That's understandable, but I think there are much better ways to do that. For example, you'll probably get better results from any program you employ if you just do a better job of communicating with people, and yourself. When there's an understanding of the need and the purpose, then folks care about what they're doing. And when they care, they will put plenty of weight behind their efforts to get the results.

I believe that where there is a clear understanding and connection, there will be plenty of effort.

This lesson is captured by a well-known, beautiful Albert Einstein quote: "If you can't explain it simply, you don't understand it well enough." Well, I might say the same thing about a program. If you don't intimately understand what you are doing, or the instruction you are handing over to some hapless client, then you are making a mistake. You might not do any harm, but at the very least a whole lot of precious time will be wasted. Progress will be squandered. Instead, I would refer to Occam's Razor as a very helpful tool. Once you have tried the simpler of any two options, and it has ceased to work with time, then and only then should you increase the complexity. That cycle repeats until the extraordinary

CHRIS MOORE – BARBELL BUDDHA

alternatives at your disposal are actually required.

There's nothing wrong with your intensity, aspiration and analytical effort. Any good training, diet, or coaching strategy will be well-defined, detailed and evidence-based. But it must make sense, and it must stand up to inspection. Sure, it takes effort and time to get your head around all there is to know, to gain the requisite experience. But we cannot lose sight of the fact that training and all that is associated with it is inherently not as complex as fucking quantum mechanics. Why should it be? Attempts at constructing a magnum opus of human performance are about as useful and valid as John Nash's famous schizophrenia-fueled window etchings. They may have once been rooted in mathematical brilliance, but they were drawn into sheer madness when his condition worsened. Thankfully, he grew to understand and cope with a new condition. Can you say the same?

I know the fear. I know that you feel as though something is missing. I've felt that feeling a million times it seems. The worry that you're not doing all that you can do. That might, in fact, be true. But the missing piece is not what you think. You are not in danger of leaving some great truths undiscovered. Rather, you're in danger of building connections and associations that are simply not there. They take form only in your mind, unexpectedly injecting themselves into your thought gears like sticks in between wheel spokes. You have likely felt the result; frustration, confusion, fear, doubt, discontent, and ineffectiveness. This is all a sort of faux-reality in your head. So, make it disappear! Remove the analytical paralysis. Remind yourself of what really matters – your appreciation.

Elevate the pursuit. Make it important to you. Love it. Give it a chunk of your day. That's what could be missing.

We should pay less attention to our egos and to how our methods and actions are interpreted. Instead, we should place the bulk of our focus on how we feel about what we're doing, and the level of importance we assign to these pursuits.

If you find little worth focusing on, then shit, you've found your problem, haven't you?

NO SUCH THING AS PASSION

"It is obvious that we can no more explain a passion to a person who has never experienced it than we can explain light to the blind." – T.S. Eliot

Have you ever been told that the key to life is finding your passion and true purpose? Have you ever been offered advice on the topic? I'm sure you have. It might have been a book. Perhaps it was a forwarded TED Talk lecture that left you all warm and tingly for all of 15 minutes. Or, perhaps it was just your well-intentioned mother offering loving advice because she's worried about you spending the next decades of your life ponderously pouring pumpkin spice lattes at Starbucks.

I've turned this hard soil over many times these past few years, and I can assure you, there's little harm to it all.

Sometimes the advice is great. Sometimes a kind and insightful word from a friend or loved one can put a smile on our face, and enough wind in your sails to carry you along for a few more hours, days, or weeks. That's the aim...to keep moving no matter what. To believe in what you cannot yet see. But you must be cautious.

There are plenty of assholes out there who also would love to help you.

What's your first warning? Good advice is never sold as top secret information. In exchange for your money, you are offered a hack, a tool, a system that will show you where your passions lie. OK, maybe it's not all the time, but more often that not this is complete and total bullshit.

I don't want to call anyone a liar, as that's an automatic karma point deduction. It does no good. I'm just saying that these folks have indeed found their passion – it's making lots of money off of your hope. I suppose it could also be that these folks just don't have any idea of what they're talking about. Or worse still, it could be a little of both.

Here's the thing. I suppose you have to beware of anyone under retirement age that slings life advice, even if you catch yourself doing it. It's tricky business. You might be surprised to learn this, but this world and this life are really, really unimaginably complicated, stunningly beautiful, and of course, absolutely terrifying at times. You should not feel as though a carpet has been rolled out in front of you at the time of your birth. There is no predestined purpose, other than the one you slowly discover for yourself, on your own terms.

Be cautious, yet relieved that you can now ignore most of this distracting, sycophantic, demotivating, pseudo-advice nonsense. You have permission to answer your own questions.

It wasn't that long ago that I believed in a singular purpose, pursuit, path, or whatever else you want to call it. I broke my bones and spirit searching around for it. I even read a few bullshit books from posers who seemed to be offering real advice.

OK, maybe I read way more than just a few.

Like most, I fell hook, line and sinker into those traps over and over for a few years. But here's the thing – once you've been through all of that and have emerged with your first few real chunks of wisdom (which rarely seems to happen before the age of 30), you realize an obvious truth...why would such information ever reside externally? In fact, the question of what to do with your life is the most important one you'll ever face. Are you going to let someone else answer that question for you?

Where would they start? How could they possibly know what keeps you up late at night on the computer, burning away the foggy midnight hours? How can they know where your energy comes from? This mad impulse.

There's a second, even more liberating realization to be had. Picking just one path or identity is a bit like showing up to the airport, pointing out a random flight, then spending the rest of your finite lifespan at that destination. I know it's exciting now, but you're sure to discover a sharp and disappointing sting on the other side of the trip. The grass might not be greener on the other side. OK, it might be brown. Dude, there's no fucking grass over there sometimes!

I know the lure was bright and shiny at the beginning, but the chances of you making a really bad decision under such circumstances are very high. Why would you assume that your life should be so rigid, predefined and risky?

Isn't it far, far better to lightly go where you wish today? Can't you just stay for a while, to visit, to learn, to burn through a few piles of energy? Maybe get to know yourself for once. Your limitations. Your actual potential, which is completely foreign to you now. As you grow and inevitably change from these experiences, so too do your destinations. So too do your options.

It all sounds so obvious when you see it typed out before you.

I think there's just one key thing to worry about here – do what's most important to you right now. Follow the energy. Work as hard as you can, with all the quality you can manage. Make an impact. Just don't take things so seriously. Be free to make a few mistakes. Embrace the errors and take pride to admit when you're wrong. Know that this is not permanent, it will simply lead to the next better thing.

But that's just it, isn't it?

Because we view our lives as being chained to this one magical, hard to find path, we naturally feel terrible when we fuck up and fail. We assume that feeling lost is a direct consequence of our presumed aimlessness. That's why we fear mistakes, experimentation, and risk. We are deluded into thinking that it's a waste of time. But really, this is just a force that controls you. It chains you down like a dog. Does that sound like the path for you? Fuck no, you can do so much better.

Do what's worth doing today, right now. Let the experiences – both good and bad – push you forward to the next thing. I promise it will be so much more lovely than anything you could have planned ahead of time.

A LITTLE BIT WON'T KILL YOU:
THE FINE ART OF INCORPORATING
VICE IN YOUR LIFE

"Happiness is not a matter of intensity but of balance, order, rhythm and harmony." – Thomas Merton

MY PHILOSOPHY

I can clearly remember buying my first computer. Well, let me revise that. I can clearly remember going along with my father to pick out the computer that I wanted. College was just around the corner, and he must have sensed that I would need all the help I could get. He graciously agreed to pay for the thing.

This story embarrasses me a bit now. Looking back, I didn't think twice about talking my dad into blowing a couple of grand he didn't have on this contraption that I didn't even know how to use. Remember, this is around 1998. As a high school Junior, I hadn't even composed my first email yet. It's not very likely, but perhaps this was an inspired moment of clarity. Perhaps my dad recognized how important this damn black box apparatus would be. Or, maybe he just wanted to have someone around who could operate it for him.

In hindsight, I can see just how brief that moment of clarity was. I don't think he has even said the word computer these last fifteen years.

All the little details of that shopping trip are still embedded in my memory. We made just two stops. The first was a visit to the local suburban outlet mall cesspool, which had recently opened a Gateway Computer shop. The air, the lighting, the whole feel of this place hit you like a heavy, boring beige wave. Giant square box after square box lined the shelves. I tried to make an assessment, carefully measuring each product against the last, but I was never going to make a choice. It was impossible. They all seemed to be the same. I clicked away at the demo unit in the corner of the showroom, I yawned, then I gathered my folks and left.

Sometimes you just know, with every molecule of your being, that something just isn't right for you. It's usually obvious, yet it's amazing how many people fail to regard that warning, and likewise, they fail to trust themselves when some inexplicable energy compels them to go down an unknown path. If you are not prepared to listen to yourself, who will you listen to?

We all hopped in the car and drove right down the street to the next shop we knew of, a local Apple Computer certified reseller. Walking through those doors I immediately felt a new sensation. It just seemed that they were selling more than computers in there. Just past the displays of software and accessories, I couldn't help but notice the gleaming display of bizarre, hyper-colorful computers in the middle of the showroom, all arranged in a large circular pattern. I paced clockwise around the display, passing by several hues before arriving at bondi blue. How was this experience different than the first? Well, as I reached out for the keyboard and mouse, looking deep into that flowery wallpaper, I felt like this computer could stare back at me. The choice was easy to make. It was natural. For the next six or seven years I cut my Internet teeth through that brilliant, flowery screen and typed countless term papers on the blue-green keys.

I miss that machine.

I now know that this experience was triggered by Apple's then highly novel, Zen-inspired design philosophy. This was the only computer I came across that was crafted with some sense of restraint, simplicity, and ease of operation in mind. The elements that really mattered were each carefully identified and executed to near perfection. The things that were simply nice to have, or that were assumed to be necessary in a computer but didn't fit the philosophy, were all stripped away. This approach removed all of my barriers. It left me at ease so I could see what I might do with this machine.

This feeling remains and is prominent every time I consider my training, write something, or map out a goal. I start by asking myself what could be stripped away so that what remains can be clearly seen. These are the essential, beautiful, impactful details and concepts that get washed out by all the bullshit beige waves in our lives. Please consider that this simple philosophy is not a passing spiritual trend, but rather a powerful toolset that can change the way you occupy space and see the world. It works with computers, barbells, business, family, everything.

Beyond the superficial lessons, I must admit that I'm no scholar on this subject. I've simply grown to love and appreciate the impact that a sitting, introspective, meditative outlook can enable. When you are still, everything looks different. But I must say, what I've grown to love even more is the notion of crazy wisdom. The term refers to an unorthodox, outrageous, or unexpected behavior that can appear to you as either madness or mind-blowing enlightenment. In terms of Zen, I see that basic, simplistic, restraint-driven philosophy as a great beer while this crazy wisdom is more of a top shelf tequila shot of wisdom to your brain.

There have been no shortage of crazy wisdom masters over the years, but perhaps the most famous of all is Ikkyu Sojun, a fifteenth-century Japanese teacher. He had a unique and powerful mastery of Zen philosophy. He was also a tremendous poet, as evident by his lean, compelling, and very provocative writings. He wasn't called Crazy Cloud for nothing.

Ikkyu is typically described as a highly eccentric, iconoclastic, overly indulgent, hyper-sexual, and anti-archetypal type of monk character. Yes, I know, how unique! He created quite a stir when he openly rejected and abandoned the local temple due to its overly pious, snobbish, and dogmatic nature. In his view, there were too many rules, too much bureaucracy, and too many barriers being placed between himself and the world.

Instead, Ikkyu proclaimed that there were many paths to enlightenment; all found outside of those temple walls, all free of impediment and undue judgment. Also, conveniently enough, traveling many of these paths just happened to take you right through the best bars and brothels. You might say the only things this man loved more than his studies were shaped like tall sake bottles and beautiful women. I don't feel like arguing with that philosophy!

Let's save the commentary on liquor and love for another time. My central interpretation of Ikkyu's work centers around the idea of profundity – of deep insight and knowledge of a state, quality or emotion. I'm sure it's something that comes naturally to some, but the rest of us develop this skill following immersion and, yes, a certain measure of indulgence.

What was that old Japanese monk after? Sure, pleasure was certainly part of it. But more than that, he was living his life way out on the boundaries. Whether it was writing, teaching, drinking, or loving, the best way to embrace the Zen philosophy and maximize a life was to appreciate the tiny details and elegant features in all things, even one's vices. These are the essential elements. You are most happy and effective when you experience them all fully and in balance.

Consider the essential elements of your day. You rise, prepare, work, plan, worry, dream, train, love, and rest. While there is always a time for moderate and restrained behavior, of course, please understand that restraint is probably the most overrated of all alleged virtues.

Do you really want to change the world around you? Do you want to change yourself? I certainly hope you do. But you must recognize that medium anything lacks the power – the impulse – to do much changing. No one gives a shit about your beige life, your beige approach to training, your beige interpretation about what's possible. Instead, why not get a little crazy and search for the boundaries?

What does this look like? Well, it starts with training hard and turning the music up loud. Let a bit of healthy anger lift some of the load for you. If you need to improve something like your mobility, what good will a few minutes of aimless and uncommitted stretching activities do? When it's time to rest, rest as hard as you possibly can, and eat what you please when the week's work is done. And sure, if you're offered something that will send fizzy wave across your cerebral cortex, a tingle down your spine, and help you see this world differently, then do yourself a favor and say yes!

Simplicity allows you to see what it is that we must do and where we need to place our focus. From here, crazy wisdom informs us that we'll never really get anywhere unless we are truly prepared to search for those boundaries.

Find and embrace your own essential elements. Respect them. Trust them. Go to where you find the energy. Don't be afraid to indulge when the time is appropriate. And for Christsakes, nurture an outlook that values pushing for progression and improvement. That's my kind of philosophy.

MAGIC IN A COFFEE CUP

Our time is sometimes difficult, always finite and fleeting. Days come and go, dropping off the calendar at what seems to be an ever-accelerating pace. While nothing is really all that easy in this life, I think this is one of the hardest things.

Midnight and dawn both come far too early. I wish I could stretch the night out a few hours, pushing back bedtime while still managing to wake up sometime before the sunlight crawls up the bed and over my still jittering eyelids. I wish I had more time for dreams. I wish I could make the day feel long again.

The wishing part is of course useless. As the saying goes, "Wish in one hand and shit in the other. See which one fills up first." Indeed. I think I'll take action instead.

This may explain, at least in part, why I love coffee so much. It's a bit of an antidote to the runaway day. The obvious answer is that its stimulating, psychoactive properties give you the kick in the ass to rouse the body from slumber, or extend those precious creative energies well into the wee hours of the morning. For that reason, I'm highly reverent towards this particular drug, that white crystalline xanthine alkaloid known as caffeine. I'm also more and more respectful and cautious with it as I grow older, acknowledging that, yes, this is a drug as powerful as any other.

This is something folks tend to forget.

Did you realize that caffeine and cocaine, when dosed comparably, both pack a similar punch? Now, I don't think you should run out for a line of blow, but there's a clear lesson in this. Drugs are drugs, just as tools are tools. They have this broad capacity to hasten your destruction, cure what ails you, or open your mind wide open for the better.

The only thing more curious than the effects of the drugs themselves is how we judge their efficacy and legality. I feel the decision to partake is a personal one, but of course, there are plenty of authority figures who feel responsible for making that decision for you. Yes, to say it all out loud is to highlight the hypocrisy of drug laws. There are certainly many, many reasons for why these laws exist. However, using reason as a guide, almost none seem to have been drafted with your best interests or health in mind.

Go figure.

I've grown to hate politics, but if I'm ever crowned all-knowing, all-powerful king of the former United States of America, my first order of business will be the creation of laws that begin with the fair assumption that you're a grown, responsible individual who can imbibe what you want without hurting or disturbing anyone else. If you screw up, it's only then that I will have you tossed into one of my many government sanctioned torture pits where you will be continually exposed to a twenty-four hour looping stream of Taylor Swift interviews. Believe me, you'll be praying for a shorter day! Following reformation, you'll be condemned to a life pushing Advocare supplements upon those you love most in this world.

Consider yourself warned!

While it's a hell of a feeling to have your brain ripple with caffeinated waves during those peak morning hours, my love for coffee actually resides in the daily ritual. The real magic is in the preparation. It begins by coarsely grinding those freshly roasted, shiny, oily beans in a grinder. See, chopping is brutal and irregular, resulting in a brew that tastes just that way. Please, if you remember nothing else here, make sure to invest in the proper tools. "Hey, I like my coffee just the way it is, thank you very much!" That's fair, and as your King, I will not judge you. Just as I will not judge your taste in Budweiser or tiny Vienna sausages. Live and die on your own terms, friend.

For my cup, four level tablespoons of that fresh grind goes right into my trusty French press. I know there are fancier tools, but few can beat this one for the price. Over the top goes a very slow pour of hot water, which is just about one minute off the boil. A gentle stir, then the timer is set for four minutes. That time is not intended for multitasking. It's for paying attention to the way the room fills with that unique, life-affirming aroma. Pay attention to the way it makes you feel. When the brew is ready, give the grinds a gentle stir, then slowly push down the strainer and pour your proper cup. You're free to garnish as you see fit. That glorious drug kick will remain. But I tend to stick with a little shot of organic half and half most of the time. This, my friend, is sheer bliss.

Sip, smile and enjoy.

Are all of these steps really necessary? No. You can make a fair cup with a far less involved methodology. Could it be that I am guilty of coffee snobbery? Of course! But you will get no apology from me. I feel that way because I clearly see the value in the ritual. The repetition and rhythm of grinding, measuring, brewing and serving provide an opportunity for relative stillness and focus in the morning, or evening for the tweaking night owls amongst us. It's a few moments where you are not concerned with what comes next, or what must be done later in the day. You are just right there, in your kitchen, still. That is nothing more than meditation in action. That's how you make the day as long as you want. Or perhaps you like your busy day just the way it is. That's fine, but my guess is that you might also make a shitty cup of coffee.

Work on that.

Act strong.

You are what you practice.
So what is it that you're practicing?

The strong place priority on the barbell. That means the bulk of the work should be heavy repetitions of squats, pulls, and presses.

Should you also work on your conditioning? Of course! But you must remember your goal. You know, that question you answered at the beginning of your journey.

As you move along, check your progress against your plan. Are you getting results? If not, why? Are you trying to do too many other things? Are you eating enough? Are you running too much?

Remember, strong is as strong does. Focus on that short-term goal. The rest will take care of itself.

SELFISH

"Your vision will become clear only when you can look into your own heart. Who looks outside, dreams; who looks inside, awakes." – Carl Jung

There was a time when I wholly accepted my corner of the world without much doubt. I accepted that, yes, there was a high degree of correlation between complexity and value. I believed that fancy, novel things and strategies were distinct and attractive to me for a damn good reason! After all, if there was a better way this world would be shaped that way. But experience has taught me otherwise. It has taught me that my distinct corner of the world is just one small flavor of possibility. While the fancy can certainly yield results, like everything else it can come with a great cost. Why not default to a simpler path if you can get to the same place, or further, without feeling eternally troubled and dissatisfied? Why not try living in a world that doesn't generate so much noise in your mind? It's our choice.

I cannot help but be reminded of an old passage I came across some time ago. If I may paraphrase, it read, "Knowledge is the process of collecting ideas, while wisdom is more about letting go of a few." Well, I would say I'm far from wise, but I've learned enough in recent years to suspect this is perfectly true. If accumulation was really all that important, you would think we'd all be satisfied by now.

Yes, the simple and the small can actually be awesomely powerful and inspiring. They are unexpected, overlooked. They manifest below your radar, ascending to give you the biggest sort of surprise your primate mind can possibly process. I don't have to dig too deep into my memory to remind myself of this. In fact, I can just think back to yesterday.

The full weight of truth in that Thai fortune cookie has yet to settle down into me. The trick was clever. My wife took the previously sealed confection and carefully removed the wrapper at its seam. Next, she exchanged the tiny fortune scroll already in the cookie for a custom one she had typed up just a short time before. But listen, when my mind turns to food I basically shape shift into a man bear. In this state, the tiny details and imperfections of a fortune cookie wrapper are about as perceptible to me as the atoms comprising it. I was the perfect mark!

The toasted coconut cookie was delicious and crispy in all the best sorts of ways. There I was, satisfied, self-centered and otherwise oblivious to the rest of the room. "So, what's your fortune say?" my wife asked. "Oh shit, yeah." Just then I read the words aloud with that tiny movie narrator voice in my mind, "Let's see here...Thanks to you, baby number two is due! What kind of fortune is... Wait, what?"

If you're reading this then you're a friend. And as your friend, I can only hope you get a few of those fortune cookie moments in this life if you haven't already. It's these tiny things that really redefine everything and bring joy. But tinier and more powerful still is that sesame seed-sized clump of cells currently dividing away in my wife's tummy. The second, more powerful punch in the combo. Of what I can recall, there was the grand initial thump of the news...The proverbial "Oh shit, really? That's amazing!" moment. Consider this equal parts excitement and shock. To think, how blessed I am to be the father of two children? Years ago I would never have guessed how happy this would have made me. It's really quite dream-like. But that excitement – the wonder, the joy – it has to fade, just like any good high. And what replaces it is this powerful sense of worry and fear.

I desperately want to be the best father I can be. And like any good Dad that includes protecting, nurturing, teaching, and providing for my children. But I also worry that I'll fucking fail! ...That I won't be there for them, won't be able to keep them safe, and won't even be able to find the right words when I need them most. No, I cannot know the dangers my kids will face in the years to come, but I at least I can teach and prepare them!

I must say, I'm feeling the pressure of this responsibility. Where do I start? What if I do fuck up and leave out something intuitive and completely obvious!? I panic, then I reassure myself that everything is fine. It just takes a moment to remember that this situation is common and need not result in chronic panic. And that's when I felt this little shift. An idea. A word. It occurred to me that, amongst a host of other things, I should teach my kids to be selfish.

I know that sounds a bit odd. I've actually never really heard that word used in a positive way in my life! The Google definition can illustrate why: to be selfish is to lack consideration for others, being concerned only with one's own profit or pleasure. It doesn't sound like something one should teach. Maybe my third eye went a bit blind this time? But let's consider the idea a little deeper. Let's remind ourselves that even ideas and words we take for granted are not only as they seem.

I can close my eyes and easily draw up an intoxicating memory of my little boy Max playing intently and joyfully. At its peak, I would say he's actually being beautifully selfish, able to block out any undue external stimuli or influence that would otherwise distract him from this joy. It's enough to give me chill bumps from head to toe because that's the same exact state of being that I've only recently rekindled in my training. It's sacred. It's rejuvenating. And you have to fight to keep and protect it. With that picture perfect vision in my mind, I now choose to define selfishness as the act of immersing yourself so deeply into a pursuit, cause or aim that you can easily lose yourself in it for a while. In a world this busy, complex and ever-evolving, you have to choose to love these things. You have to say no to something else. That thing could be a career opportunity, a loved one, a host of expectations you're being held to, or maybe even a hurt. But I hope you would say no from time to time.

I know, it's so risky, so easy to get wrong. But starting now I will whisper to Max and the one in the belly that everything is fine. I will remind my children that their innocent self-seeking nature will grow to be a tool like any other, capable of both liberating them or crippling them, depending on their motive. So I'll teach them the best I can, with a full heart, what I've only recently learned for myself. Nothing in this world could be more important than pursuing a purpose that you recognize as a mighty one. It takes a healthy dose of selfishness to resist the influence of this bustling world and its gross stimuli, especially when you already know what it is that you love. Like with any cooling love affair, it takes healthy stubbornness to get up every day and maintain this pursuit – to keep faith with your inner voice. But you must because it is worth it. Even when it gets really hard it's worth it.

The more I think this all over, the more I think I might be just fine. I'll take comfort in the uncertainty. Little boys are unique, but at the very least we will have all we need. I've been down that road once already. But what if it's a little girl? Christ, I cannot be sure of my reaction. I'll do my best to remain steady. After a few deep breaths, I realize that she will be protected and provided for. I won't fail her. But that right there is the problem! After all this, here I am, already wrapped tightly around her precious little finger.

NIGHT & DAY

"We never live; we are always in the expectation
of living." – Voltaire

The morning is a beautiful and serene time of day, but it's not for everyone. Like anyone I love to watch the occasional sunrise, but I don't find the scene any more inspiring, rejuvenating or productive than the average sunset. If anything, playing the event out in reverse might be more interesting. But to each their own, right? Right... until you run into an overzealous early bird who loves to brag about their schedule.

A saying comes to mind: lose an hour in the morning and you'll spend the rest of the day hunting for it. I'm not sure I agree with that. In fact, I might counter by saying there's nothing sillier than boasting about something that comes naturally. Lost hours, eh? Tell me, do you also brag about having the bedtime of my toddler son or ninety-six-year-old grandmother? Do you spend your free time shitting your pants and clipping coupons too?

Relax, it's just a joke.

Your ideal dawn is just a reflection of my late night. Both represent solitude, tranquility, peace and quite, and sure, heightened productivity. It's a time for getting to know yourself better, away from the hum and buzz of the awakened world. Both are beautiful, although it's far easier to justify a stiff cocktail or two if you're working the third shift.

That's the only perk that I need. You really should

try sipping booze under brilliant moonlight. It's just the sort of thing you need when you're feeling a bit heavy and paralyzed from all the hustle and bustle.

I don't want to over-sell anything here. Where there are perks, there will be plenty of downsides. As a night owl, I'm the first to admit as much. For instance, I struggle most days to assimilate into a world that's anchored to a rigid nine-to-five flow. I feel the daily pressure to comply. As I rush along, carrying this mounting pressure, I do my best to draw upon the young, tender, more enlightened aspects of my personality. What pressure? Chris, the coffee will get made, don't worry. No one will notice the wrinkled left pants leg. And those lost keys? They will show up just in time, I'm sure. Can you see that the fuss is unnecessary?

I try my best to hold onto that vibe as my wife starts with the jokes. "Oh, you can't find your keys? Why am I not surprised?" I smile, responding that such talk could be grounds for a spanking. I keep smiling, as I recall my father barking something similar years ago. "Hey, did you find those keys yet?... Finally. You know if it was a snake it would have bitten you!"

I have no retort to these accusations, mostly because they are absolutely true! I do need to do a better job of getting along with my world. I need to notice, utilize, and appreciate all that's within my reach. I must pay closer attention, as we all should. As we look for our keys – in this case figuratively – we need to remember that things are not always where you expect them to be, when you expect them to be there. Maybe the finding part of life would be far easier if we weren't so fucking busy looking around all the time! ...Maybe.

That's a pretty meaty lesson to chew on, but let's cut through the shit, OK? We all hear this, we shake our heads in agreement, we feel motivated, but then we slip right back into that bullshit habit of rushing around and focusing on the wrong things. After all, that's the thing about habits and routine. We build big complex lives around what suits us best – the hours we keep, our pursuits, our beliefs, and the Facebook wall wisdom we try and share with the world. But we're all still so busy looking and generating more hum. We can't help it.

We'll lose the lesson again, right under our noses, we'll lose it again.

Consider this the moment where a brand new cliché is born! Here's something new that we all can acknowledge but never really act on. Let's put it on the shelf right next to those other old gems, like "More will not make you happy" and "Only time will tell." That's a real shame because this is the sort of thing we really should act on. We should strip away our insensitivity. So, let's act! Let's take away the sugar coating and get a little more to the point. Perhaps a punchier, more honest shade of truth will set the hook a little deeper here.

On a recent, glorious late night ramble through the Internet, I ventured deep into the belly of YouTube. This is one of my favorite things to do. You start off with just what you wanted to watch, but then you soon find yourself presented with all these suggested links. Some are complete shit, of course, but others are little worm-holes that take you to unknown genres, cultures, styles, and topics that you otherwise would have never found. On this night, my starting point was this great concert video of Queens of the Stone Age performing live at Lollapalooza. Once that jam concluded, and I was left wanting more, I was pointed towards this little show called Guitar Moves, on which Josh Homme, frontman for Queens of the Stone Age, was the special guest. Now, I know almost nothing about playing guitar, but that hardly seemed to matter. I was as happy as a pig in shit for those ten minutes or so. Go figure.

Right at the end of the video, the host asked Josh a simple question. "What are you going to tell a ten year old who wants to play guitar? ...Something they can really take with them and use."

"To me that's easy." Josh replied, quickly. "When you expect anything from music, you expect too much. You play for yourself, you play to enjoy it, and you make the most of it for you, period." After expressing some genuine amazement that making music was actually his job, Josh concluded, "I know I'm not the best guitar player in the world, but I just love it...I honestly think that's enough."

And that's just it...it is enough. We are fine just as we are. We don't need to look far and wide for obvious answers to these everyday questions. We don't have to mold ourselves into something we're not. You should honor what you love and enjoy, and you should pursue it at a time of day that works for you. Who gives a shit what anyone else thinks about it? Sure, you can try the alternative, but it doesn't work for very long. Your soul will eat right through itself. Before long you'll be effectively dead, chained to a life where you seek only anesthetic for the pain, unable to see opportunities to fully live and express yourself.

I wouldn't hide my fear from you. I've felt that feeling, and it's terrifying. It tends to linger and haunt you even when you've done your best to wash it away. I want the gap between me and it to widen, so I'll paddle away from it as hard as I can. The words will remind me why.

Don't fight yourself. Let the day unfold as it needs to, as it will anyway. The coffee will get made. You'll find what's lost if you stop looking so hard for just a few seconds. And yes, the world will keep on not giving two shits about those pants of yours! Do try to act accordingly.

That's liberating, but remember that liberation is not permanent. It's not enough. One decision doesn't make you free forever. The chains will start to crawl right back up your legs just about as soon as you cast them off. And the catch? It's your wildly selfish, spoiled expectations that are pulling them back up. It's true, but this choice is yours. You could act out of fear, desire and expectation. You could allow yourself to grow frustrated in this little world where your path is muddy, and the rewards are not coming fast enough for your taste. But you don't have to. Instead, you could try and remember why you ever picked up this instrument to begin with.

Remember to play out of love first and you won't need the expectations.

I don't want to keep forgetting, so let me put this new cliché some place safe, where I'm sure to find it the next time I'm feeling the pressure. Maybe I'll stick the note right under that key-chain holder by the door. I'm sure I won't miss it there, right?

Abide.

There's what we want, then there's the way things are.

It would be great to have an abundance of resources to devote to training, but that's just not always possible.

However, let me assure you, you can be strong with kids, a career, limited equipment, injury, or wear.

You don't need to struggle to get there.

You just need to put these limitations down on paper. Accept them. Plan accordingly. Do only what you can! That's all that's necessary.

That is a very simple solution, but you'd be surprised at how many people struggle against circumstance.

All we need is simple.

EVERYTHING IS UNDER CONTROL

"I'm selfish, impatient, and a little insecure. I make mistakes, I'm out of control, and at times hard to handle. But if you can't handle me at my worst, then you sure as hell don't deserve me at my best."
– Marilyn Monroe

Losing control seems to be the scariest possible thing. Despite all of the effort, planning and absolute best of intentions, sometimes all you have to show for it is worry and doubt. I think the question then becomes, so, what now?

I think two scenarios are likely. First, the disappointment will feel quite crushing and demotivating for many. They will insist that they took their best shot, but things just didn't work out. By default, they will then shuffle down the path of least resistance.
That's a goddamn shame, man.

So, what's that other potential outcome? Well, those that remain will be boiling over with piss and vinegar. They will remain in the fight. They will gnash their bloody teeth, they will arch their backs, and fists will clench once again. Sure, it would be easier to roll over, especially after a few rounds of getting your literal or figurative face smashed in by someone with heavy hands. But they don't. They pursue and struggle until there are no more shots to take.

That's impressive, and a quality that is so priceless later in life. But still, we might have our best chance at success if we refine this gameness.

The force we're up against here shares a key physical quality with water. The harder you slam into it, the harder it slams back – an equal and opposite force. It's a humbling experience to go through such a fight, but like most things that cause frustration and pain, the outcome is usually far better than we expect. Actually, it could very well all be for the best.

I know my tendencies. Like most humans, learning to delay gratification is perhaps the hardest lesson I've tried to learn. My default setting is to expect learning, adaptation and progress on my own timetable as if the flesh was listening to my conscious wishes. I came up with the fucking plan. I worked really hard to figure it all out, identifying and considering all the known variables. So where is the result?

I think that perspective is driven by our awareness that life and the world all around are big and complicated, but also finite. From that place, the very next step takes you right towards a full-on zero-sum perspective where everything is governed by a ticking game clock.

It's now or never, unless it's not.

Maybe I can blame some of this conditioning on my still smoldering grade-school hangover. Do you remember any of those trips to the guidance counselor's office? Do you remember the multitude of framed, clichéd quotes hung across that office wall?

Carpe diem, baby.

I want to be careful not to disregard or downgrade the value of the daily fight. Between us friends, I hope you never unclench your fists! The world needs you, dear reader, to stand up and answer the bell. Keep your piss and vinegar on the boil! But, please remember something. At all times, you remain in control.

That last line certainly doesn't feel all that true during the day to day grind. The physical world around you, including the laws that govern its inhabitants, will never bend in the direction of your desire. Still, you control your response. With that knowledge, does it make sense to burn priceless time rolling around on the floor in a fit? No. We must put our effort into constructive action.

I'm sure your life will get really heavy from time to time, but most of your days are going to be more like sparring matches. This is simply training for the main events sure to come later on down the line. It's practice...a game. It would do us good to think and act in those terms.

The seemingly insurmountable push-back, as lame as it may be, actually serves to train you. It helps you become whoever it is you might be one day. So, why be so fussy about it? You are not a toddler being told no. Rather, you are right where you need to be, doing what you should, perhaps not getting the results you want, better still, you're getting the results you need.

When I feel that familiar burn begin to settle into my flesh and bones, I remind myself that there's no need to fight with full force right now. As the Buddha taught, "the wise control their body, control their tongue, and control their mind." No, I won't bullshit you. Control in this case is incredibly challenging. You're right to feel the full weight of that struggle. After all, this is no easy task. But luckily for us the actual result doesn't matter as much right now. Rather, what does matter is the intent. The more often you fight for proper perspective and measured reservation, the more often you'll achieve it. I assure you, that's something worth fighting for.

THIS WILL ONLY HURT A LITTLE WHILE

"Reject your sense of injury and the injury itself disappears." – Marcus Aurelius

I've been injured badly and debilitated once in my life. I'm lucky. This history is marked by silly mistakes and frequent close calls. I also carry around all of this baggage, which is filling year by year with wear and tear.

The singular incident in question occurred about thirteen years ago, the last day of my collegiate athletic career.

During winter breaks, all of our time outside of the classroom was devoted to lifting heavy things and eating all the food we could find. Our mission was clear and well defined – we needed to put on a thick winter coat of fresh muscle mass that would last us straight through the months ahead. No barbell or buffet could be left unturned!

This is just the kind of thing you would expect from a group of young, ascending, excitable meatheads. And it's all true. Our only real concern was getting to the gym on time. Of course, that perspective and motive is naive, but what else would you expect from college-aged kids? Still, there was also a clear, well-reasoned strategy in play here. Some twelve weeks of high-volume spring training sessions are more than enough to wear you down. The surplus was simply our strength reserve. The true motive was inconsequential.

But that's just the thing about motives. Once an action goes from your brain out into the world, it's no longer bound to you. Let's agree that this much is true and obvious. Out there it mixes with everything to create something beautiful and new, something with its own effect. Who knows, maybe it will return to you years later as a key lesson during the time of the great Miley Cyrus chicken-ass scandal of 2013.

Yes, we were all painfully unaware and uncouth, but at least we recognized that strength was critically important to the outcome. I guess that's why I was trying so hard when things went wrong.

The close of winter break was just a few weeks away, and I wanted to finish on a high note. For a few months, I had really been working hard to improve my pulling strength, focusing primarily on partial range of motion movements. My reasoning was that more was better. I could lift more with the barbell elevated, so it had to be a good thing, right? Well, I suppose it was initially, but the shine wears off quickly when you're talking about unnecessarily heavy barbells. I was about to be taught that more is not always better.

I was getting stronger and stronger by the week, which was a very good thing. But I wanted a bit more, one final record.

The load was really more than I could lift, even under the best conditions. I can see that now! As with most challenges we face, the better path is crystal clear in hindsight. It comes after the pain, after you've replayed the mistake a few hundred times in your head.

I approached the load with a bad attitude, fueled by vacuous turn-of-the-century Nu Metal blaring from the weight room speakers. I set my grip and pulled with everything I had, at the expense of my spine, at the expense of my future as an athlete. The weight shifted, then elevated towards my belly. While the record was within reach, there was a slight cramp, then a bursting sensation in my back that washed everything from my mind. I could not breath. I could no longer stand. I was a scared kid.

It is amazing how quickly pain and fear cut right through posturing and tough guy demeanor. This is largely why I've abandoned such behavior in my own life. It's the kind of thing that growls loudly, but packs neither tooth nor claw. It will abandon you when you need it most, leaving you terrified and feeling cold on bended knee. The path towards real strength starts with a smile, of course.

Nothing can disarm that kind of pain, at least acutely. If you are pushing your body hard and experimenting to find the absolute best path, then there's a high probability that you will face injury at some point. A real injury. Being open, patient and measured will certainly limit your risk, but still, nothing is promised. Sometimes we suffer. That said, you can be prepared for everything that comes after the pain. This much I can promise.

Lots of different emotions flooded my mind as the pain from that burst disc began to subside. At first I felt disappointed, maybe angry. OK, I was quite angry. "I don't deserve this! What about my plans? My goals? What will I do? What should I do?" Those questions sound absolutely silly to me now. While I have no real memory of what I wanted exactly, it likely didn't stretch far beyond next football season. But then I started to feel different. I started to see the value in this injury.

That tidal wave of acute pain washed away everything I had built over the previous five years or so. Every edifice was revealed as a hollow, shaky structure that really wasn't worth rebuilding. The bare ground itself was the truth. I could now admit that I didn't want to be a collegiate athlete anymore! The problem is that it was always a decision I was afraid to face on my own. There were all of these expectations from friends, family, and coaches. I felt trapped.

The injury wasn't random. It wasn't misfortune. Rather, it was inevitable. It was a consequence. It liberated me from a path I couldn't leave on my own. It was there to show me just how out of touch I was with my own body, how reckless I had been, and how empty my motives actually were. We always treat injury as the scapegoat, right? But the truth is that I was already debilitated. I was already injured and in pain.

Injuries come in all sizes and flavors. Some are quite obviously worse than others. But they all have a primary side-effect. They cause us to ask the same questions. "What about my plans? My goals?"

I think I have an answer for you.

Would you ever guess that injury and writing are a lot alike? Yes, both involve fair amounts of pain and suffering, but what else is there? Would you guess that both only take shape outside the mind? I think that's true. My injury is actually no different than the story itself on this page. The former only exists now as memory. I can draw out the emotion, pain, frustration and even the eventual sense of liberation. That all appears bright and clear to me now, even after thirteen years. But it all remains in my mind, in stasis, idealized and unprocessed. If I could just download that onto the page, right? No, that's wrong. It's not that simple. Sure, you can download a song, just as an example. But coming to terms with your unique story and complex history is actually more like writing the lyrics and composing the music yourself. That's something else entirely.

Here at the keyboard, I can lay down these words verbatim as I imagine them, but my memory is far from perfect. Everything comes incomplete, out of order, and in abstract form. But there on the page it mixes with my current world, my new experience, resulting in something previously unknown. Something brand new and burden free. That's the moment where the story becomes real.

I know it sucks to feel pain and have your best plans crumble in front of you, but you need to understand that these plans aren't all that real. They are just ideas, memories, biases and assumptions sitting firmly between your ears. Sometimes it works out, but it's OK if it doesn't.

Your story will still take shape. The pain will pass. In its wake, you might be left with something better, something new.

TIDE IN, TIDE OUT

There sits Forrest Gump, patiently waiting on his bus, warmly and honestly sharing a truly amazing story with anyone who happens to sit down. Of course, not everyone appreciates what he has to say. Such is life I suppose.

The tale is similar to what we all face between sun-up and sun-down, albeit on an amplified, cinematic scale. It's a series of glorious highs and wounding low points. There it is again, the defining, inexorable ebb and flow that defines all aspects of our lives, from work, to training, to relationships, everything.

Forrest's take on things is as pure and wise as any philosophy or academic theory I've ever encountered. In the face of it all, he replies that life is similar to a box full of chocolates. There's no assurance of what one will get.

I love that scene for two clear reasons. First, no, you never know what you're going to get. Some days are filled with fudge truffles and salty caramel, while others seem like nothing but dark chocolate covered orange cream.

Fucking disgusting!

Second, the story is powerful because of its extreme simplicity. It's powerful enough to displace any convoluted philosophical take on the subject you might otherwise entertain.

This is Occam's Razor in action, ladies and gentlemen. That's your first sign that this is a sure keeper. Among competing hypotheses and explanations, it's foolish to choose the complicated answer. Make as few assumptions as possible, always.

The top layer of the lesson is the obvious bit. No, you can never be sure of what the tide will bring in from day to day. Life will always be turbulent. That quality can work with you and against you, but it's your job to show up with a smile on your face and do the best fucking job you can. That's what makes you a decent human being. But there's a second, less obvious and really intuitive layer underneath. Let's scratch a little deeper.

I actually just learned that Forrest's famous line was inspired by the book *Norwegian Wood*, by Haruki Murakami. Well, this is what the Internet tells me at least. I trust Google would never purposefully lead me astray.

The original prose goes further. In reference to this illustrative chocolate box, a character states, "you know, they've got these chocolate assortments, and you like some, but you don't like others, right? Don't you eat all the ones you don't like as much? I always think about that when something painful comes up. Now just polish this off and everything will be OK."

If I may paraphrase a bit, is it so bad that there are a few less than perfect chocolates in that box? Isn't it true that one person's disgusting is another's bliss? Would it be beneficial, Chris, for you to just shut the fuck up and give this particular confection a fresh chance? It's not like you're turning big rocks into small stones at a North Korean prison camp. Lighten up!

I believe that kind of attitude can change your life.

Let me lay myself out there for your benefit. I work, cook, clean, read, write, train, love, etc., all on a daily basis. The common element between all of those wildly varying things is this predictable cycle of ups and downs. Things barely go at first. There's this inertia that I have to force myself through.

But once I do get moving things start to go pretty well most of the time.

I feel at my happiest knowing I'm creating good things and helping the situation, not adding to the burden. But after a short time, I start to lose my momentum. The inertia bites back and I feel that familiar resistance setting in. I get bummed. I doubt myself and what it is I'm trying to do. The world goes gray around me. But here's where that beautiful attitude comes into play.

While there will always be struggle, without fail the cycle will repeat. The good times always return. This knowledge strips all the power from those gray times.

You don't know what life will bring, but if you keep moving you can be sure that something beautiful, righteous, and worthy will come back around. You just cannot afford to be the asshole who lets the bad times stop you. Keep stepping. Lean forward.

Here's my challenge. The next time that the cycle dips down (and it will over and over again) separate yourself from the predictable emotions. You know this is coming. The pain is familiar. Isn't that enough to disarm the alarm? Can't you let go of your predictable response?

I think you can.

Don't avoid the bitter, fruit-filled bits. Just

polish off those chocolates as soon as you can, and enjoy the wild, sweet ride ahead. Everything will be fine. There's plenty of salty caramel ahead, trust me.

GIVE THE MONKEY WHAT IT WANTS

"Mud-pies gratify one of our first and best instincts. So long as we are dirty, we are pure."
– Charles Dudley Warner

"Fuck."

That's the only thing to say when you shake your stupor at 11:30 a.m.

Splash some warm water on that face. Wipe away the moisture with a clean, dry towel. Peer deep into the steamy bathroom mirror with blood-shot, tequila-pickled eyes, then ask, "Who am I?"

This is the moment where cliché meets the crossroads, friends. Or if you prefer the pop-culture terminology, this is when shit gets real.

That's the question to ask if you are a higher primate cursed with a neural cortex. Consider this to be a primary side-effect of all that abundant gray matter horsepower. We worry about shit! The job we might never land. The girl who'll probably just say no. The missing passion. Those less than sexy ass-dimples you find embarrassing.

Baby, the dimples are fine. Don't listen to anyone who tells you otherwise.

I spend plenty of time struggling with questions, but luckily I have a pretty good idea of what I am and why I'm here. I love creating things and sharing ideas, so shockingly I try to place just about all of my poker life-chips on these bets. I do my best to define my life on these terms. That said, I do a much worse job at controlling my impulses.

I'm quick to laugh loudly, to smile, to roar at trolls, to counter, or to interrupt. I rise quickly to meet any challenge, regardless of imposition, but I'm easily wounded by unexpected attacks, especially from friends or loved ones. I also have no patience for medium. If I need rest, I try to be as lazy as possible. When it's time to work, I burn the candle from every end. And when it's time to imbibe and consume, fuck, I'll take a double!

Fancy cortex or not, I'm a primate. I've accepted this, and I recommend you do the same. If nothing else, you'll feel a whole lot better about things when you cut yourself some slack. Also, once you accept this truth, you can start to put together a plan for keeping the more primal portions of your tinkered mind pacified.

We should start with some science.

Delayed gratification is a well-developed area of study in the psychology literature. I suppose the most famous work in this area is the seminal Stanford marshmallow experiment. Here, young children were presented with a single marshmallow and two options. First, at any time they could ring a small bell, summon the experimenter, and have their sugary reward. Or, second, the children could choose to wait for fifteen minutes (which sure seems more like an eternity to a hungry four-year-old), at which point the experimenter would come back and double the reward.

This is such a simple, yet powerful and illuminating study design. But the really fascinating bit is this – those same kids were assessed years later as teenagers and young adults. Surprisingly, the children who demonstrated the capacity to delay their marshmallow reward also demonstrated improved academic success, physical and psychological health, and social competence. Outside of love and affection, it could very well be that this capacity for waiting is one of the single biggest predictors of success in life.

More fascinating still, there are countless studies that point to similar capabilities in a wide array of primate species. The lesson is clear. Discipline is a good thing. I try to keep this truth in mind during the week as I prep *paleo* meals and do my damnedest to pour just one finger of liquor. Even then there's the sweet tooth to contend with. "Fuck, Chris, if a Capuchin monkey can learn to say no to those Pepperidge Farm pumpkin cream-cheese cookies, then why can't you?"

This is another good question, one I'm not prepared to answer during the month of October.

Scientific evidence and observable, testable, reproducible truth make up one side of our coin here, friends. But the other balancing force is our personal experience. This is vital, and anyone who disagrees with that can simply fuck off. We have no time for being unreasonable. The great clock in the sky is ticking away, after all. If we want something to happen, we act. When that action doesn't yield the desired outcome, we act differently. Who gives a shit what the evidence has to say. You keep flipping that coin to find your path. So, let's flip it now and answer that other great question. Why should we indulge?

If you don't mind, I'll close this particular story out with another monkey example. Picture yourself on a pristine Caribbean beach. The water is crystal clear. The weather is perfect. The waiter keeps bringing you those dangerous Mango Daiquiris. In a scenario like this, things can't get much better.

Well, aside from the pests.

You look over your shoulder and notice a small pack of alcohol and sugar dependent monkeys gathering at the tree line. They know what you've got, and you know they want it. What's the smart play here? Should you teach them some discipline, shouting and beating them back as they encroach upon your beach towel? Sure, you can give this a try. You might even find some success initially. But then you get complacent. You let down your guard once that waiter comes back out with the coconut shrimp. As soon as you walk away those little furry bastards are going to get what they came for, discipline be damned.

Don't be afraid to admit what you are. Embrace it, baby. Keep it under control. Give the monkey what it wants.

CORRUPT

"Corruption is a hobby of mine." – Josh Homme

It really is all about balance, baby. Yeah, call it that ying-yang thing.

For years I thought that common symbol was little more than boring computer clip art designed for tacky Lisa Frank 1990s era grade-school trapper keepers. Consult Google if you don't remember. Yes, you loved this shit, so bite down hard on the shame!

The truth is that this symbol, this idea, has been crafted, refined, and painstakingly considered over thousands of years. A minimal, perfect explanation for this dualistic world that is simply electrified with good, evil, joy, pain, boredom, exhilaration and every possible emotion in between. Call it a pulsing hive of energy.

The perfectly suitable definition from Wikipedia states that "ying-yang describes how seemingly opposite or contrary forces are interconnected and interdependent in the natural world, and how they give rise to each other."

I know that particular truth sucks harder than an angry Jillian Michaels anti-toxin enema cleanse, but this is the way it has to be! Struggle gives rise to satisfaction. Toil gives rise to skill. Pain gives rise to euphoria. And my personal favorite, fuck-ups give rise to true wisdom.

Lots of fuck-ups, baby. That's the key bit. That's how you get to where you're going quicker. Just be willing to take some notes along the way, you know?

Let's drill a little deeper. Why is meditation and the acquisition of mindfulness such a good thing? Yes, it's a powerful means of reducing our frustration, craving and self-imposed suffering. Further, the practice fosters enduring happiness. If you ask me, that sort of training is just as important as any other. I hope you would agree with me.

Here's the thing. I can calm down, but I cannot change my hard-wiring. I'm bubbling over with piss and vinegar. I can't be satisfied with the prospect of finding my Nirvana (the state of consciousness and/or the classic albums) only to crawl off and fold into the corner of a hermitage for the rest of my life chanting fucking mantras. I'm sorry, but that's just not my kind of thing. But I do find it beautiful. It's worth observing. But I have to abide by the energy that my meditation practice gives rise to! With all the random thoughts drawn away, all that's left are the interesting bits. That's the stuff that inspires me and boils my passions. And no, I can't forget about all those sacred little molecules and compounds that add layers of shiny polish to life.

You name your drug, baby – caffeine, alcohol, little chocolate donuts, puppy-dog farts, what-have-you. Regardless, my thesis is that you should set aside time to savor every second of it. Notice how thoroughly enjoying your vices is about the most natural thing you can do right now at this late hour, and how they only give rise to a deeper, more informed level of mindfulness.

OK, I know that sounded like some guru bullshit! Let me rephrase the thing.

You can't fully appreciate a good time until you've learned to sit still in a quiet room, happy and content in your own company. That said, I wouldn't wish that on any of my enemies as a permanent state of mind. No, I believe you go back out into the world with a focused, disciplined view so you can imbibe harder, immersing yourself fully, and wisely, and responsibly, and learning more in the process than you ever imagined.

Yeah, that's powerful shit. I've got tingles all over.

I know that there are many kind, good people out there that would really disagree with me. After all, they walk with really straight spines, avoiding sugar, caffeine, and all drugs, either hard or soft. Their tongues never grow salty, and no, of course they don't watch porn! What are you, some kind of deviant, sex-crazed weirdo?

Hey, let's not call each other names. I respect where you're coming from, really, I do. And for Christsakes, I can appreciate the dedication! But I can't help but let you know, it's very likely that your dinner party stories are painfully boring. Also, I would guess you suffer from stiff hips, which, incidentally, makes you both a terrible dancer and a really disappointing lay. How close is that?

No offense intended. Also, you do not have to be this way forever, friend. Trust me. Have a beer. I promise to take things slowly.

Do you know why I talk about vice so much? Yes, the notion seems a bit out of step with mindfulness, compassion, discipline, and all that. But of course that's just how it seems at first. That's just the conditioning, the training, your bright-pink Lisa Michaels bad-LSD-trip-inspired perspective.

The truth is really simple. I want to see you be still, be kind, have a good time, and to keep the proper perspective, rain or shine. That's a righteous thing if I've ever seen it. But let me be crystal clear. I'm not here to motivate you. I don't want to give any bullshit pep-talks and pose. What I really want to do is corrupt you!

I want you to strut hard with a smile, train wisely, eat well, slam tequila, dish out high fives, seek out that sacramental buzz, and shit, most importantly baby, I want you to keep smiling when things go sour. They're never sour long, anyway.

Yeah, that's the sort of vibe that can really spread around. Seems like a worthy mission to me.

Getting really strong is all about lifting heavy weights and managing the resulting fatigue.

Manage it better, you'll get stronger.

A great technique is to rotate exercises based on the part of the body they target most. For example, a partial deadlift will really fatigue the lower back. You should only do such a movement once a month or so. However, if you change the type of pull, you can lift heavy again the very next week.

In this case, you could deadlift a heavy barbell with a wide grip and straight legs to shift the burden onto the hamstrings.

This sort of complimentary rotation is the key to making strength gains quickly, and keeping the fatigue really low.

That's a good thing.

WHERE YOU COME FROM

Every perspective is shaped by personal history.

Here's a bit of mine.

Deep in thought, Memphis, TN, 1983

Teenage log work

Sexy

975 lbs.

Halloween, nailed

Just weeks before deciding to loose over 100 lbs.

Where Barbell Shrugged began

Skinny

The moment I learned I really was more of a lover

Return to strongman

Return to fundamentals

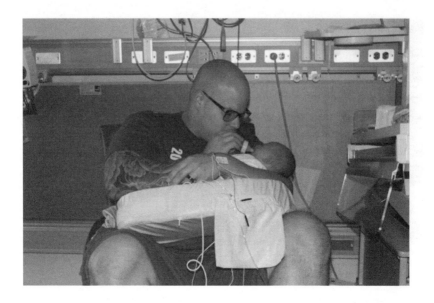

The day my mind was blown

The very first show

Chatting before the show

Unscared donut stare-down with the champ

Homies

All of my reasons

Never be afraid to try something new. Even if it's on the Internet forever.

Set and setting

SET AND SETTING:
IT'S ALL ABOUT THE
WHERE AND HOW, BABY

COMPANY KEPT

"The key is to keep company with people who uplift you, whose presence calls forth your best." – Epictetus

Science was always my favorite subject in school, especially Biology. The subject came naturally. It was engaging. And in contrast to some of the other imposed, seemingly useless courses, this stuff seemed to carry a real purpose.

The scientific method gave you a set of tools that allowed you to go out and test the world all around – to answer all kinds of impactful questions. I've always found that to be amazing.

But if I'm honest, I'll admit that I don't actually remember very many specifics from all those years of study. This is stuff I just don't use day to day. Not that it really matters all that much. After all, it's not what you think that's important, but rather how you think.

I'd like to consider that an original quote, but I'm quite sure this has been turned over the tongue, in some form, countless times before. But there is one exception! It's a little theory that I repeated under my breath many days during seventh grade physical science class. Osmosis – the tendency of water to pass from a low concentration solution to an area of high concentration. I got it. The lesson of balance made perfect sense and stuck with me through the years. And what's more, beyond the classroom I've observed this effect play out many times, albeit from a much higher, metaphorical view.

Let's consider the barbell.

For the last year and a half, I've trained exclusively on my own. No training partners. No coach. Nobody around at all. In many ways, this has been absolutely fantastic – a break after two decades of immersion into hyper-competitive, continuous dick-measuring climates. It's this isolation that reveals training to be a true craft as virtuous as any other. That said, this path is not optimal if the goal is top-shelf performance. As virtuous as it might be, optimal training requires a large, enabling social influence.

The best example I can think of involves a recent training session in my home gym. A few close friends joined me for a speed squat session, which was an amazing experience. After a quick warm-up, we turned some Queens of the Stone Age up loud and attacked the squats in a rapid-fire flight. I happened to be the strongest squatter in the group, which I'm sure would be impressive in some other training circles. But not here. I could feel the heat as Mike fought to match me pound for pound, set after set, at close to a hundred pounds lighter bodyweight! This came as a bit of a surprise. What else could I do but rouse myself and fight for separation?

This cycle repeated for some eight sets, with the distance remaining pretty close. All the while, CTP, completely new to this particular movement, is motivated to improve rapidly so he can join in the fight soon. The utility is obvious. This is the sort of climate that is essential if you want to maximize your performance. It's the only place where you can experience this very real flow of energy from that area of low concentration right to your body. I'd wager that effect cannot be replicated on your own.

The weak should be bold and chase the strong, nipping at the heels while the strong fight desperately to preserve their ego and position. Everybody can improve in that sort of environment, all at the same time. However, everyone has to buy in, contributing their share of the energy. If not, nothing can be optimal. There will just be this high concentration point pulling energy away from the group until everyone is on the same mediocre, bullshit level.

If you want to make the most of this time, this space, then you'll have to engage with people who are prepared to fight for every single pound, round after round. You'll also need to confront and potentially step away from those who are not prepared to grow and flow with you. That same energy extends far outside the gym, although perhaps with a bit less of the dick-measuring.

I hope you find yourself surrounded by a group of really smart, trusted, hardworking friends. Treasure that. The sort of people who engage with you frequently, who continuously seek out opportunities to learn and share information, and who are never afraid to admit when they are wrong, are such an asset. These are the folks that keep the energy flowing in your group. They provide the impulse you need to reach your potential. And just as in training, if you find yourself befriended by an energy leech, you should do all you can to pull free now, or else you might be drained and in retreat to the garage in no time.

I would bet we all have at least one of these relationships that we could, or should step away from.

But for whatever the reasons, good or bad, this is not an easy thing to do.

There's a paradoxical truth in training. When it comes to reaching your potential, an immaculately constructed program is certainly a very great thing. However, a rough, simple program injected with a large dose of piss and vinegar will always yield better results. That willingness to fight for a better version of yourself is what's most important. It's vital.

Amongst great friends, you don't have to worry about being the smartest, most capable guy in the room. If you're up to the challenge, you'll step your game up and reach that balance point in time. And if you are not getting the results you want – if you feel as thought you're on the wrong path – then I think you should stop and reassess your climate. Take a look around and spot the influence. And please, keep this in mind. They say you are the company you keep, so who is it you're hanging out with?

BRIGHT FLOWERS, HEAVY BARBELLS

"There were fifteen years from the knowing to the doing."
– Peace Pilgrim

That particular quote sums up my experience exactly. Only for me, the journey has been more like ten years. That's how long it has been since I graduated college. That was the moment I was rubber stamped and officially labeled as, supposedly, a very knowledgeable person.

I'm sure I behaved accordingly.

A decade on now, I can see that I was still just a fawn on fresh, wiggly legs. I had never really been out in the world on my own, fending for myself, navigating the waters without guidance. I held nothing unique or impressive between my ears, only a few naive beliefs and memorized test answers mostly. I did not understand my own emotions and motives at all. Yes, there was a giant, obvious, critical gap between the knowing and the doing.

To think that it has taken me over ten years just to get comfortable with who I am and what I know, and to be able to communicate that to others honestly and with my own voice. Whenever you find yourself feeling discouraged, just remember that this cannot be rushed. It takes time to bloom and make sense of it all. To move beyond only knowing.

Like most folks fresh from the mold, my primary limitation was that I could only repeat the things that I had learned. I had no ability to critically assess and challenge that information. I could not draw out the important themes, contrasting against my own experience and developing the ideas further. Maybe that's because I had no real experience!

It took some time to realize my academic existence was only an incubation period. That rubber stamp at graduation was actually not a certification of knowledge. No, it's nothing more than a gesture of approval. The start of the real journey. From this place, you have to go out and earn that experience.

Maybe it's time that universities and colleges started to be a little more honest with what it is they're actually selling. What do you think? It would go a long way towards managing expectations. That in and of itself is part of our problem. We've been taught that if you follow the syllabus and do as you should, then the desired result will follow. We might be underdeveloped, underexposed and uncured, but our expectations are grand! We view the life unfolding ahead of us as something we can capture in a cook book. Follow the recipe and you can find the sure career path towards the American Dream, or the next great diet, or the training program that will finally deliver the body and performance you deserve.

Here's the upside to this problem. Regardless of the inevitable frustration and pain, the fog will begin to lift in time. For me, I think I noticed the sun growing brighter with every new book I read, every fresh page that was written, and every heavy barbell that I lifted. These are the daily tools that honed my edge, helping me to draw in the boundaries of my gap.

Recipes, programs, and strict ideologies only serve to strip away your options and provide a false sense of assurance. Some people prefer that, as it keeps them from having to deal with complexity and excess choice. I don't think that's always a bad thing, mind you. Sometimes you need a break from all the details and planning. Sometimes you just need for someone else to fight on your behalf for a while. That said, any program of any kind is going to have its limitations. For all they might contribute, they are still just recipes. They are instructions written down on paper. They are only knowledge. To get the most out of the doing, we need some depth.

Sooner or later you will realize that variables, numbers, plans and all manner of memorized facts don't mean shit on their own. They only represent the highest level view. The effect remains in the doing. I'll illustrate that point with flowers. Yes, flowers! You can admire a brilliant red rose during a nice garden stroll (at least you should). But what's amazing is just how little of that rose you actually see. To the passing pollinating insect, that same flower presents as an irresistible, brilliant neon target awash in ultraviolet light. We pass right by that extravagance every single day, never thinking twice. I guess we can blame our tinkered primate eyes for all the missing beauty in our lives, but we'd likely grow bored with the light show anyway, no? That seems to be the case with everything else.

It could be that one of the most important variables for us also happens to be one of the most obvious. It's our experience, our senses, our happiness. It's the stuff that doesn't come wrapped in a bunch of abstract numbers. We need to see more of the flower, so to speak. Training is as good of an example as any. Think about the things you would typically do in a gym – a warm-up and mobility session, some heavy barbell work, maybe some jumps. From the top, can you see the difference between a well-reasoned, targeted mobility routine and simple self-flagellation? Our first rule is that we don't do things just because successful people say so, or because we have fun mobility toys to play with. We do things only when we understand our limitations and what needs to be done to fix it.

What about the barbell? What do you see when you look at that heavy load? Do you view it as your opponent? I know I was certainly guilty of that for the longest time. I would snarl and growl my way through death metal sound-tracked training sessions. That kind of intensity seemed to be necessary, but it was ridiculous. What I really needed was to learn how to be focused, highly aware, and while roused, calm under stress. The barbell teaches best right there, at the very edge of your failing posture. This is a skill that is developed one heavy lift at a time. The load is nothing without that feeling. So, our second rule is this – sets, repetitions, and percents are all meaningless until we learn to feel and connect with the barbell.

Finally, we should recognize how critical our happiness is during training. Above everything else, we need to have a good time. I've heard countless times that it's not what you do that matters, but how you do it. Well, if that's true, then the best stretch, lift, diet...whatever...is the one that you truly enjoy. So, our final rule is a simple one. Please keep in mind that a little passion and a smile go a long way.

Balance and rotation are great for movement.
So why not do the same thing with loading?

Perform a workout, something like 5-10 sets of 1-3 reps on a given exercise. Use as much weight as you can safely manage.

Next time you train, use moderately heavy loads for 3-5 sets of 3-5 reps. The third time around, try a light load for 3-5 sets of 10 or more repetitions.

Rest for the set week, then start over with just 5 or so more pounds.

That's the proven path to strength.

This solution is so simple, yet it's such a great way to keep training interesting and effective.

COLLABORATION

"We are all apprentices in a craft where no one ever becomes a master." – Ernest Hemingway

I don't mind being an emotional guy. In fact, I think it's a very good thing. The ups and downs can wear on you, sure, but on balance it's more than worth it. For all those times I've grown paralyzed with frustration, intense doubt, anger or willful resistance to possibility, there were countless other times where a rush of pure and productive creativity has plucked every sub-atomic string of my being, leaving me about as happy as a human can be.

Of all these daily emotions, there are a few I rarely experience. First, I cannot remember the last time I was really angry. Well, perhaps I should clarify. I don't consider shit-talking, raised voices, or one of my favorite pastimes, ranting, to be real products of anger. In fact, shit-talking is fun and relatively harmless if you surround yourself with level-headed folks who don't take themselves too seriously. Further, raising your voice and ranting a bit can be a super-duper effective communication style for those who understand how to do so skillfully.

I might point out that if you have any doubt whether you have this particular skill, I recommend you avoid that tactic altogether. As I often write, where there is any doubt, there is no doubt. Don't be that guy.

In my mind, anger rarely looks for any kind of resolution or productive outcome. Instead, it's out to cause harm. Just a bit of fear can satisfy. For these reasons, I've worked hard to erase this particular emotion from my life. That includes the manufactured anger I relied on during my Powerlifting days. Head-butting barbells, yelling like an idiot and throwing fits can help you lift a few more pounds from time to time, but I can hardly look back on those days without blushing and feeling embarrassed. Yes, that happens to be one of my most common emotions, but I'm OK with it.

An optimist would say that this is just evidence of how far I've come.

I also rarely find myself feeling surprised. Like most people, I'm guilty of building up a barnacle-like layer of cynicism as I age. I'd say it's voluntary as I'm actually a bit proud of my particular hard-headed brand of skepticism. This has served as a very useful filter over the years. But sometimes a notion comes across so intuitively that it just blasts right through any and all filters. Instead of capturing and examining the idea before making a decision, this surprise had me smiling wide almost instantly. I learned something unexpected.

While recording a recent podcast, a friend and I got onto the topic of programming training. I was discussing how the pursuit of the perfect training or diet program is a fool's chase. Simply put, your training climate and the company you keep are just far better predictors of success. This is actually not that different from the idea of set and setting, where the exact psychoactive effects of a particular drug seems to have as much to do with the imbiber's immediate mindset and surroundings as it does the pharmacological properties of the drug itself. In other words, never take anything and then make your way to a crowded, over-heated, overly-stimulating night club. You are almost guaranteed to have a very bad ride, especially if it's your first rodeo. Instead, park yourself on the floor of your living room, head wrapped with headphones and a flowing assortment of your favorite tunes. Stay in the fucking cocoon.

We are so addicted to the idea of ever-improving programming formulae that they might as well be administered in pill form. We forget that our progress is equally dependent upon the mood and motive of those close to us day in and day out, particularly coaches, training partners, colleagues, and friends. In my view, you should actually be worrying about your set and setting first.

This brought me to the moment of surprise.

The friend replied to my story line with a crystal clear and perfectly timed allegory, adding, "Man, it's just like playing the guitar. No one ever sits around talking about the best method for learning how to play. You just love it so much and so hard that you practice it all the time! You act with intent. You jam with other awesome players all the time. That's what makes you a bad ass, not some method!"

I replied quickly, smiling wide from ear to ear. "That's exactly right! I've never looked at it that way. Come to think of it, I'm sure even Stevie Ray Vaughn and Eric Clapton could teach each other a thing or two, had they ever found themselves in a room together and some spare time."

There's a Friedrich Nietzsche quote that seems to sum-up that lesson perfectly. "You have your way. I have my way. As for the right way, the correct and only way, it does not exist." Let that be a liberating fact!

We all remain apprentices in this journey. We never outgrow the need for refinement and growth. Whether you are a beginner or very skilled, you should always seek out the best people you can find that will illuminate dark, underdeveloped areas of your life. Find people who are stronger, faster, smarter, harder-working, and more successful than you, then spend a lot of time with them. Regardless of what it is you're after, this is probably the most important thing you can do to encourage rapid growth. It's the best possible investment you can make in yourself.

Get used to working hard, really hard, to keep up. In time, these new and demanding behaviors will ripen into entirely new habits. Rapidly expand your awareness and leave your old perspective behind. Let go! Realize that you will only reach your true potential after you calibrate yourself to a brand new standard. Do that, and in just a matter of months you may find it hard to remember the old you, even if you were pretty damn good to begin with.

SH*T MY BOOKS SAY

"In nature we never see anything isolated, but
everything in connection with something else which is
before it, beside it, under it and over it."
– Johann Wolfgang von Goethe

My opinions are stubborn and quite loud. They wield
hairy barrel-chests and greasy handlebar mustaches, and
they don't go light on the Axe body spray. In other words,
I can't hide them. Nope. I can only hope to contain them
before they take over my party entirely.

My apologies in advance. Well, I apologize for all
but one of these burly opinions – I think everyone should
read more, especially me.

Naturally, lots of folks are inclined to agree with
me, but in turn, they usually ask me for a few good book
recommendations. The first is usually whatever it is I'm
reading at that moment.

My view is simple. If I've picked the right book, it
should feel like one of the most important books I've ever
read. I figure that's the sort of thing you experience when
you're exposed to the right ideas at just about the right
time.

Because I usually don't make the obvious
recommendations, the typical follow-up question is
something along the lines of, "OK, cool. Um, are there any
good training books I should read?" Honestly, this is a
really tough one for me to answer.

I actually cannot recall the last training book I've
read. That's not to say there aren't a lot of good resources

out there. There are. Rather, I just feel that once you get most of the physiology and theory under your belt, these texts definitely seem to lose their impact and relevance. At best they are just an additional voice added to the already crowded discussion. There's no growth there, only confusion. Don't be surprised when you find yourself amazed by the sheer number of opinions that have somehow come into being.

Fuck, how many ways are there to skin a cat, anyhow?

I'm inclined to seek new company. In fact, I only gained a deeper insight into training once I started to consume a wider array of nonfiction. This stuff had nothing to do with the gym, but still, I can never separate training from any other part of my life. So it makes sense to seek more diverse knowledge elsewhere. It has to apply because good advice is good advice. The specific circumstance is not always consequential.

I think you can dig that.

This is a more efficient way to learn. It reminds me a lot of the study tactics I used in school. I can still recall one specific example. Gross memorization is not really one of my skills, so I always struggled with generic terms like "solvent" in grade school. Specifically, I could never recall whether this was the laboratory powder I was measuring, or the water stirring in my beaker. So, I just told myself that you could double the V in solvent to make a W, and with that you could spell Water.

This is very silly, I know, but I never forget shit like this.

The very same effect seems to be at work when I read edgy, honest, non-pasteurized nonfiction. When those knowledge lines cross, the jolt of deep insight leaves quite the impression. That new association is what powers my memory and understanding. That's the moment where a little wisdom seed is planted.

Do you want to learn a thing or two about your relationship with the barbell? Try reading something like Christopher McDougall's *Born to Run*. Yes, a book about our innate and unique endurance running capabilities might change your approach to training forever! Also, I can't help but recommend Amy Cohen's *The Late Bloomer's Revolution*, a book that makes me smile every time I draw it from my bookshelf. These are the pages that told me I didn't have to apologize for feeling unsure and shaky at times. Amy assured me that, no, I wasn't the only person out here worried about missed opportunities and past failures. I was OK. Everything was OK. That view changed everything.

Of course, it is perfectly fine to read just for the pleasure and curiosity of it. In fact, the book I enjoyed most this year was probably *Sex at Dawn* by Christopher Ryan, an expert in sexual behavior, and Cacilda Jetha, a physician and Chris's wife. The tag line says it all, "This is a book about why we mate, why we stray, and what it means for modern relationships." That's pretty useful for those of us looking to better understand the motives of our loved ones. But no, it's not exactly running over with insightful training nuggets. But what that book did was introduce me to Christopher and his unique philosophy, his other writings, and his podcast, *Tangentially Speaking*. And as the universe would have it, that's where

I found my most recent essay-provoking nugget of knowledge.

I think Chris was talking about divorce rates, just how damn high they are, and what could be contributing to that. He mentioned that one serious mistake people make is that they go into a marriage thinking that it's just one really long relationship with one person. However, the truth is that they actually end up having a long series of short, unique relationships with that same person. Yeah, it can be pretty challenging to grow along with someone year after year. I might say the same thing about the relationship I have with myself, as odd as that might sound.

This is something that changes all the time just the same. My great central truth is that I struggle when I fail to honor and respect those burly opinions of mine. That's what I am. It's my foundation, even though it is still raw and ever-maturing. And it only occurs to me now that the equivalent of divorce in these particular types of relationships is my own history of failures, failures that taught me some essential lessons.

My future rests on these foundations. They are mine. They are worth defending, but can always be improved upon when damaged. This is why we seek out good books. They give you a good grip and a kick in the ass when necessary. And to that end, might I add that you should never be afraid to put a bad book down. Instead, go out and find your next great insight.

GETTING USED TO IT

"We must learn to reawaken and keep ourselves awake, not by mechanical aid, but by an infinite expectation of the dawn." – Henry David Thoreau

It's silly to feel certain about anything. There is just too much tough, greasy truth out there to chew on. The wise among us simply read and digest what they can, celebrating this stupefying complexity with a smile and a few margaritas alongside curious friends.
In the end that is what's best in life.

Still, I'm pretty damn confident about one thing – most of us are operating well below our capability. This immediately sounds bad, but that is not necessarily so. We can't expect to maximize everything all the time, right? This is when it helps to be realistic. The ends do not always justify the means, the labor, or the risks. Battles must be picked carefully.

I'm not sure where our characteristic restraint comes from. It must be some mix of calculated laziness and defense as if holding back is the safe and surefire path towards a stable and injury free future. Who knows? But in any case, this is hardly a guarantee. We need to learn to dismantle this inherent mechanism if we want to achieve our best, whether it's in business, barbells or all-you-can-eat hot wing competitions. We need to get used to more.

For now, think of your brain as a picky toddler at the dinner table. No matter what is offered, she will turn her head and shout, "No!" Your job as the parent here is to get that food down, with coaxing or trickery where necessary. Sure it's a bit of a hack, but if you can get just a little bit of food in that mouth, the toddler will quickly realize that this is really something they want. Our minds are no different. Give a taste of something more and the defenses and inhibition will start to come down. At first you start to believe that more is possible, then you will grow to expect it. That's a big deal.

Let me regress to my meathead ways and share a lifting story with you. I'm terrible at the front squat. Blame it on years and years of assuming a less than ideal bent-over posture during lifting, or simply call it laziness. Say your worst.

I've always hated that lift, so I never gave it any measure of focus. That all changed recently. As you might have gathered from my writings, I think it's a damn good idea to face your goats head on, dismantling the weakness entirely, or at the very least, learning to suck less with time! I changed my mind for one simple reason: it's too easy to keep doing what you are good at. Also, it's pretty unrewarding. The wiser, more fulfilling, more virtuous path requires that we pick up a fresh chunk of wood and shape it into something new and useful. Here, the wood was my bad posture and the front squat was the razor-sharp tool.

The first few sessions were predictable – I hated it. Progress was coming very, very slowly. I was talking myself out of this pursuit. But that's when I changed my approach.

First, I started front-squatting every day to

something heavy. Well, at least five to six days per week. Because I'm such a novice in this lift, I knew my brain was in the way, holding back effort, using dread as a weapon against me. I was completely untrained in the lift, so there was no way I could overdo it! So, I turned this disadvantage around. A shot of frequency gave me time to practice my positions and get used to the activity under an accelerated timetable. To be honest, I started to look forward to the front squats within the first week or so of the change. That's how quickly things started to shift.

Second, I use overload as my quick and dirty hack. After my heavy work sets, I perform an extra three or four rounds, adding about 30 to 50 pounds per set. Do I try and squat this? No! That would be a terrible idea, for now. No, all I do is pick up the weight, step back, and hold. The focus is on position and my breathing, and maybe not shitting my pants. With an extra 150 pounds on the barbell, this would probably start to happen in just about ten seconds. So, just before the inevitable sets in, I return the bar to the rack and add a bit more weight.

So what's the point? Simple. If I can show myself that holding extra weight is no big deal, then squatting just a few more pounds above my top work set is surely possible, if not expected by now. That has turned out to be true. While I still have quite a long way to go, I've managed to add 50 pounds to this lift in just a few weeks. I need more time to adapt and grow, but my brain is now out of the way. All it needed to know was that there was nothing to be alarmed about and that this adaptation and expense to the body was worth it.

It's OK if you're not always at your best, or if you

sometimes do not try to be, really. Pick your battles carefully. But I would encourage you to find your goat. That thing that you really want to improve – that you should improve! Start with two key steps.

First, make it important to you. Elevate the issue, creating a set time to work on it during your daily regimen. And yes, work on it daily.

Second, find a quick and dirty hack that sets this task into perspective. Show yourself that it is possible, and should even be expected.

Let me tell you, expectation is an incredible thing.

THAT DESERT QUIET

"Whosoever is delighted in solitude is either a wild beast
or a god." – Aristotle

I made my very first visit to the desert earlier this year.

Well, that's not necessarily true. I have been to Las
Vegas a few times, but that hardly seems to count. That
place really is more of a zoo cage display, rather than an
authentic habitat. No, what made this trip much different
is that I was stepping out into relative nothingness
for the first time. No buildings. No chatter or buzz of
any kind. I suppose that it met my exact expectations.
It seemed plenty desolate, not unlike the imagery I
remember from thousands of *National Geographic*
pictures over the years.

If I were a lazier man, I might just start believing
that if you've seen one desert, you've seen them all. But
that of course is not true. Also, to my fascination, this
place wasn't really deserted at all.

We watched every step carefully to avoid brushing
up against these menacing little cacti dotting the
landscape, armed from top to bottom with tumbling,
barbed clusters of gnarly thorns. One swift breeze
would be more than enough to send this little bundle of
damnation rolling right into your calf meat. I was told to
avoid this outcome to the best of my ability, so I slipped
right through with all the nimbleness I could muster.

Still, I didn't want to avoid the little plants
altogether as each was stunningly lit up with bright pink
fruit. On closer inspection, you could see tiny track marks

all along the trail beneath me. These were likely from some little creature carving out a living by plucking the juicy prize from those needles. And of course, you do also notice the occasional ominous hole in the ground. If I had my guess, this would be home to the higher, venomous member of the food chain that just happens to be very interested in all those little creatures.

Amongst desolation, there is an abundance. You just have to know what you're looking for. I was able to catch the signs because they were not being drowned out by the unrelenting, nearly ubiquitous sounds and sights of civilization. Only by unplugging and stepping away did I see. I might add, there's just as much life around you right now, right where you are reading. It's just that, well, we're too caught up in madness and bullshit to notice.

The absence of stimuli within this place brought an immediate sense of calm and ease. I can easily see why desert landscapes have held such a righteous position within so many cultures. There is an illuminating and palpable vibe here, especially if you've been making your way through said desert full-on *Fear and Loathing* style.

If that reference draws a blank, then I recommend that this seminal Hunter S. Thompson book should be your very next Amazon purchase.

Thomas Merton captured the spiritual qualities of the desert beautifully when he wrote that it was "... valuable in the eyes of God precisely because it had no value to man. The wasteland was the land that could never really be wasted because it offered them nothing." You may consider it holy ground – a place where, depending on your immediate hydration and psychedelic mindset, you're very likely to meet whatever it is you've been praying to. Imagine experiencing absolutely nothing between your flesh and the endless universe staring down from above. This is the kind of experience that makes you feel very, very small in all the best sorts of ways.

This reflection points me towards something obvious. We seem to operate under the assumption that the bulk of the world around us should be scooped up as quickly as possible. We are proud primates drawn to shiny, gigabit-rich gizmos, no money-down guarantees, the promise of rapid ascension, and rightfully so, the amazing abundance of knowledge in the age of Wikipedia.

While I never see myself fully relinquishing my iPad mini and WiFi in the interest of solitude and disconnection, I can clearly see how rapid access to huge amounts of information is not always a good thing. Let me phrase it this way – if a truly wise person understands that there is still so much out there to learn, then a truly foolish person must believe they'll figure it all out in time. But this is only a lure, a trap. The truth is that more knowledge is only better once you have a good understanding of what you're looking for.

But here's the trick – you'll never know what to look for if you never change your landscape, either literally or figuratively.

You should be able to empathize with people who are disabled. Because you are fully capable, you realize just what would be missing if you lost, for example, your sense of hearing. You realize that a huge chunk of life as you know it would vanish. The ghostly memory of sound would be there haunting you for the remainder of your days. But this wouldn't be true if you were born without the ability to hear. Sure, you would soon be aware that something is different about you, but having never known the sensation, you could not detect what's missing. But that's not to say you wouldn't experience your own personal big band expansion when given the gift of hearing. We are lucky to have such real life moments captured on video, where we can witness a life change forever before our very eyes.

While some are more disabled than others, we are all deaf in some respects. I know that sounds bad, but I believe our intentions are really good. Most of us are doing the best we can, but the buzz is so damn loud! The sooner we can learn to shut out the noise – to filter out the appeals for our attention and focus – the better off we will be. It might seem that we will learn and progress less, but in the long run, the opposite is true. We acquire so much more when we take the time to be still, quiet, and look deeper.

No, disconnection is not the same as deprivation. I once again must defer to Merton, who reminds me that my own version of desert quiet only serves to enhance, deepen and fortify. In that place, I am "strengthened against the appeals of falsity."

Look for yourself. Listen closely. What are you missing right now?

Balance is great for movement and loading. Is that it?

No.

We also need to consider balance between our strength work and everything else we are going to do.

A common scenario is the deadlift. After a heavy strength session, many might be tempted, or asked, to participate in a WOD that includes a very high volume of pulls.

Instead, spread out your punches. Whatever you beat up with the barbell during your strength work, take it easy there during everything else.

Remember, it's all about making recovery as easy as possible. Be kind to your body.

YOU'RE A HOT PEPPER, BABY

"Do what you can, with what you have,
where you are." – Theodore Roosevelt

You could say my thumb is less than green, but in all honesty, it's more accurate to say that I just have no clue of what the hell I'm doing yet.

There's no shortage of potential here, I can assure you. My family contains plenty of competent gardeners. I've seen it all done countless times before. Sure, I know what to do. So why am I staring now at a patch of dwarfed and decimated vegetation?

It's simple, really. This was my very first garden, and as far as I'm aware, I think everyone fucks up a few times before they grow championship-caliber tomatoes, you know?

I get it. I can start again.

At times like these, I'm reminded of an old lesson from a former coach. I was running through some drills, and perhaps to his surprise I didn't look nearly as bad as he had first expected.

"Hey, nice job! You know, you've got potential, Moore."

I smiled, right until he qualified that abbreviated pat on the back. "But you know, potential is just a French word for ain't done shit yet!"

From then on all I recall is the sound of that garbled laugh fading slowly as I shuffled my fat-kid flesh down the field.

Anyone can know the thing, but that's the

easy part isn't it? Of course it is. In comparison to doing, knowing doesn't require failure and pain on any level. Yeah, that coach knew, barking bloated vitriol from the shade as we all just sprinted by. I wish the pain of those practices would have delivered me sooner. It would have been a much easier path. But no, potential seems to mature into wisdom and skill at a frustrating, painfully slow pace that can usually be measured in units of fuck-ups and failure.

I look on the bright side. On balance, this garden misadventure is about the least painful failure I've ever experienced. Right now I feel no urge, other than to take note. You thought a little shade wouldn't be that big of a deal. Well, as it turns out, you were wrong. Make a better decision next time.

In fact, that was the issue. While my perfect little garden spot sure seemed quaint in springtime, a few tree trunks were actually blocking out most of the sun during those precious afternoon hours. Not all the sun, mind you, that would have been an obvious thing. No, the sun was blocked just down the rows that now contained my would-be crops. Well, most things died. Bummer, I know. Of what remained, the vegetation never really grew more than a few inches.

But this all started to change a few weeks ago.

Late summer in Memphis is a pretty miserable time of the year for all living things, but that seems especially so for plants. The days grow shorter with the approach of autumn, the rain is scarce, but the burdensome heat holds on. My garden might only be mostly dead, but it has now taught me a practical lesson about the seasonal shift, one I've never noticed before.

The sunlight is now flooding in at a slightly different angle. What was once covered in shade and left underfed is now bathed in raw energy for most of the afternoon. My dwarfed plants now had their shot at doing something. But I didn't get my hopes up. "There's just not enough time", I told myself. "Too little sun, too late."

Well, as it turns out I was wrong again! Perhaps this is an emerging, repeating pattern in my life? No, that's just the easy thing to see. The failure usually brings along some of the most fascinating little stories and lessons. It has its perks. I've kept watering those little plants just about every day, mostly out of guilt I must say. It was my fault, after all, that they were in this less than stellar situation. The least I could do was keep them from dying a terrible drought death!

Consider it a karma-salvaging maneuver, if nothing else.

But just the other afternoon I noticed something extraordinary and beautiful. Yes, we are all guilty of overusing those words, but they really fit this scene. One of the tiny little plants, a hot banana pepper plant, had somehow produced fruit in just a matter of two weeks or so, without my notice! More than that, this little pepper was actually just about as large as the plant itself!

Here was one of those rare moments where I have nothing to say. I just stood there and admired the accomplishment for a few minutes. I paid a small tribute. It is odd, I know, but it just felt like the right thing to do, you know? I didn't pick it. The plant's got a bit more work to do yet before that pepper goes firecracker red.

Walking away I realized that this plant – against its fate, my ignorance, and a seemingly insurmountable lack of resources – still grew a pepper that was far bigger than itself. And yet, here I am carrying around the greatest mystery of the Universe right between my ears. I'm writing a story about a plant, on an electronic gizmo that is capable of answering any question I can conjure. I am fed. I am fortunate. My body is healthy and able.

Despite all of those precious gifts, I'm guilty of feeling cheated. I want what I want. I don't always feel as though I get my fair share of the sunlight. That's when I take down the second batch of notes.

What are you waiting for, Chris? What more do you need? What's your excuse? Why not do something different? Why don't you shake your red pepper instead?

GETTING MINDFUL

"You have power over your mind - not outside events.
Realize this, and you will find strength."
– Marcus Aurelius

MASTER OF THE MOMENT

"Do not dwell in the past, do not dream of the future, concentrate the mind on the present moment." – Buddha

At times, I am fully capable of giving the present the attention it deserves.

Just a few hours ago I sat perched on the side of a wide open restaurant balcony, overlooking a ridge of the Rocky Mountains gently blanketed by the brilliant orange rays of a fading sunset. Before me, there was a perfectly cooked hamburger, topped with a freshly fried egg, and accompanied by a fine pint of Colorado Indian Pale Ale. "This is amazing," I told my wife. "You know, we are so damn fortunate to be here, right now."

We both smiled, which was all that was necessary.

I took the final burger bite, washing it down with one last swig of ale. I allowed my mind to break from the moment, marveling at the ability of a simple fried egg to transform any dish into something delicious and decadent.

To the first human being that realized that crispy, runny ovums made for the best sort of condiment, I can only say thank you.

Yes, I am thankful.

Like anyone, my life is pinned to the outer edge of a big winding wheel. That wheel churns at all hours, as steady as a ticking clock. Predictably, I find myself at the bottom of the arc from time to time. Call it the bad day, the shit training session, the moment where I don't quite feel up to the challenge.

If I could sum it up in one word, I would call it doubt. But each visit here gets just a little bit easier because I am now aware. I know that these days are nothing to fret over. They are natural. They are necessary. I remain the one who's in control.

No matter what, the decision of how to react is always my own.

But like I said, I'm feeling fortunate right now. While things are not perfect (an expectation that is not all that desirable anyway!), that winding wheel has brought me near the top of the arc. Life is good. Training is good! My body is once again responding to my demands.

I have no complaints.

Is that just an artifact of the cycle, equally predictable as the bad stretches? Could it be luck? I can't say for sure, but I suspect it has little to do with discovering some new approach or method. Really, I just started to acknowledge where I was actually standing, aspiring only to take that next appropriate step, not the one I'd rather take. I also reminded myself that, no matter what, I must always have a good time under the barbell. Above any other method or scheme, this would provide the requisite energy and focus. This is how I would keep my axe sharp.

I know that Conan the Barbarian had an answer for the question of "What's best in life?", but I have my own – nothing is better than being physically strong, present, and at peace in the moment. This is best because the feeling is so fleeting and easy to let slip away.

Five months ago I realized I had failed. I was in pain, both emotionally and physically. I was weak. I was flooded with doubt. What was the cause? Well, it feels like such a dumb and easy mistake, but I allowed myself to abandon the present. I had developed this habit of inspecting and scrutinizing the past, which is fine as you are learning, and sharing the lessons. But in reality, I was being too critical. I also became intoxicated with the future and all that it promised (as if anything can ever be promised to anyone). This was my opportunity to make up for my late bloom. While there's nothing wrong with planning boldly, that's not all I was doing.

I was actually looking to will my way towards the specific version of the future I had envisioned. I was reaching out, ready to grab tight.

How silly and destructive is this? You might as well try and pry open the petals of a flower because you want to know what it looks like right now.

The reason that the present is so damn important is this - It's the only thing you own and control. At this moment, you can choose to be happy, attentive, detached from everyday drama, or to train in a manner that satisfies you deeply and makes perfect damn sense. But you don't own the past. None of those embarrassing and frustrating mistakes can be taken away. Yet, nothing in your history is worth beating yourself up over. These things brought you to where you are now, and that's perfectly fine.

Even if you are not where you want to be, you still have this moment, right now. Please, don't rush the bloom! You cannot correct your course by prying open a new, better path.

You have no ownership over the future either. Oh, you can try and take what you want as soon as you can, but life tends to frown upon that kind of shit. It seems to act as a large body of water – the harder you dive into it, the more violently it resists.

We are stuck on the fucking winding wheel, for sure. These are the terms of the lease on life. You are born, you get the ticket, you take the ride. The track is laid. But that doesn't mean you lack control. You – complete with those limited genetics, a scarred history, your current struggles and doubts, and this desperate impulse to create a better version of yourself – you are in control.

Marcus Aurelius seems to be screaming out from the page, sharing words that are as relevant to me now as they were to him nearly two-thousand years ago. "What then can escort us on our way? One thing...philosophy. This consists in keeping the divinity within us inviolate and free from harm, master of pleasure and pain, doing nothing without aim, truth, or integrity, and independent of all others, action or failure to act."

The mistakes that led to my anguish down at the bottom of that arc were not a consequence of not caring enough, or not trying hard enough. No, if anything I cared and tried too fucking much! But that alone wasn't the source of the anguish. The source was my forfeit of the present, of this moment, of my own individual mastery. I thought I could beat back the past and will my future into being. I was dependent now, projecting desperately forward.

The critical oversight was forgetting that the

key to this mastery is so damn simple. It's about paying attention now, taking the next best step. This is not an attempt to step back into a former self, or to erase the last missteps. We lean forward, but not too far.

I can embrace the lessons of the past without feeling any regret. The regret isn't real. I can aspire to something better, something great, without carrying the burden of having to make it so. It will become reality, likely in some amazing way that I cannot yet see, if I just remain the master of this moment. That means choosing to be happy. It means training and working in a way that brings me immediate satisfaction and joy. That sets the wheel into motion. It creates the cascade of events and adaptations in my mind and physiology that will carry me to where I want to go. All that is required is that I remind myself daily.

Step, step.

I am the master here. This moment is independent of others' actions, and any past failure to act. While I am not immune to doubt, this is pretty damn comforting.

Let's not forget how amazing and powerful this is. As we push and sharpen ourselves against the barbell, let's remember just how damn fortunate we are.

MEDITATION, OF COURSE

"You are never alone or helpless. The force that
guides the stars guides you too."
– Shrii Shrii Ánandamúrti

What comes to your mind when I mention the word
meditation? Be honest.

Do you envision a common Indian Guru
archetype, clad in a scant loin cloth, bushy in hair and
beard, chanting repetitive drivel, legs permanently
twisted into that lotus position? I will never be in that
lotus position. Maybe you are conjuring the image
of a Hipster Westerner turned poser Yogi, complete
with proudly matted hair and a strong aversion to
any chemical contained within any common stick of
deodorant.

It's OK to have this preconceived notion.
However, the truth is that meditation is really no
different than any other area of training, or life in
general. Where possible, we tend to inject heavy doses
of assumption, association, and generalization into the
mix. Our egos are so quick to take over the internal
conversation. That feels good. It's reassuring. It makes
our version of the story easier to interpret and store.

We need to break those patterns.

Meditation is exactly what you make of it, and
nothing more. You can assume any position you like.
You can practice in any manner you see fit. And just
like with a barbell, the vast majority of the benefits
can be obtained with the simplest possible methods.

My personal daily meditation practice always centers around music. Hardly a minute passes in my day without something groovy or emotion-triggering spilling across my eager eardrums. It's a priority for me, and it makes perfect sense that I utilize this love to enhance my focus.

The routine goes like this. First, I play a favorite song, preferably something current. Yes, pop guilty pleasures are completely eligible. With the music commanding most of my attention, I just count each breath, drawing air and then blowing it out slowly and smoothly. I almost see the breaths as a long string of molecules that I draw in and out one by one. When I find myself thinking a rogue thought, I just draw that focus back to the counting and rhythm. That's it, the most basic, and probably most effective way to still your mind. Another easy technique is to imagine yourself playing one of the instruments in the song and singing the lyrics with all the passion you can muster. Really, pretend that you can feel the artist's motivation for writing the lyrics. It is a bit goofy at the start, but this is far better than focusing intently on everything that lies outside your front door, ready to claw right through those fancy noise-canceling headphones of yours to get at your burgeoning focus.

Be prepared.

I do not feel a need to even try that lotus position. After all, I'm looking to break unnecessary rules, not abide by them. So, because it's incredibly comfortable, I just lie belly down on the floor with my hands crossed beneath my forehead. I stretch out each breath as far as I can, as deep as I can, imagining that any spare gas molecule left on the end of that long string could be the one that punches my ticket to enlightenment. I can see myself nailing every drum fill, every chord, every note of these songs with perfect pitch. After three tunes pass by a little alarm chime rings. I raise my head slowly, peeling the slightly sweaty headphones from my ears.

This is what you're after. If you feel, at this brief moment, like you're waking from a dream, then you are exactly where you need to be. Congratulations! You're one step closer to wherever it is you must go.

Keep this in mind, the object of your focus doesn't really matter as long as it's positive. Just work to isolate and reject all those rogue thoughts. That's the skill that will help you get the most out of any of your experiences. It also builds slowly and surely through repetition, just like any barbell exercise. And like those exercises, we can add variety with time to keep making progress during our journey. So, what does that variety look like? What does it sound like?

The next step is visualization.

Try this. The next time you go through your warm-up drills and mobility work, actively focus on pushing aside the noise and hustle. Go through the forthcoming training session one movement at a time, jump by jump, kilogram by kilogram. This will burn an image of those target goals into your brain with a bright-red virtual poker!

You'll be shocked at how effective this technique can be.

I think the final step would be the use of mantras, which are basically nothing more than sounds, words or short phrases repeated at length during meditation for enhanced effect. Consider this to be the baking in of that thought until your mind just accepts the shift in outlook. I remember reading a Joseph Goebbels quote some time ago, where he stated, "If you repeat a lie often enough, it becomes the truth." I need not explain the sort of monster this guy was, but he was right here. So, might as well utilize this truth for the better.

Meditate on what you'd like to become and make it so.

Please believe me, that's the secret to everything. I think a lot of people struggle to commit in this way. To let go of all their attachments. They are tightly bound. They go for a quick dip, but never really work up the nerve to swim across the deep end. Worse still, all those inevitable, negative thoughts and distractions flood in freely and unabated, just as they are approaching the brink of real success. This has to be the moment where most people quit. However, if you've developed your ability to focus, even just a little bit, then rejecting these silly thoughts and emotions will begin to come naturally. You will be a happier human being because that's exactly what you're training yourself to become. It's what you're practicing.

I would also bet that you'll develop a razor-sharp sense of perspective that will remind you that your bucket will indeed fill drop by drop. To you, the spaces of time between those drops shouldn't matter. Each one is perfect enough all on its own. This development is happening and unfolding just as it should.

You train so incredibly hard. You pay critical attention to your diet. You devote little chunks of your day to mobility and to recovery. So wouldn't it be strange to devote almost zero dedicated effort towards the development of your most precious, powerful and transformative asset, your mind?

Go now, practice, practice, practice.

There's no place for negativity or tough-guy bullshit in the gym. Turn off the death metal.

Instead, play music that stirs better emotions.

Play something that can bring the workout into focus by fostering mindfulness and cheer. Next, play something to raise your heartbeat a bit.

That's a great combination.

Remember, you can have the greatest training program ever devised, but it will not work unless you're having a good time and putting as much effort in as possible.

If you cannot smile, you cannot be truly strong.

POWER OF BEACH

"To myself I am only a child playing on the beach, while vast oceans of truth lie undiscovered before me." – Isaac Newton

I'm as excited to see the ocean now as I ever was as a kid. This sight – a little too rare in my life these days – comes with this immediate sense of revitalization. It stirs me. The smell of the air alone sends me into a childish giggle fit.

Of all the potential calibrating experiences in this world, this is my favorite. This place just seems to facilitate fine and rapid meditation, although it might not seem that way at first. The cell phone still rings out here, of course. Looming commitments back home pollute your otherwise ideal margarita-fueled fantasy. The beach itself churns with activity as countless sunscreen greased primates strut up and down the shore. You remain in reach of the world. But that's just not true when you're neck deep in cold ocean water.

Yeah, it's one thing to look at the ocean, but it's quite another to be fully immersed in it, to feel its power and infinite depth. That's a startling and terrifying sensation. In that place, you are now fully disconnected. You are on your own, powerless, at the mercy of the turbulent currents and cresting waves. With that realization, you have no choice but to be highly aware. Consider the experience a remedy for chronic ego inflammation, as well as a perfect opportunity to learn and balance perspective.

I am relaxed as can be in the water. My body takes its float posture, which looks similar to sitting in an invisible reclining chair with a forward tilt. The bulk of my muscle tissue is tranquil. My form rises and falls with each passing wave.

I take care not to resist the motion.

That's where the calibration comes into play. I float peacefully, eyes glued to the horizon while I count the breaths between crests. This is perhaps the most restorative water experience outside of an actual isolation tank. No, you're unlikely to have a sensory deprivation induced hallucination (yay float tanks!), but it's just impossible to come back to shore without a smile on your face.

You are fixed, now you just have to try and stay that way!

I don't rush back into the arms of the world. No, I take my time. I enjoy the restored child-like default setting in my perspective. With the worries of my adult life stripped away for the moment, all I really care about now is finding interesting things beneath my feet. Little mollusks buried in the sand. Brilliant bright red sand dollars. My failed, yet ongoing attempts at capturing those elusive jellyfish in my bucket. An hour passes fastest at the beach. The moment was happening, then it wasn't. I cautiously made my way ashore, sunkissed and as red as a freshly steamed lobster. Here, the same thought always occurs to me. "Why not just stay?"

I've yet to mention what makes this particular beach trip to Destin so memorable. My father, a Floridian himself, first brought me here some thirty years ago. Yeah, that's the sort of thought you have to digest slowly.

So much has happened in that time, but the way I see this little town hasn't changed. It still feels small. The fishing docks stay busy. The people who work them are tough as nails. The local seafood dive on the bayside is, for me, essentially a religious experience.

All these images and memories establish the definition of "beach" for me. Sure, I've been to plenty of locations that were more exclusive, but no other place has the power to make me feel like a fucking ten-year-old kid again. More amazing still, this year – this trip – I'm showing the place off to my nineteen-month-old son Max for the very first time.

God, talk about mind blowing!

Well, perhaps I should back up a bit. He was here in a far more primitive form two years ago, at the time his mother and I had our beach wedding. That's right, we were well on our way to being a family way before the vows were shared. Jani's belly popped right out into view like a big, brilliant, white pearl in that dress. I never thought I would see such a beautiful bride. I never thought I would be so happy.

As I savor these last few moments on the sand, one particular vision occupies and illuminates my mind and heart. I can see my little boy cautiously stepping out into the sand for the very first time, with tiny grains of sand squeezing up between his chubby little toes. He's scared at first, clinging to my shoulder and neck as we step out into the waist high water. "Daddy, Daddy, Daddy..." He repeats nervously. What he's actually communicating is, "Dad, I'm really scared, but I'll trust you. It'll be OK, right?" My heart melts as I type the very words. He's not let down. Everything was OK, of course. Fear dispersed, we walked back up to our umbrellas and shared a piece of watermelon in the cool shade.

This is a rare instance where a giant loop in your life closes. It's stunning, soul shocking even. Right there in the sand I realized that I'm in my father's exact position now, some 30 years after that first visit. This is just how he felt as he watched me dig around in the sand and water for the first time. What else can you say? What words can capture the full weight and gravity of that kind of realization?

I might not experience this feeling for another twenty or thirty years, when, Dharma willing, some grandchildren might be in the picture. But let's not fast forward. The mere thought of all that stuns me further still. And I'll be honest, all of these precious moments also bring a fair amount of sadness as I know that the moment is fleeting. Before I know it this little boy won't be so little anymore, and I'll be put to pasture (if I'm lucky!).

I wish I could slow it all down, but that just won't happen. So, I'll do what I can. I'll savor the days while they last. And sure, I'll keep a cocktail in hand. May this margarita fantasy never end.

LEARNING TO WEIGHT

"Pride makes us artificial and humility makes us real"
– Thomas Merton

Here's something that seems plenty true.

No matter how experienced and wise we grow with time, we are not entirely free from those old mistakes and tendencies that dotted our past. The effect lingers. The habits tend to claw their way back into your life. At least this is what I'm telling myself now, just about a day after a training session that ended with me screaming at the barbell.

I feel a little bad about how the whole thing played out. Screaming, "Fuck you!" at the load might have been a little uncalled for.

If this was a typical abusive relationship, the sort you always see in bad, straight to cable TV movies, then this would be the time I grovel and beg for forgiveness. "I'm sorry baby. I just got a little carried away and crazy last night, that's all. Look, you know I'm under all this pressure right now. It won't happen again, I swear! I'll change."

Yes, yes, but it will happen again. It always does. Luckily for me the barbell is the best possible companion. She is far more patient than me. She lies there in the corner, cold, knurled, and ready to forgive me when my dark cloud passes.

This is something I must work on, something I must change.

Henry Rollins put this best in his classic article

"The Iron." If you have never read that piece, then please do so. You'll love it. My favorite lines read, "The Iron is the great reference point, the all-knowing perspective giver. Always there like a beacon in the pitch black. I have found the Iron to be my greatest friend. It never freaks out on me, never runs. Friends may come and go. But two hundred pounds is always two hundred pounds." There's that perfect patience once again.

As with most of these emotional outbursts, the problem started squarely with me. I had a certain inflated idea about my status when I stepped out into the garage gym. I based my daily goal on warm and fuzzy memories, not reality. Like clockwork, it was the barbell that kicked me the real deal. The raw motive was reasonable. I needed to test myself. I hadn't really tried to separate a really heavy load from the ground in a long, long time. So, what better time than the present.

I should know better, but I still could not help myself. This is such an easy mistake to make. My body wanted to slip back into that former groove, so I kept adding more and more weight. Up and up the load went, towards numbers that were once routine. I arrived at a weight that I thought would be my last warm-up attempt. "OK, now we get serious." I adjusted the radio to something a bit more fast paced, tightened my belt, then coated my hands liberally in chalk. After a quick growl and snort, I bent down, wrapping each hand carefully around the barbell to secure my grip. After one final growl, I pulled in a deep breath, arched my spinal column, then put all the force I could muster into that load.

Nothing.

You can imagine my reaction. It's the reaction most people have when they're faced with a shocking truth. In this case, I was informed as politely as possible that, no, I was not very strong. I thought it was an illusion, or a mistake. I repeated the ritual again, adjusting the music, tightening, and chalking up – then again, and again for what must have been the tenth and final time! I did what any child would do. I ripped off my belt, slamming it into the ground and releasing that very loud screaming f-bomb insult. All at once I felt a strong sense of shame and relief. At least no one was there to witness it.

The emotional discharge did allow me to return to my senses. Imagine my surprise at that moment. Here I am, diligently working at this mindfulness and meditation stuff daily, yet I'm still capable of such outbursts. I'm still capable of losing control. Yes, I know better than ever that old habits claw their way back, and they claw hard. It's OK. I'm not enlightened, I'm just me, flawed, yet growing. Traces of those ancient emotions remain, and they seem capable of rapidly germinating and sprouting up under the right conditions. But I shouldn't beat myself up over the expected. I should focus on what has changed for the better. The truth is that all of these efforts to grow and be present in any situation have really paid off, because to my surprise, I immediately came back to center after this tantrum of mine. I didn't let the weight of that acute emotion drag me down and taint the rest of my evening like it once would have done. After the flood of emotion burned for a bit, this made me smile. I can hear this inner voice smile back, saying, "see how foolish it all is? How funny? Don't worry, next time you'll do much better."

This story is a perfect example of why meditation practice is so critical, even for the lifter. We are often so unnecessarily hard on ourselves. In that blinded moment, all I could feel was this deep sense of frustration and disappointment as if I had let myself down. I hadn't felt that in a while, and for lack of a better explanation, I just couldn't fight off that burn. But it's ok. There's nothing wrong with feeling the emotion. There's nothing wrong with slipping. We just need to make sure we take that moment to reflect and learn. We have to inch forward.

Next time will be better.

I'm not what I was, that much is clear. But I think it's so important to say out loud that, no, there's nothing wrong with where I am now. It's not a condemnation or a judgment, it's just the way it is. All I need to do is adjust my plan and expectations. From here the water will turn back on, and there my bucket will sit, filling one drop at a time. I will be just fine. But that doesn't mean I have to forget about this, does it? No, of course not.

The barbell is not the only one in this relationship capable of teaching lessons. She takes this round, and I am humbled. I will go back to work. But make no mistake, mindfulness doesn't mean I won't enjoy my eventual revenge. That weight will separate from the floor next time, and I will be ready to smile wide ear to ear.

HEAVY DUTY MANTRA

Mantra: A sound, syllable, word, or sentence that is considered capable of creating transformation.

I suppose I didn't put much thought into the phrase at first. The line had a nice ring to it, short and sweet. It made me feel good. Smile. Sip. Lift heavy. Why not?

The second bit is maybe the easiest part to start with. I am a coffee lover, to put it mildly. From my view the beverage is more than just a soothing drink, it's a sacrament. It's a daily ritual where we take in this powerful, psychoactive, white crystalline xanthine alkaloid in order to set off a creative firecracker in our mind. Anything that powerful and delicious should be respected, utilized, and appreciated dearly, right?

The first bit about smiling might take just a bit more explaining. Consider an example. No one wants to get big, strong, lean, fast, fit just because it's cool. No, of course not. We want those things – as cool as they may be – because we're pretty sure they'll make us happy and content. The trick is that they do not, not while there are still humans walking around who are bigger, stronger, leaner, faster, fitter, or whatever. This contrast only highlights the fact that we are rarely happy with who we are right now, something we have the power to change.

Most of us realize how silly it is to crave more and more shit. It's a cliché for a reason, right? But this is a just another case of something being much easier said than done. Here we are chatting at a controlled pace. My rational brain is doing the talking. However, flash something I want before my eyes (like a dozen maple-bourbon bacon donuts and a pint of chocolate milk) and in an instant you'll see evidence of my tinkered primate brain grinding away back behind the curtain of this higher consciousness. You can't simply outrun your deep history. The impulse is nearly impossible to control. That is unless you take extraordinary measures and train yourself to do something better!

Everyone knows about meditation. Quite possibly you've tried it. Regardless of your experience, what do you think the purpose is, exactly? Is it all about the mantra, the ritual, the rambling guru schtick? Perhaps the goal is to trigger an actual spiritual awakening? ...Perhaps. I wouldn't rule it out. But I think that the real truth here is far more obvious and ordinary. To put it as simply as possible, meditation is nothing more than practice. You practice controlling the impulse. You practice recalling warm moments in your life, times you were overcome with joy, love, satisfaction or compassion. Times where you were genuinely proud during one of those tough, but successful lifts. To put it simpler still, this is the act of fucking practicing happiness!

I know, it sounds too easy so it must be bullshit. But this is anything but easy. This is work, and you should commit to it daily.

Every time you conjure up the imagery of that beach retreat, your child's perfect smile, or that steaming cup of spiced wine on a cool fall evening, your brain reinforces the pathway just a little. A basic training adaptation like any other. Those thoughts start to come easier in time, displacing the mad rush of random images and the buzzing that usually occupies your head space.

Really baby, this is no different from getting strong. Get your reps in and you'll have your reward.

I should point out that the opposite is just as true. If you practice losing control at every possible opportunity, then you shouldn't be surprised when you master the destructive behavior itself. After all, that's what you've been training for! But don't worry, this need not progress any further. You don't have to move on to the next level, marked by a propensity for embarrassing yourself at parties in front of attractive girls. As I said earlier, it always remains your choice.

I do understand the motive, however, to kick up the emotion. It's true that you must be sufficiently focused and roused to lift a heavy ass barbell from the ground. But rousing is not that different than putting on cologne, dear friends. Always remember that a little dab goes a long way. You don't want to go around stinking up every room you step into. Just respect the emotions you're drawing up. They can be a danger to your happiness.

It's a real mistake to manufacture anger for the sake of a successful repetition. I should know, I was guilty of the practice for many years. In my experience, a few things are true here. First, this thing, as a strategy, just doesn't work. Anything more than a quick huff and puff is only likely to distract, disorganize and prematurely fatigue you. You'll lift less, doubt yourself more often, and then you'll become really good at being miserable in the gym. Second, you should save the yelling and screaming for the rabid, hormone-enabled teenage boys currently stalking your neighborhood streets, or the classic, puffy faced meathead lifters who have been at this far too long to know any better.

That's not good enough for us, though. You and I can do better.

The obvious truth here is that the barbell can always get heavier. For that glaring reason alone, we should all temper our hubris. But more obvious still, why claim victory over something that is really nothing more than a teacher to you? Why should training be considered a sort of bloody battle, when it is really nothing more than a series of practical lessons? A relationship you cultivated and develop like any other? You should know that all the heavy emotion adds nothing to the experience, it just weighs you down. It dulls you. It demotivates. It actively labors to keep you weak.

We really can do much better.

That mantra is a reminder that happiness starts with a smile. A fresh cup of coffee can only makes things better. Sip away, because it helps the world seem even brighter and shinier than usual. Finally, when the time comes, put everything you've got into that third bit of the mantra. Lift heavy and often. My recommendation is that you use it. Remind yourself daily just how fortunate you are to even engage the barbell. Remind yourself of why it's important to you, and why it keeps you smiling.

It's not about how much you lift of course, it's about what the act itself reveals and represents to you. And sure, it might very well be a full-on spiritual experience. But in the most simple terms, it's nothing more than a daily act of personal calibration. Continual, progressive refinement of the flesh and the ego.

    Yes, indeed. The mantra has been repeated many times. And look at me, transforming still. I think I'll keep it up.

COZY AND STRUGGLING

"Character cannot be developed in ease and quiet. Only
through experience of trial and suffering can the soul be
strengthened, ambition inspired, and success achieved."
– Helen Keller

The little struggles begin at dawn.

I'm certainly aware of the unrelenting buzzing on
the table beside the bed. I know what time it is, yet I still
make the decision to snooze. You might say that, on a
subconscious level at least, there are no fucks to give.

That fifteen-minute act of snoozing seems like
a relatively minor offense, but it still breaks the well
intentioned promise I made to myself the night before.
I said I would tune out sooner, shutting down the near
runaway thought train, resting and rising fully renewed.

Not this time. As always, I cannot help but light
the other end of the candle. I pour a few more fingers of
reposado, telling myself, "Just a few more pages. That's it.
Six hours of sleep will be plenty."

Oh, how the tune changes at 7 a.m., no?

I wonder, how many weeks or years will need
to pass before this resolution takes hold? I tell myself
it's not a big deal. These are temporary actions. But the
truth is that this little acute act displaces the morning
hours just enough. The world doesn't wish to wait for
the lumbering, drowsy night owl. It forces itself through
touch-screen interfaces and demands a response.

The rush brings down the defenses. It opens the
door to resistance, distraction and frustration. So, there

must be a better way to go about things, no? Or at least, maybe there's a better perspective to be had on such mornings?

This is the heart of our perceived, personal struggle. The world presents its list of demands, yet here we are, desperately looking around for another option – any option – that will provide us with an opportunity to pursue something we actually care about, at a time of our choosing. Is this too much to ask? Does dreaming of such a thing make you an asshole?

No, so long as you pair the dream with the requisite elbow grease. You should come down to the altar and pray. Just make sure you do it every day. Also, bring a rag and some tools with you so that you can polish and work on that altar while you're down on your knees. Let me tell you, in my experience magical shit starts to happen if you keep up that practice for a few years. Real change starts to take hold. Exciting opportunities manifest. All of the desperate prayers start to answer themselves.

Yes, struggle is the right word. Past time and scope, I often find myself drifting superficially from task to task, unsure of my choices and motives. My direction. My personal value to this world. The actions start to feel like a long series of chores and to-dos. But this is no panic signal. It's just a prompt, a signal that a change has to come, the sooner the better. I might not fully grasp the solution, but at least I know the score. The world seeks to set the rules of the game. Well, let me rephrase that. My perception is that the world is seeking to set the rules. In reality, I'm only setting up my own limitations. After all, I've set the conditions of my life. I have chosen to keep the channels of excess input open. These are my worries, attachments, hopes, wishes, wounds, and aspirations. I complain from time to time that gravity seems to be riding me harder than it should, yet here I am, walking around with lead-lined Doc Marten military boots. Figuratively speaking, of course. I have no desire to churn up any relics of my high school years.

I've huffed and puffed and bitched about it all. That's not an unhealthy thing to do, no, but it's also not a productive thing. It will create no impulse. It will lead to no change. So, it's time to forge a new resolution! Something just for me, crafted with the aim of at least tamping the pressure of this struggle.

I will take new action starting now. I will practice the act of letting go of all the perceived bullshit and buzz that swirls around me. I will pay no mind to the fishing lures that dot my path that seek to snare my motives and behavior. I know, it all sounds a little too much like some rehashed punk prose, but this is not an act of aggression. This is not a rebellious thing. Really, it's quite the opposite. What we're talking about here is the act of stopping...of sitting...of just being...free of the self-imposed struggle.

Just typing that brings me relief. Also, how do I explain the words I stumble upon during these late night hours, when surely I should be sleeping instead? "Do you surf through it all, or do you carry it around like a load? If only you could throw it off." Fuck, Ram Dass, why do you have to go and hit it on the head like that?

I've been working towards a goal, as foggy and shapeless as it might be at this moment. I cannot name it, but I feel it. It fills my belly with this pregnant urge to pursue. It compels me to stay up, to search, to reach out. But the struggle is largely an illusion. Sure, there will be pain. There will be some burning from time to time, but the difference is knowing that the buck stops here, so to speak. I'm the only one here with hands to grasp. I can let go. I can keep an arms length. I can keep surfing my way through this experience, waiting patiently, painlessly for that next wave.

I'm not sure how long this emotional sugar high will last, but I'm going to bed a little earlier tonight. Right now, I can renew the commitments. I can start by getting my ass up on time, this time, if only in a figurative sense. Void of rush, each moment can be appreciated for what it is – a chance to be still for once.

I'll make sure to get started first thing in the morning. But first, where's that reposado?

It's foolish to spend countless hours training the body while completely ignoring the mind.

This is the most important thing you're not currently doing. Trust me, it could make all the difference.

Commit to practicing 15 minutes a day, whenever you want to do it. Start with slow, deep breaths. Count them. Keep your thoughts on the rhythm.

When your thoughts drift, simply bring them back to your breath, or a positive thought, or a candle flame. The object of your meditation doesn't matter. It's the discipline of thought that counts.

Meditate before and after training, after the week, month, or year. Use it as an opportunity to consider how far you've come, and where you need to go.

You'll be smiling more often in no time.

MAX'S RINGS

"Keep your eyes on the stars, and your feet on the ground." – Theodore Roosevelt

We cannot escape the numbers.

The endless series of digits are inexorable and fundamental, having been sewn into the very fabric of reality a long, long time ago by some force or energy that no one can fully conceptualize. But that doesn't stop us from trying, of course. Our species has a long, mixed history of trying. How can we stare through a clear night sky towards infinity hanging over our heads and feel truly confident about anything?

Somehow we manage to do just that on a daily basis. Somehow we are able to overlook something this striking and obvious.

Of course, I would be much more comfortable immersed in a simpler reality. I'm sure everyone feels that way. But that's the thing about reality and the elegance of its underlying mathematics. It's true whether we're prepared to believe in it or not! Like everything else in this unfathomably beautiful and complex universe, the personal preferences of an enlightened primate do not appear to be a priority.

Imagine that.

Things start to come back into focus once you reassign meaning to all these numbers. Sure, the total number of suns visible to our naked eyes in the night sky is beyond comprehension. How can we begin to understand what it all means when we say that there are one-hundred thousand million stars in the Milky Way alone? It's enough to trigger a gush of blood from the nose, for Christsakes! Still, for what it's worth, I can take a deep breath and draw down the scale of everything. Things just don't need to be so overwhelmingly abstract.

It's quite possible that you've heard this story before, in one form or another. That's perfectly fine as there's nothing wrong with a bit of repetition. That's especially true when it comes to the fundamental ideas that we often forget. Having just been reminded of this tale this week, I'm struck with just how damn applicable it is today.

We begin with Siddhartha Gautama, popularly know as the Buddha, being questioned by a follower regarding the very nature of the universe and what might come after death. We humans cannot help but ponder such things. It's kind of our thing, even though we are no closer to an answer than when we first were able to ask the question many, many years ago. Siddhartha answers with the famous story of the poisoned arrow.

Allow me to paraphrase a bit.

Imagine that you are walking along a city street, when all of a sudden a shadowy figure leaps from the bushes and shoots you right in the middle of the thigh with that poisonous arrow. The villain runs away, leaving you there to die where you lay. I know, fun story so far.

What do you there in these fleeting moments? You might feel compelled to ask why. You might also swear to track this son of a bitch down in order to exact your vengeance, or perhaps you just wish to discover the motive. Maybe the loss of blood makes you a little loopy, and you begin to question why he wouldn't have just used a gun for this job. Wouldn't that be far more practical? These are all interesting questions best saved for another time. Because there you lie, curious and befuddled, but dying all the same. What's the best thing you could do? Yes, of course, you should probably just drop the philosophy chatter and address that arrow buried bone deep in your fucking leg! Faced with the immediate prospect of your extinction, save the undue emotion struggles and ego pangs for some other time.

I feel like the wounded man more often than I would like to admit. For me, it's the common question of where I am and where I'm going. From my current view, there's little difference between a stunning milky way vista and my future. Both seem equally incomprehensible and scary as hell. Enlightened or not, it's a lot for any single primate to consider, right? It only grows worse with the realization that the arrow is actually real! Sorry to piss in the punch bowl, but death is creeping towards us by the minute, but we fight and struggle for these big answers all the same. Who wouldn't prefer a more convenient and comforting reality, one where we were not all assigned an expiration date the moment we're about to bloom?

The big numbers of life can be absolutely numbing and paralyzing. So, let's return our focus to those that are small, manageable and relevant. I might think about the number of people who will read these words, only to find some tiny bit of insight or benefit. That brings a lot of comfort, actually – to know you're not alone on this stage is awfully reassuring.

I can also take a look at the numbers in any of my bank accounts and be reminded that they are not a reflection of my true worth or value. Rather, with the appropriate amount of work and luck, these particular digits may grow to serve me in the future. They will enable me to invest in the things that I love. They will put me in a position to be just a bit more free year to year. All that is required is that I remember to be served, and not the other way around.

Finally, there are the numbers I care about most of all. Those that drive the refinement of my flesh and spirit. The digits that guide my training and make my plan – my journey – possible. Early in the day I can look out and see where it is I would like to go in the coming weeks, perhaps months. I can see the level of strength that is possible. And, I can certainly see what I must do today in order to make that future possibility a reality.

If I have a trick, it's this. I learned from Ernest Hemingway that if you want to avoid writer's block, simply stop your writing mid-sentence. When you're ready to resume the work, you'll know just how to begin. Why treat your training any differently? If you always leave just a little bit in the tank for the next time, you'll just about always set a record the next time! Yes, small numbers matter just as much as big ones.

We are all capable of driving massive shifts and change if we follow this sort of step driven path. Maybe that's the only real purpose of a good program or plan. Maybe it should simply serve as a reminder that it only takes a few more repetitions, a few more kilograms lifted to create that change, to keep us moving forward. The benefit is not just increased strength. Maybe it's the sensation of peace, assurance and satisfaction that we are really after. It just feels good to know that, even though you can't see all that far into the future, you're going to be just fine.

I'm as bad as anyone when it comes to forgetting the obvious stuff. The majesty of suspended, innumerable stars overhead is so amazing and overwhelming. How could it ever be ignored? But buried in these words is yet another thing I am missing.

The reason all of this can be so intense is that, well, it's not our job to figure it all out! It's not our karma. In truth, maybe the most important thing is to enjoy the moment and acknowledge how truly stunning it is to be here.

Just a few days ago I was doing some training out in my garage gym. Yes, as you know, it always comes back to training for me. Before me was the exact load I had planned on lifting the entire day before. The situation was simple – if I could lift that load, then I would know that I'm on the right path. I would know that I was growing stronger. After wiping the sweat from my eyes and applying a fresh layer of chalk to my calloused hands, I approached the barbell calmly. With feet driven into the floor and the flesh of my hands squeezed into the sharp knurling of the bar, I gathered my breath, arched my spine, and pulled with everything I had. The lift was an easy one, of course. After all, it's just a few more kilograms this time around (and nearly fifty kilograms more than I had lifted earlier in the year).

Yeah, it feels great to rack up these small victories – a steady march towards our dream outcome. But is this the best feeling? Is that all there is? No, I don't think so. I was pretty happy with my lift, so I stopped and sat down for a moment's rest. Just then my wife and two-year-old son came out into the garage to say hello and play. Before Max so much as notices me, his attention was immediately captured by the set of gymnastic rings I keep hanging in my squat rack.

"Oooh, oh!" he says. He's as present, excited and determined as any human being I have ever seen in my life. Those little chubby hands reach up and set their grip into those plastic rings, squeezing as hard as they can. Then, in a span of about ten seconds, the boy pulls his little feet up and holds them out in front of his body. I've never seen such a wide smile on a kid's face before. That's the shit that really makes being a parent the best possible thing.

Looking at that kid, I did the only thing I could do...I smiled just as wide. I clapped, then congratulated, "Good job, Maxie!" And maybe a tear or two of pride and joy surfaces, which is nothing I'm not too proud to admit. I just gave the kid the biggest kiss I could give. And that's just it, isn't it? The stars are impossibly beautiful, but I don't have to look up at anything to be amazed. This little boy running around under my feet is more than capable of doing that at any moment.

Max will grow up soon enough, a truth that I'm definitely not ready to face just yet! He'll do his best to make sense of it all. From time to time, he'll feel plenty small, mis-stepping more often than not. But that's OK. I'll be there along the way to remind him of something he taught his old man way back when on those rings.

"There is no poisoned arrow, Dad. There's just the moment. That's reason enough to smile extra wide!"

GET CHANGE

For Mae

You changed everything, Darling.

PROLOGUE

If I could only teach my kids one lesson, it would be Plato's Allegory of the Cave. As the lesson goes, imagine that you are a tiny creature chained down and locked away in a cramped, dark cave. Your movement is limited, you are not fulfilled, and you can barely see anything apart from the light that flickers across the rocky back wall.

The light creates crude shapes and figures that move left to right. They dance, intersect, interact. They are all you know, shaping every belief, goal, and opinion you have. You do not realize that the flicker and action are nothing more than cast images, silhouettes. An unseen puppeteer sits in front of a fire, controlling the dance, tightening your chain.

The wall would entertain, influence, and provoke, but your heart would grow heavier and heavier as the years went by and the questions piled up. Your divine side will whisper in your ear. Then it will roar. You will notice that although your chain is tight there is no lock. There is nothing stopping you from leaving that cave and stepping out into the sunlit world, the full scope of which is beyond your grasp.

When you do decide to make your escape, be careful and take your time. Tiny little creatures have tiny little eyes. The light is so bright, so hot and intense, it won't be much fun at first. It may even burn. I'm sorry that you have to go through that, but trust me when I tell you it's worth it.

In time, right on time, your eyes will grow strong. You will see for yourself a whole new world. Other kinds of creatures. A cool breeze. Astonishingly bright colors. An endless horizon. Best of all, in every little puddle of water you will see light reflect from the sun above. The cast image of a real thing, and there above in the unfathomable distance, hung within infinity, the sun itself.

Kids, listen closely. There will be times in your life where big decisions will be required. For now, it'll be pretty easy stuff. It's not easy to share your stuff, to hand over that Valentine's Day card to a crush, to live with the embarrassing moments, I know. School can be a pain in the ass. Your future feels far away. But hold on. Remember that you have nothing to lose. You might get hurt, sure, and you'll definitely feel embarrassed from time to time. You'll also recover from it all. You'll learn, and the next time around you will get it right. You'll be better, smarter, stronger and well prepared for the really big decisions down the road. You won't be such a small, blind little creature anymore.

The story I'm about to share isn't perfect. It isn't even close to finished yet. But it is honest: every thought, emotion, low moment and useful insight that I found during my hardest year is right here in these pages. It might not be everything that you expect, but I promise, in just a little while you will look down at those familiar chains and realize that there is no lock.

Open your brand new eyes, baby.

– Chris Moore
Memphis, Tennessee
August, 2014

PART 1
GET CHANGE

CLOUDY RED ROOM

I decided to sit down and have a drink with the old man. Why not? He's always around, rumbling away under his breath, peeking out at me. I thought I would say hello. And hell, I could use advice.

"Do you mind pouring me one of those?"
The old man raised a sharp eyebrow and one gray corner of his beard. "Sure," he replied. "But when did you get the taste for Scotch?"

"You should know better than anyone just how much people can change."

"Yes, I do, Baby Boy," he replied, now with a full, wide smile. "Yes, I do."

He finished his pour then pushed a few fingers worth across the table. "So, what's on your mind? And save the bullshit, baby, you know I don't have the patience."

I kicked the ice around a bit then took a sip. "I guess I'm just a little bit worried, that's all."

"Worried?"

"Yeah, so much is happening. So much is changing. I feel like I'm behind the wheel of one of those crazy-ass speed boats, you know? The water goes choppy and you're only one unlucky gust from flipping over. Worse still, what if I just fuck up and jerk the wheel by mistake? This whole thing could go up in flames, with smoldering chunks disintegrating across open water at two hundred miles an hour. Figuratively speaking, of course."

"For Christsakes, you always did have quite the imagination, didn't you? Do you know what your problem is?"

"I might, yeah. And I suppose you'll confirm it for me."

"You got that right. You're falling back on that old default setting. Social imprints and all that other bullshit people pile upon each other. The limitations that have been taught, yet are completely imaginary. That's what most scared primates do when life starts picking up steam and rumbling along too quickly. Illusion, Chris. That's what that is. The truth is that the world around might be plenty dangerous, and hard, and competitive, sure, but not as much as you'd guess. Nature isn't always red in tooth and claw. Your life isn't nearly as tricky, complicated, or illusive as that imagination of yours would suggest. Loosen your grip and see for yourself. There's nothing worth getting uptight over."

"I guess I can't really argue with that."

"But that's the problem, right there. The facts make plenty of sense, but that doesn't stop people from getting scared and denying it. Sure hasn't stopped your over-thinking, or the paralysis. It's funny, man, you go to school just about every day of your youth, and then you spend the rest of your time unlearning bad lessons and unlocking yourself."

The chat was heating up, but we took pause to tip back the tumblers.

"Do you know what really matters? You always have to search out your boundaries, the line, the edge, because it always changes. Day to day, year to year, you have to keep looking for it. That's where you test yourself, where you find endless new ideas, where you separate the bullshit from the truth. How long has it been since you've really seen your edge? I'm guessing a long time, right?"

"No, you're right. But I've been looking for it."

"Goddamit, looking ain't the same as doing. That's why you're here."

"I know."

"No, you don't, not yet. I remember that feeling, that all you had to do was wait on things. It would all happen, especially to a great guy. Yes, life would unfurl and draw you right in, if you wanted it hard enough."

"But doesn't that feeling count for something? I know that I need to actually bleed for awhile, really sacrifice, but other than that I don't feel sure of anything. I have to believe that if I bleed for long enough, I can make that dream come true."

"But see, that's just it."

"What, the dreaming?"

"No, the bleeding. How much blood have you shed? What action have you taken, man? What have you placed up on the altar so that you could make a run at this dream of yours? Dude, so many people burn away their lives waiting. There's something they love there's something they're desperate to do but people rarely define their work, relationships, their goals first by what they love. They don't do what they must, they defer all that in exchange for a paycheck, a short-term sugar rush, something less scary, something secure. Can you imagine, trading your time and ethereal self for something so cheap and corrosive?"

"I don't have to imagine it. I've done it for far too long already."

"Then I guess you get it now. Consider yourself

lucky enough. Most folks don't realize it until their ship has all but sailed. That's a goddamn shame."

I nodded, sipped the spirit, ran my thumb around the lip of that icy tumbler, wiping away the moisture to reveal crystal clear glass underneath.

"Fuck. I'm guilty."

"It's so easy to call it a temporary thing. We tell ourselves that one day soon we'll start putting that dream together, right after the current mirage has run its course. Just for a little while longer. 'I can't afford to leave yet. Just a few more years, then I will do something for myself.' Then we realize just how quickly ten years can pass by. Everyone's been guilty, man. You just have to remind yourself that you were not equipped with a powerful mind and abiding body so that you could burn away your time in the safe zone."

The old man poured another round. By the third glass of scotch I was all ears. "So, you're worried that you're going to fuck up this life somehow, right? That you'll break it. I get it, but listen, how many times have you felt this way before?"

"I guess I've always felt a little worried about it, that I would make a wrong turn and botch the whole plan, if there is a plan. Fuck, I don't know."

"Right, but why are you still so surprised when things shake themselves out? You should be smiling most of the time instead of worrying, you know that."

"I know."

"So do it, baby. There's no time for complaining about some circumstances, or the timing. There's no time but right now, so stop waiting. Take the action.

You might as well bleed a bit, there's no harm."

I was struggling to ask questions by the bottom of the third drink, but I could still manage one last query.

"Are you happy with your life? You've seen what's ahead, so, tell me Is it worth it?"

The old man managed a wide gray smile. "Worth it? Yeah, I guess it was. Every second of it, actually. All this talk of passion and bleeding, do you remember what Mr. Bukowski had to say about love and work, right?"

"Find what you love and let it kill you."

"That's it. I've gone over the boundary, the line, the edge a few times. It's not always fun, but I agree with Charles. You can't burn time worrying about what you're going to find on the other side. It all looks scarier from a distance, that much you get. But forget the fear. Instead, just fight for what you love. Do what you simply must do. Do it hard! Worship it like a voluptuous life-giving goddess, but don't run away too far when she breaks your heart. That pain is just as natural as the bleeding. Just come back to it. Let it take you away and kill you again and again and again if that's what it wants to do. Hell no, it's not always fun, but it's always worth it."

FIND WHAT YOU LOVE AND LET IT KILL YOU.

THE FORMER

It's strange to be a former something.

I'm not talking about relatively benign history, random old jobs and identities, puppy love gone bad and all the stuff that occupies slivers of your memory and spills out in dreams on rare occasion. No, your real former self is still hanging around in the bright daylight. It's captured in every family picture. It's the old nickname that really stuck, unfortunately. It might be stuffed tightly inside that closet duffle bag you cannot bring yourself to toss out.

One such bag of mine is filled with old, stinky football memorabilia. Decade-old uniforms, team pictures from games won and lost, typical stuff that once defined me. I know, it didn't take much back then. But now I'm fascinated by the fact that I can hardly recognize myself in the old team pictures. It's like a window into an alternate reality, the photos the only tangible evidence of a past life that played out thirteen years ago. Plenty of time to see yourself turned over completely. Every last atom, every motive and goal, all of it.

Those pictures are weird because that guy really is gone. The time in between was filled with incredible quantities of trial and error, though it was mostly error if I'm honest. It was no fun at the time, but now I've come to see that the more honest mistakes you can make early on, the better. It's a fair trade, especially if you consider that most of the negative emotions around failure are all optional.

More than anything else, I just want to be in motion. There's nothing like the energy and thrill that accompanies a new, exhilarating, and enlightening experience. It pushes you forward. It's a fuel, freely available to anyone willing to go for it. I wonder if I really am in motion. I hope so.

Standing still produces the opposite feeling, that I know. It's madness, really. A motionless and unchanging state is a cursed fate: sad, unnecessary, and all too common. It's fucking hell, actually, and wholly against the natural order of things.

We can do so much better, and we will. I will. Let's have the barbell tame and tune our flesh, shall we? We can make more time for slow and deep breaths to settle our minds. We can cleanse ourselves of all the bullshit that society and school and well-intentioned parents lay on us by reading more books. Yes, this is still an amazing thing to do, I assure you. Read and then read some more. We can also refill our souls with honest, unfiltered conversation with other enlightened, curious, friendly, open-minded primates. And fuck yes, we can always make room for a nice cup of coffee and a few Chuck Berry tunes on a perfectly cool late Friday afternoon. Whatever the worry may be, it can wait, right? This is the righteous path, friends. This is the sort of vibe that we're after.

*

I love stories. Nothing stirs me up like an awesomely motivating movie. My favorite film ever for such an occasion is most certainly *The Last Samurai* with Tom Cruise. I know, I know, it's probably as historically accurate as a creationist history textbook. But that's hardly the point. What I'm after is the fictional romantic thrill, of course. About an hour into that flick and I'm ready to quit my life, fly to Japan to play out my days staring at fucking cherry blossoms! Yes indeed, that would be a fine retirement. But for years I would always cap such day dreams with something to the effect of, "Someday. For now, I'll keep doing what I have to do." That's the story we tell ourselves, when in reality no one is enforcing those terms. We are free to be anything, to write our own role in our own story. We can make any change we want, if we are bold enough and have got the balls to go through with it.

This is our opportunity, baby. We can make our move right now, we can kick off the change right. When life hands us lemons, we will make something fancy out of it like Lemmon Pots du Crème with Meringue Brulée (take note of this advice, gentlemen, as the ladies really do love a man who can satisfy a sweet tooth with whatever is on hand). You've got all you need to do whatever you want.

I cannot wait to see what I become next. I can't say for sure what it might be, but that's exactly 100% of the fun here. I don't know. I don't want to know. So let there be no more delay. Let's get to studying the heroes. Let's look for things to say yes to. Let's be open. But first, just give me two fingers worth of scotch whiskey over ice. Be generous, please. On a perfect Friday afternoon like this, that's just about all I need to get things going. Oh, and a few of those tunes from Mr. Berry, please. What better hero could you ask for? He always seemed to be the coolest guy in any room.

TERMINAL

An airplane just isn't the place for proper sleep, especially when you're dead tired. At best you can achieve a dazed state of consciousness. Not quite restorative, more like stasis.

My eyes are closed tight while those off-white earbuds serve to mask the constant hum of the engines outside. Of course lying down is mere fantasy at this point, so I bury my forehead firmly into the seat ahead to give my neck a much-needed break. Closed eyelids serve as little projection screens for the strange waves of light and shapes now occupying my field vision. Yep, pressurized cabins and cumulative jet lag dazedness are a real trip.

One turbulent jostle and I'm upright once again, semiconscious. That's when I notice my hands, dry and cracked from the recycled, pressurized winter air. They are restless and shaky at every joint. They're jittery too. That's the only part that makes me worry, actually. I'm used to being tired. This is not tired. This is the ground shifting under my feet. This is what it feels like when things get weird.

I look over to Mike Bledsoe, who's sitting to my left, just to check my bearings. "I think I might have been hallucinating a little bit just now. Little shapes, little cartoons. I really can't tell if I was dreaming or not."

"Oh yeah?" he replies, not looking all that better to be honest. Call it blurry-eyed indifference. "That sounds pretty weird."

"Yeah, I thought so."

When you find yourself with that kind of acute brain fever, it's wise to just sit in your chair for a while and get your bearings about you. I was in no mood to jump right back into that horde of humanity waiting just beyond the gate. It didn't take much convincing. "Let them stand, fiddle, and rush around," I thought. "I'm fine right here, slouching and content within this tube. Baggage claim can fucking wait, alright?" It's just too harsh down there. Everyone waits around that conveyer belt, staring, waiting, feet pointed toward the door because there's just so much shit out there waiting to get done, am I right?

The feeling is temporary. Before long all I can think about is that cold stream of air shooting down into my left eyeball and the now depleted bag of M&M trail mix that was no longer capable of sustaining my existence. So I jump up at the next opportunity, just as an elderly man to my right reaches for his bag and causes a temporary break in the exodus.

Feel free to take a moment for zoning out, but understand that opportunities come and go. If you can manage it, jump right up when you've got that opening, regardless of the potential consequences. Regardless of your pissy attitude. Fear might get to you, sure. But there's always the next chance. Jump up, jump, for Christsakes, catch on!

I shuffle down the narrow aisle, clumsy, disheveled, bags and headphone cords held high to avoid the inopportune arm-rest snags, as if I were wading through murky, waist-deep swamp water. The only remaining hurdle was the stewardess waiting by the exit door. Shit, she looked miserable. "Thanks

for flying with us today, sir. Please enjoy your stay."
She, of course, didn't give two shits about the quality
of my stay. After all, this is the same exact women that
snarled and huffed and puffed just a little bit when I
politely suggested that Miller Light couldn't possibly be
the only alcoholic beverage aboard this aircraft. But I'm
not offended. Who knows what she's carrying around
with her, what she's struggling with? You can be sure it's
something. Maybe she's just sick of being in this fucking
tube every day, the terminal trolley ride waits, the shitty
airport-industrial park hotels, and that steady diet of
little gin bottles and cinnamon cookie wafers. I can't
blame her. I just look at her with lagged eyes, smiling,
answering only, "You bet!" It was the best I could do.

My pace picks up speed once my feet hit the
terminal carpet. From here on one of my favorite rituals
supplements my drained energy reserves. I cannot get
my little earbuds back in fast enough. I stretch my thumb
out a bit, then make quick work of the travel playlist
shuffle. The first tune in this new city, the particularly
fitting "Leave it" by Bombay Bicycle Club. The opening
lines seemed to soothe my frayed eardrums immediately.

I picked that tune because I know it well. I've
played the song so many times that it immediately lends
a sense of the familiar. Also, it feels like it's being sung
directly at me in this moment. That's the way a song
should feel when you're hearing it at exactly the right
time. Just keep pulling out the records during hard
times, until you find something that serves to soothe
and cleanse. My head clears a bit, enough for me to
acknowledge that a shallow three hours of sleep in an
uncomfortable hotel room the night before was no sleep
at all.

Something is bubbling up, shaking itself loose. Could it be that, as just another aspiring writer, I now find myself at the center of my own Franz Kafka-style metamorphosis? "That's far too indulgent, Chris," I think to myself, drawing things back into focus. "I just think you could use a drink."

Who am I to argue with that?

With a half hour to spare, we settle into the terminal bar.

"Good morning, gentlemen. What can I get for you? Hot coffee, tea, orange juice..."

"Glenlivet, please," Mike answers. And with only a small delay, I follow with my order of a tall Guinness. "It's been kind of a harsh morning, you know?" The man nods in agreement, then gathers the food menus. Most people have been here a few times. It's universal.

Before long I'm with beer, smiling. It's 10:30 a.m. on a random-ass Friday morning, but it might as well be midnight under the red lights. Everything is coming back into focus. I'm smiling within smoke-filled spaces. I'm playing Stooges tunes and feeling confident, perky, and not at all ready for bedtime.

I grab my pint and polish off the remainder. I set the empty, foamy glass back down with a gentle, steady hand. I stretch. I smirk. I remind myself that the last thing I need right now is another round of resolutions. I just need to learn to get out of my own fucking way, to let my metamorphosis happen. I know, it only took 33 years to learn.

I begin making my way to the connecting gate, confident as hell, pilot light shining bright. With one more click of the thumb the tunes return. I am ready to move along, just as I leave with that final thought. "Shit, if there's some sort of change to be made, then for Christsakes, let's get on with it. I'm ready for that ride."

EMBRACE CHANGE AND PINT GLASSES.

NOT GUILTY

Sometimes a story comes out all on its own.

I sat down to write a few hours ago, about what I had no idea. It's a common thing, to not know at all. But this is what came rushing out after the first few lines got painfully laid down.

John Lennon was cool as shit, but no saint. Who is? But man, he's just a little bit guiltier than some. After all, he is responsible for unleashing Yoko Ono upon this world. That's a bit of negative karma if you ask me, but no bother. I can take it, and the other offenses that are easily visible from a just cursory view. It's alright. No one's got all their shit together. The sooner you really accept that, the happier and more tolerant you'll be.

We do still have to credit John as a modern day musical genius type, right? That's even with his posthumous legend being inflated a bit, of course, by his terrible and untimely demise in New York City. I've always been more of a Stones guy myself, but I certainly believe the world was robbed and permanently damaged by the lunatic gunman that pulled the plug on John's amp. It really sucks, and it happens all the time to amazing, brilliant, genius people. I know, thinking over that low note doesn't get you far, nor will losing sleep over a guy like Mark David Chapman do you any good. But we can still let out a cathartic, "Fuck you!" That goes a long way, right?

For all his flaws, the Beatle was a hugely impactful teacher of sorts. I'll always remember his famous statement that, while we make other plans for our futures, our lives happen. That rings true every day.

We have to deal with that paradox. When it comes to making plans, what's apparent to us now might not be so a little bit later. On one hand, we all understand and accept that research and planning greatly reduce the odds of us fucking things up. At its best, that diligence makes our success more probable. But how many can say that life has turned out just as they had planned it out a decade or two before? I would guess just about nobody. Further, how many successful people out there right now wish that all of those old plans would have worked out? That's right, just about nobody.

The lesson seems easy enough. Plan properly, but remain flexible. All the really good shit in life will probably come along when you're not even expecting it, despite your plans. I think that's a useful approach that will keep you from missing out on some of the wilder and more-rewarding rides life has to offer.

Come to think of it, the very best example might be travel itself.

One of the worst things you can do when visiting somewhere new is to overplan. Rushing around like mad checking off targeted destinations is no way to experience a place. At best, all you do is catch a snapshot, a series of blurs and shadows, a dirty reflection, a half note. If you ask me, you're better off dropping those bags at the hotel and going out for a really long walk. Sniff out the street food and listen to the local music. Grab one of whatever the locals are drinking. You'll do just fine.

People are pretty great, all things being equal.

I promised myself to stick to this approach when I first visited Europe back in 2009. As cliché as it might sound, you only get one go at that first experience, so I wanted to nail it. That didn't keep me from making a blunder on my very first night in Paris. My wife and I visited a massively popular tourist attraction at sunset. Fuck, I know, right? It seems like a great idea to go see blood-red sun rays draped across the edges of the Eiffel Tower. But no, it wasn't so beautiful when we were essentially cornered by a group of bold men selling tiny knockoff key-chains and tacky little bracelets made of bright green, yellow, and black strings. I did the only sensible thing I could think of. I took out a fistful of cash and brought it slowly to belly height, peeling off a ten Euro ransom and forking it over. "There you go," I said as I traded for a shitty wrist ornament. "I'll make sure to treasure this forever."

Transaction complete, I fold the cash up neatly, keeping eye contact all the while. That seemed terribly important to do. Just as the moment couldn't grow any more tense on my end, I took my wife's hand and we continued on our way. I really expected to be cracked over the dome with one of those metal souvenir towers, but perhaps my puffed chest and confident gaze was deterrent enough. Maybe I never had anything to worry about at all, as the danger could have been totally impinged, the product of some subconscious judgment or prejudice. You'll be surprised to know that most people are terribly kind and polite, even in a place like Paris that's somewhat notorious for its attitude. If you are polite as well, of course. Strange how that works.

Make a note – be mindful of those who can only offer shallow criticism in reference to other cultures, people, or ideas. This is the signature characteristic of someone offering useless insight or advice.

My Parisian wandering was for the most part amazing. I drank coffee. I ate everything I came across. The constant caffeine-and-pastry-fueled marching up and down city streets and subway lines eventually took me to the Pantheon, an incomprehensibly beautiful church turned secular mausoleum I would have otherwise missed. At first this place came off no different than any other famous museum spot. That is until we made our way down through the central, ancient stairway, into the belly of the structure. A crypt, to be specific. Here lay the mortal remains of some amazing people, including Marie Curie, whose pioneering research on radiation has saved more lives than she could have ever imagined. It's so unfortunate that her gift came at the cost of her own life.

My primary person of interest down in this crypt was Francois Marie Arouet, otherwise known as Voltaire, the French writer and philosopher. I could not deny the dude's presence as I stood next to the sarcophagus, even though he's been dead for over two hundred years. The feeling was entirely imagined, but it hardly matters. The moment was real enough to be impactful on a young, recovering meathead only starting to figure his shit out.

In my view, Voltaire was at root all about freedom of expression. A right mostly taken for granted now, but an act that surely would have had you imprisoned or murdered during the better part of history. There was duty and honor in preserving this right. In 1752, Voltaire commented on the topic of sin and judgment. He stripped away all the typical dogma you would expect in such a discussion, proclaiming, "Every man is guilty of all the good he did not do." That was a powerful, crystal-clear doctrine that ripped the curtains back and spilled bright light on everything in my life. A key consideration, the question on the table: was I going to be happy staying on the comfortable, easy, quiet path? Or, should I seek out a wilder ride?

The answer was easy. I didn't know where to go, or what to do with the coming years. I just thought I would keep the thought in mind. I would whisper it under my breath during tough times. I would be reminded, "No, not today. I will not be guilty."

YOU ARE GUILTY OF ALL THE GOOD YOU DIDN'T DO.

TURNING ON THE CHARM

I scribble down catchy music lyrics and punchy lines at every opportunity. I snap quick pictures of impactful paragraphs for later reference. And like any domesticated ape with a smart phone, I enjoy my fair share of pop quotations from famous people. Authors, philosophers, actors, musicians, it doesn't matter so long as the person is interesting and thought-provoking. The authenticity of the quote actually might not matter to me that much, either.

Who cares if a quote is 100% accurate or not? Did the words move you to take some action? If so, there's no harm. Consider this the intellectual equivalent of popping a breath mint, a wintergreen jolt of perspective to get your gray matter moving. Now, if it compelled you to take action, then those words would gain immeasurable power. In that case, who cares how accurate it is?

The Muse has whispered the same inspiring lines over and over again, in countless forms and languages, a million times before. You are the next to receive it and carry it forward. Consider this a blessing, a really amazing opportunity to push the idea further.

I guess you do get a bonus bump when the material is authentic. You can tell. The words seem to be richer. They bend the air differently. Case in point, I have a neat little tome called *Leonardo's Notebooks*, a compilation of Leonardo da Vinci's personal sketches and ideas scribbled down something like 500 years ago. It's got some truly mind-blowing sketches coupled with interpretations, and even handwritten study notes and corrections from the man himself.

What better source of quotation material could you possibly ask for? We might as well agree that this man was a true genius amongst geniuses, eternally impactful and masterfully skilled at...well...just about everything. And I do mean everything. He was brave as hell to boot, as he's rumored to have been a homosexual at a time when just trying to be a fucking artist and a scientist for a living was really more than enough to get you killed, or at the least be imprisoned. Also, he appears to have enjoyed a little wine in the morning. I certainly can dig that. The morning light is really bright and harsh when you've been up all night "painting," believe me.

Consider this topic for starters. Of all those pesky human traits we could name, what's the most destructive thing? To the environment, to society, to ourselves what causes the most damage, suffering, dissatisfaction, and ultimately, the most lost time? It could be the constant craving and wanting. More is never enough, you know? I cannot count the cravings I've had this morning alone. Something new. Something better. Something more in line with my expectations. Something crunchy, or something just a little more sweet. Just one more cup of coffee. It's always something. But more is rarely necessary.

*

Leonardo's notes seem particularly impactful during recent rounds of reading, coffee and craving, especially these lines:

A painter who has clumsy hands will paint similar hands in his works, and the same will occur with any limb unless long study has taught him to avoid it. Therefore, O Painter, look carefully to that part most ill-favored in your own person and take particular pains to correct it in your studies. For if you are coarse, your figures will seem the same and devoid of charm. It is the same with any part that may be good or poor in yourself; it will be shown in some degree in your figures.

I'm coming to terms with the fact that we basically always have two options. First, we could push for more and more all the time, or we could become less coarse. Better still, we can work to balance the two options. For myself, I want to be the kind of person who pounces on an opportunity as soon as it pokes its furry little head from its desert borough. I will knock it over the head and slap it on the barbecue because it will feed my family and help me sleep easy.

But for all those times where the action will not bring more happiness, or more value, or more freedom, then I really want to do a better job of saying no. I must do that because my future depends on it. I'm much too coarse.

I could go on and on doing the same old things working the same job, living in the same town, creating the same types of art, training and pushing my body for more and more records. But the truth is that I, you, we always stand to gain just as much by going back and unlearning countless destructive and limiting ideas. The Muse whispers to me right now, "Take those ill-favored works and do your best to correct them. Show the best side of yourself in your works."

That thought is much more than pop-quotation motivation porn. It's a real lesson. Go back and study a decision. A situation. A progression. Your training. Your craft. Think for a while. How could it be done better? How could it be improved upon? What can be corrected so that there will be fewer limitations down the road? Replace your beliefs and sacred cows with something new. Something read or stumbled upon. Something learned late on a Friday night after damn good conversation and a few proper pints of ale. More is not better, only better is better. And better works both ways, back and forth.

Go back and study yourself, Chris. What points of view are holding you back? What do you assume to be impossible that's anything but? In what areas of your life are you devoid of charm? Fix that. It's the only way to move forward.

PROGRESS WORKS BOTH WAYS. DON'T BE AFRAID OF A LITTLE BACK AND FORTH.

HIT ME

10:00 a.m., the day my world changed forever.

No one likes coming here. You walk right through the front door wearing a heavy coat of dread, passing through a branded lobby carefully designed to remind you that humans are just little ceramic coffee cups bouncing along life's granite countertop. "But we can take care of you at times like this. Just sign here first."

Luckily I don't buy it. I've never bought it. Dad did, I guess. He seemed to embrace this ending, although to his credit he never blinked one goddamn time under the fading lights. He was reassured and calm, for whatever that's worth. I don't know that I could embrace any of this. I'd much rather follow behind Mr. William Henley and be the captain of my own soul. At least I will try. I will fight for the chance to shuffle off to the next realm with my ass parked on some white sandy beach, well-tanned, holding onto a warming glass that once held that perfect red grapefruit margarita.

I really do hope for that, because all I can feel right now is my father's struggle, and his pain, and his desire to be any place other than this. That feeling just piles up higher and higher as I pass by the gift shop, the cafeteria that's serving pseudo-hamburger substitute, onto the elevator that will take me to the third-floor intensive care unit.

The doors open into a raw, menacing environment, as scary as anything you could ever see. From out in the hallway, I can look in and spot Dad's big boney leg. Even in this state he's a pretty heavy guy, never all that shy of two hundred pounds. I have the same frame, which is one of the positive things we share. I'm thankful for it every time I almost break a bone doing something silly. But I'm also still learning to overcome a lot of the less positive things. Right here, at the foot of the bed, I'm reminded of how hardheaded I can be. Sometimes it's a good thing, but often times it's not. That's the quality that put Dad here in this bed before he needed to be. It would love to do the same thing to me, but thankfully I'm trying to learn from all this now. I'm here, looking for something to smile over, opened up and unafraid of what's going down.

My words start to fail me. There's my Pop, alive but locked in a zombie-like state of consciousness due to the steady propofol drip. "Well, at least he's moving and coming around," I thought. But that's when something really extraordinary and intense happened.

He unexpectedly opened his eyes wide, like he was spooked by some dark spirit. His eyes locked onto my mother who was already standing beside the bed. His face then absolutely exploded with raw emotion, every kind, from highest to lowest and back again. That was the last time I ever saw his eyes open.

I didn't want to hide from the intensity of the moment. I couldn't. I had to see the circle close.

WHY ARE YOU WAITING? THE TIME IS NOW, NOW'S THE TIME.

1:00 A.M., THE MORNING AFTER

I've always struggled to define my taste in music, to explain just why I dig what I dig. I don't really have a single favorite genre or style, and I certainly cannot bring myself to rank and choose between favorites. That's such an impossible task, one that begs swift retribution from the celestial Muses. It's more just a matter of picking the best possible tune for the given situation, project, mood or life crisis. That shit's variable.

In simple terms, it's about listening to what makes the most sense to you right now, in perfect moments or at a time like this when everything seems upside down and broken.

I often find guidance and inspiration in the lyrics and rhythm, but all I really need, the only thing I must have on a daily basis, is the restoration and soothing qualities of the music. It's precious and sacred to me, as essential as food and clean water. That's really how I've come to understand music and any kind of art, really. Where the world sullies and spoils, art will cleanse and restore. That's why I need my music, now more than ever.

The next artist up on my playlist was Bob Marley, who really was a true force of nature behind the microphone. I felt his lyrics scoop up and cradle my little baby soul the night of my father's funeral. Of all the tough moments I've known, this was the toughest. I had Bob's ethereal, eternal spirit right there in the room with me. I'm simply grateful to have this to turn to, and to love it so. I just owe too much to it.

It'll be alright. Hit me again, baby. How bad could it be?

But of course, where music will soothe a beaten soul, it will also expand one that's just beginning to bloom. At least this is what I accept as true after listening to one of my all-time favorite Pearl Jam songs this afternoon, "Rearview Mirror."

To be honest, this song is really intense for anyone who's ever endured a tough relationship, whether with another person, a job, a substance, whatever. The key is the idea that we can see things with greater clarity when they appear behind us, in our rearview mirrors.

Now I can hear Eddie Vedder mumbling away in my imagination, bottle of red wine and cigarette in hand. "Shit man, you know exactly what you need to do. So what are you waiting for? [*lights smoke*] Dude, the time is now and now's the time. If this whole death thing has taught you anything, it's that."

Eddie is always right in my book, even when he's conjured, so I'll have to have faith in that advice. I'll have to act. I will. I'll break the cords. I will unplug. I will slow down. I will take notice. I will be there, right there, where I need to be every day. I will not chase after shit I do not want or need. I will not sit back and wait for the circle to close.

Until I shuffle off this mortal coil and "Magnolia Mountain" plays me off the stage (this is stipulated in my will; I'm not taking any chances), I want to seek out amazing people, learn their story, and hopefully do a decent job of sharing that experience with the world. For everything that music has given to me, this is the least I could do to return the debt. I'm sure Pops would dig it too.

It's time I went full-speed with this now. It's time I showed the world just how stubborn and brash my father's son can be.

STAY ON TOP OF THE TRUTH.

TRUTHS

I don't think I carry around much regret, but in general I suppose I could have spent a lot less time searching around for well-defined truths. Like anyone, I take up my shovel daily and go digging around in some direction. Sometimes the effort is well planned, sometimes it is random and desperate. In any event, I find value in the constant motion. As they say, you don't win anything with unscratched lottery tickets. I'll take the shots. If nothing else, it's good form to stay busy.

We are all looking around for something worth biting into, something real for once, a gold chunk amongst the gray gravel. Until we find it, we're more than happy to go on fidgeting, worrying, imagining ourselves as the very first primate ever to have experienced such trials and tribulations.

Cue the hurt feelings. Bring out the lollipops.

Let's put down our collective pacifiers and remind ourselves that this struggle we're feeling is universal. Everyone has to deal with this constant searching. But that's the gig. You only begin to sort your shit out, heal and go on, once you've realized that the whole sensation of struggle is totally conjured. I find myself asking the question, "If you're so tired of digging all around, why don't you stop?"

Things get easier once you realize that the digging and the searching isn't all that necessary. It's work for work's sake and doesn't really lead anywhere. It just leaves you inflamed, wanting. It helps to realize up front that truth isn't a permanent thing. It shifts along with your ripening perspective. But don't freak out over it! Not yet, at least.

Remember, you knew this aspect of the truth already. Things change, and change is scary as fuck. It's also the key to everything, so we might as well get used to it.

When we are willing to change with everything else, we are alright. When we resist, we are fucked. The longer we hold on to the bullshit the more intense the fuckery gets. How rare it is that the best thing to do is also the most convenient?

I'm sitting here typing with a long list of beliefs in my pocket. I have an understanding of what it means to be an athlete, a hardworking employee, an artist of sorts, a husband, a father, you name it. And here's the scary part – I know this is the best I can do right now and I don't think it's going to be good enough.

"Take a deep breath, Chris. Sip some reposado and apple juice. Draw in one deep, hot breath. Be cool."

I'm constantly worried that there won't be enough of whatever it is I've got to find, and that I'll fuck up the game in some permanent way. That stings deep every day, but I also have to remind myself that this is a tiny little divine kick in the ass. It's a blessing to be aware that I'm not unique and isolated and that my discomfort at this stage of life has been felt countless times over by many a primate before me.

That's the sour but reassuring side of the truth. The second, truthier, motivating side is that it's a damn shame to be selfish or ignore the struggles of those around you, all lives you could easily affect for the better, even if in a tiny way when all it takes is a small step. If you can know and accept that then you can drive yourself forward to wherever you need to be. It's guaranteed. It can be a bit painful, but that's the fuel that will keep you firing, carrying you on to the next day. And shit, every new day comes with so many new steps you could take if you decide to.

I know I'll be capable of more because I can look back and see how much farther off track I used to be, which is a nice and cozy reassurance. A few years ago, last year, even last month... I'm way different now. What I did. How I trained. What I taught. What I believed. What I was prepared to ask and say out loud.

The things I believed to be possible. Every truth has been radically redefined and will be again.

To paraphrase Eddie Vedder, we all have different ways of thinking in our individual brains, and that's okay. Fucking-a it's okay! Look back and see just how much you have really changed. It's scary, eh? So keep that in mind the next time you whip out your dick and slap it across someone else's point of view. Think of it the next time you make a judgment against yourself and what's possible for you.

We're speeding along, baby. Everything is in rapid motion, impermanent, so let go of the rails. But before you go zooming along let me leave you with one more little pearl. The only thing you have to worry with believing is this: when it comes to your philosophy, your work, your family and friends, just go full speed in the direction of what you love most. Not an easy thing. Not the thing that always rewards. The thing you feel you must do, do that. That's your truth. It may change and shift from time to time, but it will always be true because it will change with you. As everything shifts and churns you'll be right where you need to be. Scared shitless, of course, but how boring is the alternative?

Staying out ahead of what you believe is tough, and takes some getting used to, but it beats the hell out of what we had before. We don't need filters over our eyes, ears and minds. Let's push on. Let's work hard to stay on top of the truth.

YOU'VE STILL GOT A CHOICE, DON'T YOU?

TRUST

Overall, I'd say the experience was much harder than I had first imagined.

I expected to drive in to to the office, park my Jeep, and then burst out into the cold winter air ready to kick ass. The cave's illusions shattered, a menacing cloud of desert rock would be at my back. It was time to pull the dream down from the cloud. Push the chips in. Take a real risk for once. Final victory and vindication. A clean and bloodless transition.

But that's not what's waiting for you on the back end. Instead, things only get more intense, with your being reminded of obvious, terrifying things. Some miserable guy with the glazed look of the damned is going to look you right in the eye and explain that you should think twice. "Have you considered your family at all in this decision?"

Is this guy just trying to fuck with me now? Is this the first play they teach you out of the Human Resources playbook? *Scare Keanu back to his battery cage by invoking images of loved ones. This always seems to do the job.*

I'll be honest. All I could think of in that instant were all the times I had daydreamed about doing something else. All the times I had fantasized about changing my life. All the times I just sat there, hoping for shit as I continued to push action items around my work space. *Just a shot at the dream, some kind of a lucky break. That's all I need.* If I'm honest, this hoping wasn't action at all. That's exactly why the decision took eight years. I had to work at it and learn the truth the hard way.

The suit spoke back up, "Hey, times are tough, you know? The market out there is not what it used to be. It's a hard industry. Look, you've experienced a lot this year. Your dad passing. You have a new baby on the way, is that right? Yeah, it's a tough thing. Have you really thought about what you're doing? In the end you've still got a choice here, you know?"

Right there is your test, friend. At some point between right now and your dream really coming true someone might ask you whether it's wise to sacrifice so much for what you love. Your security. The pleasing mirage of having a good thing going for you. All that you've worked for leading up to the fateful moment. They're going to make you say it all again out loud, to make you feel like you're somehow renouncing god and country. Then they'll ask you to write it down on a big official form, with the final signature cross your heart, hope to die. So, what do you say to that? Here some guy takes out a heart-shaped shiv and jams it straight into your soft under-belly, figuratively speaking. The sensation is not pleasant. It sucks out just about all the breath you've got...almost.

With the acute pain fading, you will gather up just enough air for your reply. "Yeah, I've considered my family. That's just about all I've done. And you're exactly right about one thing. I do still have a choice."

I'll never forget the conversation I had in that airport terminal. "Burn the boats. You'll make it, you'll have to!" And this is what the flames look like right up close. They are hot, they are intense, and I have to admit, the water is chilly and scary as fuck! Luckily my next choice is perfectly obvious and far easier to make. "I think I'll swim."

The drive home afterward was surreal. I felt numb but at peace. Sort of like the feeling that comes over you when you're lying on the floor after a tough training session. It's a cleansing feeling, a humbling thing. It helps you to cast your eye back on what matters now. "Please Do Not Let Me Go" was playing over the speakers. There were no storm clouds, only the sun getting brighter and hotter as it rose overhead. I caught myself smiling. So far, so good.

I wish I would have learned the lesson sooner, but oh well. Better late than never. As the old saying goes, the absolute best time to plant a tree was twenty years ago. Then, you could be lying in the shade today. The next best time to plant is right fucking now. It's time to take action. It's time to take the risk head on.

The fear feels very real, intense, crushing at times, but I've put in the work. I'm on the other side of that decision now.

Your shot at the dream, the break, your faith, it's all great and fine. But the action is all that matters. You have to demonstrate to yourself and all of creation that you truly love what you say you love, and that you will not live apart from it, or ignore it, or delay it any longer. There's no time for that, friends. We have to go for it. That leap will surely get the Muse's attention. She will have to see us through to the other side.

At least, this is where I'm placing my faith now. Repeat, repeat, repeat: So far, so good.

SOME THINGS MIGHT NEVER HAPPEN, BUT THEY ALWAYS COULD.

WHAT DO YOU BELIEVE IS POSSIBLE?

ANYTHING IS PROBABLE

Look, I know the Internet is dipped in bullshit, especially when it comes to idiotic sources of information and quotes of questionable authenticity. I have to think, "Believe nothing you read, and only half of what you see." That policy might be a little bit aggressive, but cognitive caution and critical appraisal is not a widely cultivated skill. Let's not discourage it.

There is a way to know whether what you're reading is of any real value. It's quite simple, really. If that little string of words kicks over a few dominos in your brain, sparking new thoughts or insights, then you've found something worthy of your consideration. It doesn't really matter who wrote it, or whether they were a scholar or a con man (not that these are mutually exclusive).

I have learned that while some things are unlikely, they could, at any time, become possible. The higher levels of your primate brain bark back predictably, "But dude, like, things can't be likely and unlikely at the same time." Well, as it happens, you are both right and wrong! At first glance, no, we cannot simultaneously observe the impossible and the possible. But when it comes to all of the probabilities and potential outcomes in your everyday life, the odds are not a matter of mathematics or logical reasoning. No, they are determined by what you are prepared to believe.

What are the odds that your dream, regardless of the scale, will come true? Perhaps you want to open up your own high-end dog grooming business, specializing in artisanal anal-gland expression. That's great. The world needs people just like you. Or, you could have a more common sort of dream. To break away from your shit gig, to write a book, to lose fifty pounds, to find someone to love. It could be anything, but the question is the same. How exactly will you make this fucking thing happen?

I'm big, so I'm qualified to comment on the plight of the fat guy. I can make the jokes. You get into this club by simply demonstrating the burden that is tying your shoes. But I'm also human, which qualifies me to comment on our general condition. Here's the big problem. In my humble view, we spend too much time waiting around for a fucking breakthrough. It just doesn't work.

Many people assume that chasing their dreams is a lot like the game *Frogger*. You wait around alongside the busy road of life. As soon as you see an opportunity, you slip out into traffic. At first there is excitement, like when you land that new job. But then the pressure sets in. Make your next move quickly, or you're going to end up flat underneath something very heavy. Also, as in the game, there are those dark times where you must take a few steps back to save your hide. With enough patience, skill and good fortune you might make your way all the way over the highway, just in time to cash out that retirement savings account and move to Florida. With any luck, you'll be happy, but don't count on it.

If we wait around for our dream, we'll be waiting forever. That's where the math comes in. It's not that the world doesn't care, it's just that there's too many variables that do not include you right now. This is especially true if you spend the better part of your days and evenings eating Chunky Campbell's soup right out of the can while playing *Grand Theft Auto 5*. No! What we're going to do instead is improve the probability of our dream becoming reality.

There may be an infinite number of ways to do this, but three come to mind. First, find the damn thing. Start with your dream, if you know it. What do you love to create? What would you love to do most, right now? It doesn't have to be your destiny or some overwhelming passion, it just needs to elevate your pulse and bring a smile to your face. That's all. What do you want?

Now that you know the thing, place 100% of your focus on helping others with the same goal. It's important to make money and establish your name, sure, but this shit takes care of itself if you start with the right motive. And please understand the only thing that really does matter is using your skills to help others in some way, even if you're inspiring them to say, "Hey, look at this bitchin' hand-crafted bottle opener! Wow!"

The final step is repetition. Repeat, repeat, repeat, because your dream life doesn't come down to breakthroughs, dear reader. It's about improving the odds – the possibility – that you'll be able to touch and positively affect more people. You do that through practice, endless practice. Fueled by love.

Forget lucky breaks, you will make your mark by working the pump. Every day you will churn away at this thing you love. Don't worry about keeping it up.

That's what the second step is for. If you think of others first, they'll do the same, and you can give each other the energy you need. And because it's there, you'll get up every fucking day ready to churn those gears and flood the world with this little thing of yours. With every turn, the dream gets closer and closer.

Don't let your life come down to chance. Work for this. Bleed for this. Make someone close to you smile. Help them with this skill of yours, and watch as the impossible becomes more and more likely every day. This is the battle plan.

TO BE YOUR BEST YOU HAVE TO GIVE A SHIT.

T-SHAPED

Hurried airport conversation is the best. The rushing around is like a weird form of exercise, it wears you out but is really stimulating to the mind. You can't help but get new ideas when all of your senses are pointed at something brand new.

Doug and I were rushing by a terminal bookstore on the way to our departure gate. The thought occurred to me that, "Two of the most powerful urges I can think of occur right here in the airport."

"Oh yeah?" Doug replied.

Yeah. First, I cannot imagine a scenario where I would fly sober. The edge of it is just too sharp. Why not a pint or two, a magical pastry perhaps, or at the absolute very least, the largest cup of coffee you can possibly balance as you shimmy your way down the airplane aisle. Life is full of boring moments where you have to just sit around. I'm pragmatic. Why not get your brain a bit frothy and use that imagination?

Second, I can't get on a flight without something new to read. It's almost impossible to pass by that store and not pick up a new release. I do a little reading on my electric devices, but you cannot rely on these fucking things for anything. Delays can be unexpected, and you can't count on the presence of functional power outlets. If my phone goes and gets itself dead I need good, old-fashioned print media to give me something to think about. I need a distraction from the Starbucks cookies that won't stop giving me the bedroom eyes from behind that display glass. What's a good man to do?

Non-fiction paperbacks are always my preference. The more punchy, terse, segmented, provocative, and bat-shit gonzo, the better. I just need some strong words to grab my attention. I need to feel the purpose of the prose pretty quickly. Like the feeling you get when you start listening to a tune that is very good, this shit shouldn't take all day. When it's good you should be able to tell quickly.

Maybe it's my attention-deprived mind. Or, maybe I just don't feel like being bored to death by a long, burdensome, indulgent story when a short, entertaining, sexy tale is an option. "Get on with it!," I reply with a faux British accent.

My current selection for passing the time was a pretty good one: *Jony Ive*, by Leander Kahney. It's nothing earth-shattering, which is fine. Magic is rarely necessary. It's just a simple and direct account of one of the most successful product designers the world has ever known. I learned a few things from his story.

First, you have to remember that something like the iPhone doesn't happen by accident. Something that big and impactful isn't the product of a whirlwind brainstorm session. Rather, some of these gizmos' best design elements began in Jony's head over 25 years ago with the advent of addictive click pens and radical phone concepts. He toiled away at his craft every day for decades and was never satisfied with a particular design, holding himself to the highest possible standard. But there was no magic required.

That's how you get good enough to make a thing

capable of changing the world if we are to believe the story. The skill you see there is no accident. Without it, you wouldn't be able to watch iPad porn in your bathtub. You owe this man!

Secondly, Jony's story carries a very powerful lesson that should inform the way you work, create, train, socialize, basically everything. It's the specifics that don't really matter all that much. The objective of the design, the shape of the gizmo itself – it can all vary. What matters is shape and how that affects the function.

The most interesting thing I've read in this book so far is a little pearl from Alex Milton, a Professor at Heriot-Watt University in Edinburgh. To him, Jony is a classic T-shaped designer, meaning that he has both mastery of a specific discipline and also depth. It takes a special sort of designer to work closely with engineering, marketing, logistics, and everyone in between so that the product comes out close to perfect. After reading those lines I scribbled away madly in my notebook. The lessons seem quite useful:

1. The only standard that matters is your own. Set it extremely high. Do your damnedest to exceed it. Do not cut corners. For fuck's sake, why would you cheat yourself?

2. If you have trouble with the idea of setting the bar high – if you lack the impulse to take action – then you're probably doing something silly and not worth the time. Go find something that is fun but allows you

to burn hot with energy. Don't worry about the pay and reward, just burn. Do that and people will start paying attention, quickly.

3. Understand that you cannot ride all of your horses with just one ass. Think about being T-shaped instead. Pick one thing in each area of your life that needs to be moved forward, taken to the next level, or elevated. Drill down as far as possible and give it everything you have. After you've made your progress, stop, then reach out and get an appreciation and understanding of what others are doing. Their craft. Their point of view. Their sources of inspiration. Think hard about why they do what they do, how they go about it. Have a conversation. Pretty soon you'll find that everything else out there only informs and enriches your work. It keeps it fresh, like a never-ending energy source. Look outwards from yourself and you'll never run dry.

No, there's nothing magical about people like Jony Ive. He's just a super nice guy who loves to design cool, beautiful things. He's plenty smart, but not a genius. I don't see evidence of revolutionary tinkering or construction abilities. But in the end, the explanation for all that incredible skill is obvious, and elegant, and open to us all. If you want to be the best you really need to care about and love what you're doing. It has to be your thing. You must bleed for it. Take risks for it. To be your best, empathize. Care. Really care. Don't stop till you're damn proud of what you're doing.

DRILL DEEP INTO WHAT YOU LOVE DOING.

THAT'S WHEN THE MAGIC HAPPENS.

EMERALD GREEN

I get it. I can look through the same peeling, speckled fence posts and spot endless emerald green grass just like you. It's more than enticing. It's enough to make me feel desperate and inadequate. Fuck, maybe I should go back to school and learn some fence-climbing skills? Luckily, this isn't at all necessary.

You think humanity would have cracked conundrums like this by now. After all, every warm-bodied ape such as myself loves the fence-hopping tactic, and every single one has landed on dry brown earth more than a few times.

It's not that it's always bad. The strategy can work, like anything, I guess. But jumping over every fence is not a very efficient way to move on up. It was Robert Pirsig who taught me that systems are sustained by their structure and mechanics, even when real purpose and meaning are absent. His most relevant example: how could overthrowing a bad government or ousting a corrupt leader possibly lead to any real change? How could it do any real good? The answer is that it can't, won't, and never will. Not while every other condition that gives rise to corrupt empires and shitty politicians remains in place.

I'm not the sharpest knife, but this makes plenty of sense. If we wait for any system of our own or someone else's to change itself, then we'll go to our graves waiting. I say empire and politics, but those messes are obvious to anyone who's spent decades voting, hoping, and pleading for real change. Let's take the time to see how it might apply elsewhere (hint, it's so damn common it's scary).

What are we really doing when we jump from one shitty office job to the next, from one hyped diet or training program to the next, or from one city to the next while chasing our passions? It's hard to see how it differs from our political systems. The thing has changed, but none of the behaviors, the beliefs, or the fears have. Hopping is not jumping forward, it's a hard reset. Progress can never be made so long as the conditions remain unchanged.

We take those leaps and hops because we demand a change. We do. On the other side of the fence awaits reward, contentment, basically everything we currently crave. The motive makes sense to everyone. Make the jump, get what you want. But new gigs start tarnishing and looking like old ones in just a matter of weeks or months. Somehow the assholes, idiots, and oppressive bosses you've known have followed you in different guises. Or, somehow this program has also failed to deliver the supreme fitness, impressive strength, and deep abdominal striations you crave.

It's the hopping. How can you make a change take hold if you won't even wait around long enough to see what happens?

Do you know the other characteristic of a system? It's related to recurrence, I suppose. It's predictability. The system is structured to spit out a predictable outcome every time. So, it does seem pretty damn silly to blame the structure when we're unhappy with less-than-stellar outcomes. We shouldn't expect to be happy, or satisfied, or empowered later down the road while we're miserable right here where we are. That's an impossible change.

The best example of this comes from lifting. It's a common thing to crave strength. It's also pretty common to want it sooner, rather than later. The program hopping junkie that wants their dessert right now might start and stop programs in rapid succession, basically looking for the magic combination to their strength lock. But of course strength doesn't come, mostly because strength is not the sort of thing you can just find. It's something you have to build, and that takes time. You have to get real good at using certain tools. But also it has to do with the conditions. Look for your combination all you want, but it will hardly matter if you're sleeping only five hours a day and chronically under-eating.

What else would you expect from these systems? To complain about such things is like fussing at a scorpion after it stings you on the hand, or getting mad at an orange overalls-clad redneck reality TV show host when they say bigoted, dumb shit. That's kind of their thing, no? They are what they are.

Let's look for a better solution, rather than jumping back into the same old behavioral loops. How could we really change our lives? What can we leave behind? What do we need to hold on to? It's a tough problem for sure, especially when you're desperate for something new. When the current circumstances are crushing and just won't do. But maybe we start by backing away from the fence for a while.

Let's consider our options. Maybe something new, fancy, or radical isn't required at all. Maybe taking some things away and sitting down for a while are actually the next best steps. Maybe we should consider our conditions first. Like asking whether one more rung up the ladder even means anything to us anymore or whether better results would actually come from training less often, more simply, or just with more passion and energy. In other words, maybe all we need to do is go back and remind ourselves that the kind of change we're after begins with having a good time.

Maybe, but we're going to be tempted anyway. We'll be walking along, minding our own business, when, all of a sudden, some future possibility will shine right on through those peeling posts. Big, bright, and green like the city of Oz itself. We'll be curious to hear more. But at least we'll stand a chance of making a better decision if we're already smiling wide. Maybe we'll be inclined to go for something better or grander, like all that which hangs in the clouds above our heads. Isn't that where the real goals belong? Isn't that the only change really worth going after?

THE OTHER SIDE IS EXACTLY THE SAME. GET HAPPY NOW.

PLUM

There have been stretches of time where I stayed on these long, straight lines. I couldn't tell at the time, but I had stopped evolving and learning, I had fallen far behind my leading edge for a number of years. Pointing out the long lines is an enlightening exercise, and sure, comes with just a touch of regret, but maybe that feeling is necessary, useful.

I remember a time when nothing in my life felt predictable or linear. My days were random messes, video games, daydreaming, trouble-making, all that. The times advanced in blocks and stages, grades, seasons noted by the turnover of little league uniforms. In general, this was a pretty bitching time for me. I ascended from birth to "maturity" with only a reasonable amount of fuss. I was never bored. I never felt dread or worry. Most of the time I was very happy and perfectly content. My life never took a clear, predetermined direction, and I felt no need to enforce one. I'm grateful for that time, and I want it back.

Extra degrees of freedom give you room to breathe, space to get your bearings greased. A chance to be you. So it's hard to believe that, at some point, I decided to forfeit that freedom. I took the deal for whatever reason. It could have been the expectations I placed upon myself, or my ignorance. Shit, maybe it's simpler than that. Maybe it was just the best option at the time. At that age, it seems alright to do something else because a better option would surely come along later on. And of course, this would be better than being a bum.

In any case, it was a choice. You live with it and focus on what you've learned from it, not on what you've lost. Too much regret becomes a spiritual drain that sucks your introspection and momentum down with it.

In all fairness, I should disclose the less-romantic aspects of my youth. Yes, hand to God, I did at one time own multiple Limp Bizkit albums. This is something I try desperately to atone for every Friday and Saturday night by playing plenty of Joe Strummer and Jimi Hendrix tunes. And yes, it does get worse. I did also once proudly prance about with a bleach blonde buzz-cut hairdo and fucking Dr. Marten military boots. All I can say is that the 90s were very, very strange times.

I never noticed my life flattening out. Going straight, edgeless, dull; fuck it's painful to admit that it took nearly a decade to see. Better late than never.

You might have heard the myth once or twice. "Mother nature never draws in straight lines." That certainly sounds romantic and true, just the sort of thing that spills out during dull dinner-party conversation. It passes unfiltered, right into the trivia-loving centers of the mind and embeds itself. There it remains, next to the bit that still believes that 90% of the brain is actually never utilized, except during morning Sudoku puzzling, of course.

If you ever needed evidence that we are a very strange species, then look no fucking further. Here we are, so confident in what we believe and where we're going, happy to consider ourselves refined and reasonable most of the time. All of this, despite the fact that most of what we accept as true – as reality – can be easily challenged and likely uprooted with little more than a casual Internet search. Ideally, one would read a book or two. That alone would make you more knowledgeable on the given subject than a solid majority of the population. Better still, why not pay attention to and give a shit about what's down there between your feet and all around you right now. Yes, pay attention.

Is nature really so squiggly? No, not all the time. There are plenty of long lines out there in the world, most people are just too damn busy and numb to notice large chunks of it. Stone formations yield to time and pressure, fracturing along clean and true edges. Crystalline forms are innumerable and astonishingly complex. Many plant and animal structures are as straight as a young, freshly shaven Wilt Chamberlain decked out in a hand-cut black suit.

Look back and see things as they were. There was nothing easy about being younger. The pressures were no less intense, they were just different and really fucking lame at the time. They came from different angles. But at least you were getting your start. You were finding a direction in life and figuring shit out. And with that came this sense that you could survive anything.

How powerful.

The lines were all short. They had their edges. Nothing lasted long. There was no reason to believe that you wouldn't survive the climb. Every new stage, grade, challenge, or period of hormone-fueled existential upheaval was only a brief period of high pressure. It released and propelled you forward to the next thing. Somehow you were right on time.

My moment of forfeit came when I traded all the edges, the corners, and the challenges for a sense – illusory as it was – of assurance and arrival. That's when I jumped on that long line. The frustration shouldn't have felt mysterious. Imagine, you have this amazingly complex, variable, angular life with literally limitless possibilities. There's so much cool shit to see, to do, to take on, but you cannot stack it all up and make it fit on just one clean, sure, riskless path. How could you possibly achieve that?

Real, heavy-handed change is necessary because it reminds you of what you are. It cleanses, wipes away the old titles. Hey, I know how destructive a title or label can be. It's nothing more than an assigned seat. Its only function is to shape you into a form and hold you there, by the throat if need be.

Stone edges and crystal formations may be plenty straight, but not for long. That's the real point. They are only linear for a short time. So maybe I shouldn't try to be so straight, or anything for that matter. There is nothing to chase, no mold that needs to be stepped into. There is nothing keeping me on this too straight, too long path other than me. With that, I'll kindly take back my edges and corners. I can decide right now to feel really fucking young again. Reset. In proper form. I have only one goal: maintain and amplify this high-quality life.

DON'T STAY ON ANY ROAD FOR TOO LONG.

DETOUR, BABY. LEARN SOMETHING NEW.

THE LEADING EDGE

I can draw a line straight down from the age of 30. To the left lies everything that came before – Chris' life B.C. (before children). Everything I used to obsess about. All those times I was so selfish and absorbed in my pursuits, I could have never imagined the life that was ahead.

A tsunami of emotion crashes over you the moment you meet your first child. It's a love like you've never known. It's scary as fuck, and there's absolutely nothing you can do about it. I can now say that my father's constant worry is justified. It's tough. I can appreciate it now, and better later than never I guess.

And there it is, the mortal joke. We so often strut away our youth feeling pretty damn confident about most things. We do what we want, despite what our parents might suggest, because we know better. (Cough.)

The poets laureate of Philly, DJ Jazzy Jeff and The Fresh Prince, said years ago that parents can't understand. Of course, we do understand. We've lived that life before, and now we see the punch line. My, how the world can change around you, and look at how hard it can be to keep up with the times as the years tick on by...tick, tick.

I have witnessed my world shift radically several times. The Internet became a practical, useful thing during my high school years. I sent my first email during college registration (Gasp!). I saw the iPod turn my epic, expensive CD collection into a burdensome eyesore, then my iPhone made my iPod look like a goddamn Betamax a few years later. The pace of change is startling.

I understand why my parents always equated the Internet and related gizmos to something like black magic. Their brains just were not like mine. They never felt the pressure of rapidly evolving technology like I did. The plasticity of their brains was never really fully challenged in that way, not even close.

Fortunately, this doesn't have to be true. We can harness an idea called reverse mentorship to keep our brains supple and up to speed. Well, as supple as they can possibly be.

Consider the idea of multitasking. Depending on who you ask, this is either impossible or an essential skill in modern, data-rich times.

So, who's right? Well, both ideas, to some extent. First, attempting to do two things at once doesn't work all that well for most. What feels like increased productivity is really decreased efficiency. It will take longer to do both things, with an overall decrease in quality. Fuck, you don't want that. But there's a twist. The less obvious bit is that some people are actually quite good at quickly shifting their working memory and focus between two disparate tasks. Where some are unskilled and clumsy at this exercise, others (usually the younger and more mentally pliable amongst us) seem to be quite comfortable with the task. The matter is relative and skill dependent.

I can see that phenomenon clearly with my young son. At the age of two, he can already pick up a touch screen phone, unlock it, open his favorite app, and then start playing all on his own. His relationship with technology will always be more savvy and intuitive than mine, which really pisses me off. But there's no point fussing over it, or challenging it, or taking my ball and running home. It's what it is. Fucking reality.

I see two choices. First, I can call the phenomenon silly, ignore it, and remain comfortable with what I know. I would end up like my folks, unable to turn on a fucking DVD player if my life depended on it, figuratively speaking. Alternatively, I could pay close attention to what my son becomes interested in. I can look to him for mentorship, about what's new, what it could do for me, and how we can utilize it together.

It takes some humility to let a kid teach you, but it only makes sense. How else are you going to find the best waves? Go to where the most energy is.

I have to think that this strategy will only help the father-son relationship in years to come. At best, Max will be able to look up to his Dad and say, "Well, at least he's not a total idiot. He's got musical taste." (In this scenario, those Limp Bizkit CDs have been erased from my history.) The idea of looking back to the young for knowledge is not just about technology. It's really about how we can find inspiration and information year after year.

As you get older, you will be more and more likely to settle into what you know. Your fences will be high and your garden just as beautiful as you had imagined, planted exactly to your standards. But the view is limited and too comfortable. I don't care how sure and safe it feels.

The young have their goals, their rules, a blank slate to fill. They are ready to experiment and push the line forward. There's no better example of that than the revolution of CrossFit. For the last twenty years of my life, I have thought long and hard about strength and performance. I've put in countless hours under the barbell. I've researched and dug deeply into all the science, ad nauseam. I felt sure about what works and what doesn't. What's possible and what's not. But I'm not so sure anymore.

We have something new to consider now. In this sport some of the younger athletes are breaking established rules. They are highly conditioned but also strong enough to compete on the national level in Weightlifting. What's more, they have bodies that would make any physique competitor envious. We've only seen the beginning of this shift, and I couldn't be more excited about it.

The older we get, the more valuable our experience becomes. But we cannot yet afford to get comfortable with the gardens we've built. We have to always work to get back out to the leading edge. There's no out-growing it. There's no stopping. There's no time to delay.

WHEN'S THE LAST TIME YOU FOUND YOUR EDGE?

BETTER IS BETTER

A few days ago I went out into the garage for a little
barbell practice. That's really all it was, a quick, fun
opportunity on an otherwise lazy day to practice my
all-time favorite hobby and bring up a few parts of my
flesh that might be lagging behind just a bit. Alright,
maybe a lot.

I sat and stretched for a while, mostly my stiff
ankles. They need the extra attention. The same is
true for these bound-up shoulders, which are still
plenty strong, sure, but they are about as tough and
inflexible as old bull leather. I have some twenty years
of football and competitive powerlifting to thank for
that.

I can't wipe away all that wear and tear.
The damage has been done. But I can stop it. I can
certainly still improve where I need the work most.
I can strive to move a little bit better every time I
practice. I can take back some of what I forfeited years
ago. Fortunately for me, all it takes is a chunk or two.
Just a few minutes to stretch when I would otherwise
just be sitting around. A little piece of time to do a few
good snatch reps, to pick up something heavier than
my body, to tune my nervous system, done whenever
I have the opportunity. That's all that's required, all
that's necessary.

The whole secret here is the fast and fun part.
I'm not alone in wanting to get better quickly and
reconcile past blunders. But that's just the problem.
We are driven by the goals that we dream up and slap

on our inspiration boards, whether they take the form of our bathroom mirror or refrigerator door. There's no shortage of initial effort and initiative, but I think there is a natural tendency to assume that lost ground can be made up in double and triple time. We all want to believe in a short-cut, a quick way around, especially when we're more than willing to do the extra work. Isn't that what's important? Isn't that what counts? No, that's exactly the problem. It's much easier to accumulate work than it is to adapt to it in an enduring, productive, satisfying way.

It could be that the problem is all in the name. Call it an extra workout and you set a tone that more is actually better. But as I was taught years ago by one of my coaching mentors, Louie Simmons, "More is not better, dude. Only better is better." So why not just call it practice then? Why not make "better" the only goal?

Lifting and coaching is one way to demonstrate this point, but music may be a better example. Consider what it takes to get really good at playing. Someone who wants to master the guitar, for example, will pick up the instrument and play whenever they can. At least they should. But that doesn't necessarily mean that mastery is the motive. This might just be a pastime, a way to impress chicks, a pathway to popularity, stardom (if you're very lucky). But as the record industry's fortunes dim, so too should the old-fashioned notion of rock stardom. You may not be able to snort coke from the flat stomach of an aspiring actress at Keith Richards' beach house, but what you can do is master an instrument purely for the love of music.

It might start with nailing that brand new chord, to get it to ring just right in your ear. Maybe you can then tie a few chords together in that same perfect way. You work out the riff. You have a fucking blast jamming with some friends. At each stage, it's pretty easy to get lost in the moment. To flow, to be powerfully present. Time stretches out and flows forward at a relaxed pace. You cannot help but be satisfied with the effort. You only get more and more comfortable with your ability in time. That's the proper beginning.

There's no rush to this journey, friend, don't start with the end in mind. Precisely because there is no rush, the mastery will start to take hold all on its own. The result comes before you even notice, and the practice itself then becomes renewing and empowering, not a drain on your motivation.

If you want to make up lost ground and perhaps find a higher point of view, then take the opportunity to practice what you love and enjoy it. Don't rush it. Don't pile shit on top of it. All that ground will cover itself, don't you worry.

EXPECTATIONS WEAR YOU DOWN.

THERE IS NO RUSH TO THIS JOURNEY.

JAM OUT OF LOVE, BABY, NOT REWARD.

TIPPY TOP

Everything was fine for the longest time. I only remember the pleasant act of drifting around, seeing what there was to see and getting to know the world without much expectation. But nothing lasts forever. Things do change, and I didn't do a very good job of staying adrift and in motion.

Every once in a while you arrive at a full stop, like a flipped coin coming up heads or tails. You end up right on top of the goal, which is a curious spot. Expect an immediate, "Wow! Fuck, dude. Yeah...So, what's next?" That's always a tough question, because you have to keep answering it over and over in life. No reward is certain or forever. The best we can do is make our efforts more of a climb than a dig.

Where are you now? Flat open ground? A dead-end, sun-baked savannah? That place where our species originated so long ago, and not all that different from our current concrete and glass habitats. We can still see just far enough to know that there's something better out there worth shooting for, and yet we cannot get over the powerful fear of what's lurking out in the tall grass. It could be nothing, or it could be the sum of all your fears. Simply put, we all know the price of a careless step. There's no forgetting that. Fear is sewn right into our genetic fabric.

Nowadays, you walk along, you stop, your foot dangles with doubt over the next step. Ultimately, any step could be a careless one, nothing but a wager based on little more than a hunch, or far worse; the crushing pressure of those goddamned expectations.

Fear is a bitch. Don't take it lightly, but don't back away from it either. Start by making yourself more mobile. Put down your baggage, any embarrassing, painful, burdensome thing that you've already carried around for too damn long. Don't be tied down. Wake up. This is the moment when the lights come on.

Consider the peculiar, volatile, impossibly rare features of your unique personality. Isn't it cool? No one in the world can be you. It's your gig. So imagine the nightmare that is the submission of that gift. Imagine a lifetime spent learning facts, figures and trade skills in an effort to become something else entirely, a generic thing to be set inside a marketplace, bought and sold by the fucking pound.

Okay, that's a little dramatic. But it's still a goddamn shame to see someone work hard to become something at the expense of who they really are and what they love. I know, I know, cash and shit. There's that fear of the future again. "Go for the sure thing." I know how it goes, but is it so sure?

Even unique things can become easily replaced in time. The shimmer wears off. They go ordinary but get no less costly to maintain. Stop the digging. Turn and walk away, run, right up the nearest mountain. There you'll see things more clearly than ever. So climb, climb, even if it's been years since you've done so. Even if you think it's too late to start. Climb because it makes more sense than anything.

If you choose to stick around in your hot little savannah, it's probably because you're unsure of just how long or how hard the climb ahead could be. It's understandable. After all, everyone gets struck by that emotion when they're deciding on a future. It's not always easy to step again, to climb some more, but you have to.

In my case, the climb lasted ten years. Every spare moment was a chance to read more, to coach, to grow, to philosophize over pints of beer, to stay up late so I could write about it all, to chatter into USB microphones. It hardly seems like work at all when I consider my likely fate back on that savannah.

It might have been just fine I guess, but still, I would always be anchored there. The climb would only get harder and harder. Reaching a higher level of awareness, productivity, effect, and significance would get less and less likely.

The view from the top of any mountain is much different. These are dividing points in your life. Drop a stone, then watch it roll right past every challenge you've had to overcome, every sacrifice and investment you've made in yourself, every late night that you've illuminated by burning candles at both ends. Now, turn around and drop a second stone. Watch it roll away, towards innumerable opportunities and possibilities, all the way down to a bitchin' shoreline.

Until this moment every single stone you dropped rolled back down the hill, towards that same flat, boring, repetitive, ambition-sucking spot. But not now. Not here. Not anymore. From this point on gravity will pull you downhill, towards great things, and plenty of pain and resistance, to be sure. We can't forget about that. But there is an important difference now. Even the stuff you drop manages to roll your way now. There's nothing to force. Nothing to fret over. You just need to keep going. Everything you build, create and put out into this world will only take you closer and closer to a wide-open ocean view, and maybe, if you're lucky, a burnt orange sunset coupled with a few top-shelf margaritas.

That's my dream, anyhow. So far it's only halfway real at best. I've done the climbing, and now I'm looking down the mountain towards a beautiful but steep and scary slope. Just like before, I'm leaning forward and dangling with doubt. It's never an easy decision, but I remind myself that this is just the fear talking again, just like before. The only thing real here is my choice. So, I will choose to go for the shore.

CLIMB, CLIMB ALL THE WAY TO YOUR TIPPY TOP.

EYES TO SEE

One of the most important things you can do is pay super close attention. Practice the skill of looking closely at every passing moment, every beautiful detail underfoot, every little lesson that you stumble upon during the routine day-to-day grind. I say this for practical reasons only. This is where you find the most fascinating and illuminating stuff.

I spot most of my tiny lessons in my various daily rituals and routines. They are comforting patterns, sometimes efficient and productive, but not necessarily so. They are at least constant, a sort of measuring stick against which I can quickly spot the changes and shifts. For example, during routine training sessions I note all of the deviations from my "normal" when the barbell feels lighter than air or heavier than a pile of rusty anchors and scrap iron. Each and every repetition is an opportunity to collect new data and learn something. A better, more accurate understanding of my status, my trajectory, my success. "Why would this be? What has changed? What could I be missing? What did I add too much of too soon? Was it even enough?"

The same thing goes for my reverential, obligatory little coffee habit. If I'm honest, this habit of mine is far more consistent than any other, including the training. Yes, that is mostly true. This most-constant thing of mine sets the tone. Coarse grinds are measured out one spoonful at a time, four in total per cup if you were curious. The cold-filtered water comes up to the perfect temperature in its own time. The minimum four-minute brew itself should not and cannot be rushed. All that procedure makes for plenty of in-between spaces. Measure, measure, think it over. Take your time. Pour, pour, wait for a few minutes and think it all over. Consider what should be done. "What's the next best thing I could do, the very best place to start?"

Don't forget about the downtime and recreation. This is not time for pure recreation. It's a chance to dig up some interesting, educational, inspirational stimulation.

I have my morning ritual. First, I must check the front page of my Reddit feeds. Random, informative stories, endless meme images, surprising facts that I learned today – what a great way to burn an hour. But the stimulation is more than fun. It's the start of something.

I'm learning more and more that, in this life, nothing ever changes without stimulus, or without something brand new in view. Every day there's a search for provocation, new mentors, scary challenges, debatable points of view, what have you. For the curious adventurer and aspiring ass-kicker, there's hardly anything that should stay true for long. We should always maintain the forward lean.

I will admit, I'm a complete random pop-quote whore. I love it. It's the best sort of sugar-rush stimulus. A quick perspective bump that pairs so well with that third cup of mid-morning coffee. A great line is from this cat Desiderius Erasmus, a fifteenth-century teacher, humanist, and theologian from the Netherlands. The quote, which you might be familiar with, goes, "In the kingdom of the blind, the one-eyed man is king." That feels true for me right now. Even though I'm fully capable of sight, I often feel as though I'm walking around with one good eye closed. That particular random element stirs up a memory now.

My life has always felt like an ever-accelerating learning curve. Around every single corner, underneath every step, there is only more and more to learn. But of course it helps if you can literally see. In school I could never read the chalkboard. My mother would ask me nightly to stop squinting so hard at the television, and I resisted her recommendation for years. She was right to ask, "Maybe you should consider going to the eye doctor?" Of course, I didn't agree. After all, I am my father's son, which means I have X-Men-strength powers of stubbornness. This head is as hard as Adamantium. But this has changed with time. After all the years spent squinting like an idiot, I finally agreed to go for that exam and not a moment too soon. Being able to actually see for once was an amazing performance boost during my final year of university, in life, in being able to gawk more efficiently at passers-by in airport terminals. It's a good thing.

I still remember the very first time I put on my shiny new spectacles and jumped into my Jeep Wrangler with fresh eyes. The drive was fairly unremarkable at the start, as if the benefits of sight were somewhat offset by the awkwardness of wearing the frames. Then ten minutes in I was struck by an astounding vision. All along the avenue I was driving along there was this sea of trees decked out in vibrant green leaves. This was my first chance at such a sight.

Not that I hadn't noticed leaves before. Close up they stand out to even my dull and squinty eyes, but you have to really stand back to catch the full view. Before that moment every tree was nothing more than a blurry Bob Ross painting, little trees dotted with broad green brush strokes. But after the revelation I could see a whole new level of detail that changed everything. I just needed to accept the fact that there was so much more out there to see.

Here's a helpful reminder, for myself most of all. Seeing all there is to see is a skill. You have to work at it very hard. You have to go into every situation assuming that there's far more data hidden from view, and it's freely available – if you can stop being stubborn and rushed for two seconds. If you would only look. We only see a fraction of the world around. A small, blurry, shallow sliver. So, look very close. Look up. Try and spot what you've been missing. Never ever be afraid to put on those shiny new glasses.

THERE'S A WHOLE NEW WORLD RIGHT IN FRONT OF YOUR EYES.

PULL THE TRIGGER

There's nothing permanent in this life. The world goes changing all the time, unstoppable, vivid, and alive. The same goes for you. If you're living right then you're not the same person you were a few years ago, last month, last week.

You're addicted to learning, hopefully. You ask interesting questions during dinner conversation. You're excited to study your mistakes so that you can maximize tomorrow's possibilities.

You train, searching for and exposing weaknesses. You refine yourself, always, at every opportunity because you're alive, and lucky, and able, and pretty goddamn powerful if you consider it.

Test the theory. Send a quick message to a close friend. Tell them you were just thinking of them and hope that they're doing great. Tell them you miss them. You can see that this is a nice thing to do. It feels good, like an opiate. You know that friend will carry on with a smile, spreading a groovy little vibe to the next hundred or so people they contact. That's powerful.

Even with an act so simple and effortless you can change a tiny chunk of the world. Imagine if you put the full weight of your voice and body behind the effort? Imagine if you made it your work, committed fully? Gandhi nailed it, saying that we should all be the change we wish to see in the world. We can't all be sitting still wishing and hoping, right?

No, don't sit back and wish. Don't pray for

anything. Don't pout, piss, and moan over it. Don't put it off any longer. Make a better decision. Initiate change. Show others that it's an okay thing to do and doesn't automatically result in death, chaos and annihilation. It's scary as fuck, sure, but it's okay.

The whole trick to life might be getting comfortable with the incessant shifting and churning as quickly as possible. No, it's not all about ability, talent, education, good fortune, fast-twitch muscle fiber percentages or good looks, although I must say I have been told I bear a striking resemblance to a fat Matt Damon (I'll take whatever I can get). If you're willing to change, to shift, to act boldly, to listen more closely, to let go of what you were trying to force into place year after year, then you're going to do very well at something very interesting. Worst case, even if it never quite works out for you, just think of all the light you will have shined all over everything. The change can't help but happen, and on a much larger scale then you are prepared to see now. Countless little things will grow up to shift the entire world in lots of strange and weird ways. How divine.

Nothing's permanent, sure, but some patterns do seem to keep repeating themselves in new forms. We always struggle with moving on. The list of what we want to do is long and beautiful and inspiring and rewarding and all that shit. We should figure out how to do it, but we delay and stay where we are. Because the dental and vision plan is good, the florescent lights don't always seem so bright, and the 401(k) contribution matching program is quite generous, if you compare it against the market average.

There's nothing wrong with it. The job is good. You need that fucking job! But no, not forever. You don't know what you want to do but it was never this.

Still, things remain okay. Just do something, on the side, for kicks. Do it because it's fun and rewarding. Do it to attract the right kind of woman. Do it because it's fucking cool! You know, make more art. No matter if it's grand or small, get stirred up and spill your light. Get to paying off all that karmic debt. In other words, wake the fuck up!

Close the gap by working as hard as possible, whenever you can, even if it's far too late. Once you're within jumping distance, jump. Pull the trigger. Punch your fucking ticket, take a ride, let go, have a sit, calm down. Here, take a big pull and blow it out slowly. Realize that if you can just keep up the momentum then you can accomplish any goddamn thing you like. How's that sound?

Strength is built and sustained the same exact way. First, we recognize that some things are set firm in their foundations. They are the rules of the game. We must lift heavy. We must march forward, because as Mr. Klokov said, "The best way to get stronger is to get stronger." Keep marching. Be patient. Get what you're after, and then don't be afraid to try something new.

I know you don't want to give up on anything. You've worked so hard to be something, why toss it all away? But this only seems like it's true, kind of like the world sure does seem to be flat and motionless. But the actual truth is that you can only push in one direction for so long, before you get tired, bored, or injured. Even in the best-case scenario, we end up forgetting to have a good time. What a shame.

So change. Find challenge, pleasure, and reward working on something you love doing, but are terrible at. Try backing down and making the quality of your effort the most important thing. Let go of your ego. Embrace being a beginner again. Be a little baby and end up far better for it. Learn to take yourself and your pursuits less seriously. Smile, feel lighter, walk with a righteous swagger, and then realize how women find these qualities sexy as fuck and impossible to resist. Send me a thank you card later on, but please, always be a gentleman.

Be kind. Show compassion. Only slap weasels as a last resort. I keep on changing, getting older and older, more and more different. But I feel like it's for the better. With any luck, I'm heading in the right direction.

DON'T FRET, POUT, PISS AND MOAN OVER IT.

PULL THE TRIGGER.

WIDE OPEN

The morning hours are just as harsh as they've ever been. I come to terms with it the best I can, grunting, mumbling, and tossing my flesh about like a grumpy toddler.

Momentum carries me towards the edge of the bed, where I slide onto the floor, right on down the stairwell towards the kitchen door. The mission is time-sensitive. Momma needs her bacon and eggs before she rushes out the door with the little caveman in her arms, and it's Daddy's job to do the frying. So I fry and smile with blurry red eyes.

I was solo for many years, until I met my wife, until I knew my son. It's just as my father taught me so many years ago over breakfast: "One day you'll see how much everything can change."

I've now seen and felt that in the deepest part of myself, and I cannot imagine living a single day without it. The world has never seemed more beautiful, even at 7:00 a.m., even before my morning coffee finishes brewing.

The a.m. rush gives way to perfect silence, as well as the first big opportunity of the day. This is a chance to be still, to light a candle and have a seat, to think about the day ahead and what can be done with it. A moment to just be yourself for a while, before putting on an alternate identity and rushing out the door.

I have all of these identities. I'm a part-time fry-cook and cooking show addict, an often-times clueless dad, a writer and radio rambler of sorts, a Saturday night inebriate and music-worshiper, a washed-up lifter desperately looking for ways to stay in the game, a gelato and coffee fanatic, and on and on we go.

That's the hook, actually. Everyone feels the pressure to be something great, right? Everyone knows that weight intimately. Because of that we hunt around like mad for years and years in search of a single golden ticket to the chocolate factory of our dreams. Of course we have an idea of what to expect, and just how big and golden this fucking thing should be, so we toss out more than a few shiny tickets along the way. It's also far too easy to lose sight of yourself, and who you really are, the longer you hunt around. You are, after all, only seeing the world in one specific shade. A woefully incomplete view.

There's no sense hunting, or even looking until you first know what you've already got.

The mission must be to keep the balance. To always start with what you are, and to not go out too far or too long in any one direction. Yes, it's what's best for you. But I also think it's the only effective way to take on more of this endlessly complex and open world, and know it greater in return.

We don't ever have to be just one thing. We need not give up any part of ourselves, or make apologies for what we love to do. We just need a better perspective. Just this morning, I was fortunate to stumble upon a line by William Blake, a nineteenth-century English poet and artist. I understand he was also considered quite mad by his colleagues due to his highly eccentric behavior, which I suppose explains my interest in the man. In *The Marriage of Heaven and Hell,* Blake writes:

If the doors of perception were cleansed,
everything would appear to man as it is, infinite.
For man has closed himself up, till he sees
all things thro' narrow chinks of his cavern.

Every time you wear the cap, you see the world
from that vantage point, with certain eyes, under a
particular bias. That bias is necessary, as it allows you
to have some reference point. It gives you a way of
measuring yourself against this specific version of the
world you're experiencing. But, as Mr. Blake reminds
us, without that bias, that door of perception, then the
possibilities and potential paths are truly boundless.
Anyone can do anything. Not without fear, of course.
Not exclusive of pain. Oftentimes uphill. But still,
the doing is possible. So why not do more of what is
possible?

To exist as just one thing, or just a few things,
is a very narrow view indeed. To place the same value
on the same things year after year is impossible if you
are changing and learning as a person should.

There have been times when I've looked
back with some regret. It's just so easy to notice all
the things I could have done better, or completely
differently. But it's also far too easy to forget all of
the good shit that those past experiences have left
me. I carry around all that data now. It gives me some
powerful filtering options. I can still see and feel what
I knew back when I was a clueless student, aspiring
researcher, a wholly average athlete, a full-blown and
highly viral meathead, a true business greenhorn. But
I can measure myself now against where I've been,

which only gives me a deeper sense of what's possible, which is far more than I would have ever imagined. But I have to remain open to it. I have to be willing to consider the perspective. And I am. In fact, I've never been more excited and blown away by what's possible. I'm reminded every time my son speaks with massive toddler attitude. I feel down in that deep central spot every time I feel my daughter kick from within my wife's stomach. These are all reminders of just how wide open and amazing this life can be.

What can I say? I want to know more of it.

IF THE DOORS OF PERCEPTION WERE CLEANSED, EVERYTHING WOULD APPEAR TO MAN AS IT IS.

INFINITE.

UP AND ALL AROUND

Stephen Fry is one of my favorite human beings.

Honestly, I've never heard him utter a single sentence that wasn't funny, charming, poetically poignant, engaging, educational, or empowering in some significant way. Of everything I've heard him say there's one thing that stands out: an English accent can fool Americans into thinking the speaker is more intelligent than he is. This is something I think is true. It's also why I get such a kick out of doing a British accent.

Tell me, if Patrick Stewart drove right up to you in his dope Professor Charles Xavier wheelchair, but introduced himself with a pronounced New Jersey accent, would you not be disappointed? Still, would you pay a couple hundred bucks to see him act out fucking *Macbeth* at your local theatre hall? No, I suspect you would not.

Why not nail down a passable British accent? Be ready to pull it out of your back pocket once you engage the cute redhead at the end of the bar. Ask her, "May I buy you a drink, love?" She will say yes, of course. Who are we kidding? You will then sprout a slight smile and say, "Waiter, a few fingers of tequila with red grapefruit, please. Pinch of salt. Shaken."

We all love a good accent because it does imply brilliance. It's more complex and fancier than the garbled nonsense we hear fumbling from our own tongues. Our brains cannot help but believe what is only implied.

Before we move on, I should make it clear that Stephen Fry and Patrick Stewart are both true geniuses that will hopefully serve as our human ambassadors in the event of a hostile alien invasion.

I suppose this false detection of brilliance might have something to do with shit they teach in school. It's what we all assume learning is, right? The indelible imprint.

Look at how it all begins. You start off this imposed journey at the very bottom. You know nothing. You are utterly confused by the day to day rigors of existence. At school, you'd rather run outside and play. You spend most of your class time ignoring the fat kid beside you who threw up in the hallway after lunch.

Fast forward ten or fifteen years and where are you? Burning midnight oil, cramming for the very last college final separating you from your divine corporate calling. This is the product of a long escalation.

Class by class, year by year, more and more shit gets added on top of your pile. The course numbers keep climbing. You are riding a two-dimensional arrow straight towards graduation, at which point you are tossed out on your ass in a quantum, ten-dimensional world. It's shocking that we're shocked, to be honest.

More is not the only thing that matters. In fact, it's hardly important at all. Not because it can't bring you love or happiness (it won't, by the way). Rather, it's because more is often the harder, less-effective path.

We can look for inspiration and wisdom in far more directions than just up and to the right. Yes, you could spend the next few years of your life poring over philosophy and guru texts of all sorts, which is cool. But don't forget to go back and have your mind blown, and passion renewed by *Oh, The Places You'll Go!*

Yes, a fucking kids' book is one of the most incredible sources of knowledge I can think of. It's the kind of book you might have tossed around your little race car bed or blanket fort when you were a kid, and have likely not considered reading since (but you really should). No, instead you read *Fifty Shades of Grey*, firmly convinced that, "No, of course, this isn't porn!" In your head, when Christian Grey asks you whether you want a regular vanilla relationship with no fuckery, he always sounds just like Daniel "007" Craig himself. And he's got your stir stick in his hand, baby.

I'd like for you to keep something in mind. Always look up. Learn all the cool, wondrous, mind-boggling shit you can. Stretch your mind till it throbs. Seek out those who are much better than you. Grind your bones in pursuit of your chosen craft. Just don't miss what's in plain sight. Understand that illuminating, inspiring lessons are everywhere. Everything, everywhere is potentially a mentor! A children's story. That class you've dreaded because it has nothing to do with your major, or the book you never thought you would read, these things shape your new point of view. It could be an athlete from another sport, a musician, a physicist. That documentary you saw about the famous sushi master with a tiny restaurant tucked down in the Tokyo subway, you know the one. These are all brand new influences, voices, and philosophies. They come from unexpected angles, are often simple, and could be just what you're missing. It's a whole other kind of learning experience once you see how everything is connected, and how one discipline can inform and radically reshape the other.

Do start making it a habit to look up, down and all around more often. Way more often, all right? The best example is the dream. The great pie-in-the-sky goal. We take classes and read books our whole lives in order to acquire the knowledge and skills we need. We listen to audiobooks, attend seminars, watch awesome documentaries during glorious late-night munchie sessions. We plan. We work that job that we swear will just be a temporary thing. We wish. We hope. We follow the plan that has been imprinted upon us. And what does that get us? (Cough.) Mixed results. Maybe it works, but it often doesn't.

We have to remind ourselves about the intuitive, obvious lesson. Write this down and stick it in that same back pocket. Are you ready? If you want to do something great in this world, as you define it, then go fucking do it right now. There, that's it. Nothing, and I mean nothing, is stopping you. And if you want to become someone great, then go surround yourself with great people and adopt their habits, from big to small. Look at the world from their point of view for a while. Shift yours. In time you'll become more and more like them.

Incidentally, the opposite is also true: practice the same old thing over and over, and you will cement yourself in that shape. You will turn into concrete, dulled. The pie in the sky drifts further and further away.

Let me make it easy. When in doubt, use that British accent. Go practice.

THE ESSENTIAL HABIT IS TO ALWAYS LOOK UP, LOOK DOWN, LOOK ALL AROUND.

MENTORS ARE EVERYWHERE.

OFTEN PAINFUL, NEVER BORING

Oscar Wilde once said that most people were boring and stupid. He might have had a point, especially given his situation. I can't imagine it was all that easy to be a genius writer and exuberant personality far ahead of their time in late-nineteenth century London.

Where would you go for engaging, open, revolutionary conversation? Not many places. How long could you hide your true self and privately suffer? Not long it seems. Oscar caught a ride to someplace better after only 46 years.

The truth about his statment is that it's not a judgment at all; it's a warning. Avoid both labels with everything in your being. You can do it, and so you should.

The written word is humankind's most amazing party trick. Books and knowledge remain our most powerful tools by far, allowing anyone to hone their edges razor sharp. Sure, there are limits. Let's not pretend that everyone is blessed with a dope Samurai blade or five-pound Claymore from birth. I'm convinced that I was born with little more than a butter knife, or a good all-purpose chef's knife on a great day. But as any decent cook will tell you, there's no dish you can't make with that blade. You just need to keep the thing honed and clean. That's on you. You're holding the fucking blade, no one else. You make the decision to care for it or not. Sit, let it go dull, and you'll never cut another tomato again.

I think being boring is pretty much the same type of thing. No one has to be a bore; sure, your shitty jokes may lack punch and your stories may fall short on panache, but anyone can learn to at least keep it brief!

The only tip you need is this: say half of what you had planned, and with twice the confidence! At worst, they'll say you were too intense, and every fucking person in the room will remember your name afterward.

You don't have to be a bore. More to the point, you shouldn't allow yourself to be bored. The philosopher Soren Kierkegaard wrote, "Boredom is the root of all evil. The despairing refusal to be oneself." I see his point. To be bored is to be wholly motionless, uninspired, and effectively dead. You're not playing when you should. Not working as you could. Not training and growing stronger for what is yet to come. And you're certainly not resting. Don't kid yourself. Resting requires the cessation of something.

Remember the warning. But also remember that there is no crime in feeling bored, or worrying over whether you're capable. You feel that old feeling and you remember that there's just so much cool shit to do, and so shockingly little that's keeping you from doing it.

That's a pragmatic view. The even more pragmatic, scary as fuck, awe-inducing, mind-ravaging view is that right outside your chamber door, a world is pulsing with endless energy and possibility. And, what's more, all of that energy forms little more than a thin bio-film on the surface of a small rock.

A rock suspended in an infinite vacuum, tucked in the back corner of an ordinary galaxy just recently found to contain at least one billion similar rocks, each likely populated with tiny sentient beings with nothing better to do than burn their afternoon away on Buzzfeed.

Boredom should be impossible. Life is plenty harsh and turbulent enough when you're plugged in, engrossed in whatever it is that gets your rocks off. But to be caught off guard, completely idle and indifferent? No, fuck that.

Life drops this lesson randomly. First, it calls on the second day of your big-city vacation to inform you that your mother was almost turned into a memory by a careless teenager merging into traffic. Yeah, how's that perfect macchiato with the caramel tones taste now? Better yet, you get this news just as a man dressed as a giant vagrant Elmo offers you a 20% off tour bus coupon and then crowds your wife and kid for a picture. I might kill the Elmo man.

This is the dark side of things, sure. It's the side that makes you feel scared shitless when you think of the future. It's not all bad, that side. It's what gives art its meaning, after all.

Even when the dark turns funny, there's plenty of pain. Just a day after that call I was enjoying a perfect moment with my little boy. We were tangled up on the sofa watching *Toy Story 3*, maybe for the tenth time. I don't mind. I could never mind, even after a thousand views. That's because I'm not really watching the screen. I'm watching the boy. He is amazed and his smile is endless. And I'm amazed at the fact that he even exists and that he'll grow up to be capable of so very much, far more than me. It's too much to fully consider, so I stop it with the fucking considering for once.

I lean in and kiss the chubby cheek. I say, "Hey, I love you, Max." But there is no reaction. Just that same smile frozen within its frame. "Max, did you hear Daddy?" I ask. Just then the boy turns and embeds his plastic Buzz Lightyear action figurine right between my eyes. Whack!

One flash of brilliant white light later and I'm left cradling a gnarled brow ridge. "Ahh, shhhhit, what was that for?!" What did the universe offer in return for my unexpected anguish? How about the ceaseless chuckling of a proud toddler. Yes, the boy found this to be about as funny as anything he'd ever seen. I was far less amused, of course, but I get the joke.

Sometimes these things happen. Sometimes they are really bad. Sometimes they are just too damn funny. It doesn't matter. Anyway, when it comes, I need to learn to deal with it. I need to learn to smile about it.

My context, my perspective, my being compels me to move on. There are plenty of books to read, so why not pick up another? With so much to do why not stay in motion? Even when I am not able to move forward, why not be in motion?

Mr. Kierkegaard, thanks for the lesson. I may bitch and moan from time to time, but there will be no refusal here. And to Mr. Wilde, I'll keep the quote in mind. And if we ever meet on some other plane, I promise to keep it short.

GET SHARP.

BRAND NEW EYES

We know the power of a label. As soon as you start thinking of yourself as something specific you start taking on that world view. It's a defining action.

The stressed-out office worker sees the world as mostly bright fluorescent lights and quarterly deadlines. The bad-ass athlete sees the enormous challenges and requisite training schedule ahead and eagerly smiles, knowing it's only a matter of time and effort. The chef constantly searches for new, exciting, unexpected flavor combinations, always tasting and thinking and testing. The frustrated and wayward will have trouble looking out and seeing much of anything at times. That feeling is unique, in that all get it. We know it. We've felt that.

In every case, the world is what it is: endless and indifferent. It's our eyes that filter through the data. Our minds do the piecing together and simulation, which can certainly be both a good or bad thing. Fortunately, this is something we can control and refine with practice. As Nikos Kazantzakis said, "Since we cannot change reality, let us change the eyes which see reality."

Let's consider two sides.

I recently came across an illuminating idea from Dan Pauley, a biologist who wrote a paper back in 1995 called "Anecdotes and the shifting baseline syndrome of fisheries." Yes, a scientific fishing paper – there are many of them. In that report, Pauley makes an interesting point. A generation of researchers studying the number of fish in a particular reserve will operate from a certain set of assumptions. They will assume that data they know is all there is to know. Each will measure from a distinct, temporal baseline, the one they learned and became comfortable with at the beginning of their careers.

These researchers might note a population dip or shift from year to year, decade to decade, whatever, as measured against what they consider to be normal. Fair enough. That's good science. However, as Dan points out, the real story starts to emerge when you look further back, perhaps through the eyes of a historian. When you do that, you find many documented accounts of a time when the fish were so plentiful in that same region that you could just reach into the water and grab one, like pulling a cold beer from the fridge. The problem here is awareness. You don't know until you've seen something in reality.

If you are only aware of one view, everything you can see, know, or experience will be capped and permanently shallow. You will be numb to any other version of reality, unless you are willing to change the view from time to time. Unless you make an effort to get some elevation.

We cannot afford to take a shallow, limited view. So, we can learn from this Baseline Syndrome, and maybe reverse it via some kind of plan. Maybe we should flip it on its head and use it as a powerful tool instead, one that pushes our reference point forward and upward.

We will upgrade our eyes so at last we can see new, brighter realities.

You have to plan, right? You have to think about where you want to go and how you will get there, but there is this pesky, baked-in limitation. The plan encourages you to start reaching out for things, and when you do so you run the risk of getting ahead of yourself. Maybe you reach in the wrong direction. Maybe you reach too far, or not far enough. It's tricky, until you think of your reference point.

It's okay to want shit, but instead of reaching out immediately for it, focus on changing your reference point first. With that comes a new set of possibilities never before considered.

I know that I have three clear wants in my life. I've always wanted to be as strong as possible, but now I want it with as little wear and fuss as possible. I also want to teach and help others in some meaningful way. And most importantly, I want to be the best husband and father I can be. So, the question becomes, how can I make that all happen? How can I see beyond what I currently think is possible, to all of those other levels?

Time has allowed me to try and toss out most of the silly moves. I've mimicked the training programs of the most strong with mixed results. I've attempted to reach out by being more like other people, working like them, creating like them, planning as they plan. I've also tried miserably to push this world back so I could spend more time with those I love the most. But none of that works all that well, at least not for long. These are pathways to numbness. They fatigue. They frustrate. They undo that plan you worked so hard to put together before you even find the real target.

I now accept a better reality, one that really does work. And it's dead simple. If you want something, focus on shifting the baseline first, and the best possible result will unfold automatically. If you want to be really strong, focus on moving, living and thinking as a really strong person. That's a high-quality existence that leads to strength. It should be the first focus. You cannot get all the way there by obsessing over what you can lift now, versus what you think you should be able to lift.

If you want to connect with someone and teach, start with what you are. What you feel. What you fear. What you actually know. Talk about challenges and how you've dealt with it. What you have learned from the process. You are human. If you can connect with yourself first, honestly and openly, without conforming, open ears and hearts will find their way to you because humans are hardwired to appreciate such a thing.

This is all fine and good, but that last baseline is what's most important to me. It's also been the absolute hardest thing to try to master. I need to figure out the path forward. I need the balance back. But I know the balance is usually short lived, no matter how hard I fight. You cannot push back against that noisy, pressing, loud version of the world for long. It's too big, too heavy.

The deadlines, the email alerts, the bureaucracy, some reference point that cannot be moved. I tell myself to let it go. I stop reaching for balance and instead let it happen on its own for once by giving myself room to breathe.

The problem is not an effort deficit. There's no lack of love there, or dedication, or force of will. It's a matter of giving it a chance. By stepping away from the pressure, balance happens all on its own. At least this is what I trust to be true now. Even in the foggiest times. Even when everything seems slow, burdensome, heavy, and absolutely impossible, we have to remind ourselves that new realities only appear to those who are prepared to look. We have to remember that there is always plenty to see around us and overhear, well beyond what we now know to be true. That knowledge should keep the fire going.

START WITH WHAT YOU KNOW, WHAT YOU FEEL, WHAT YOU ARE.

CAPITAL PINK

Mae, we were plenty excited.

That's just how it goes when you're riding out a big chapter change hand in hand with the person you love most. So far our story has been anything but boring. And yet, as if things couldn't get any more interesting, the very next page begins with your name, baby girl, right there in capital pink letters.

I want you to know that we were sufficiently scared, worried as hell, and quite mindful of what happened the first time around. We were right there in that same hospital, a few doors down from where your mother blew my mind. A full fifteen hours of natural child labor was the preamble to your brother's arrival. The grand finale was a solid two hours of all-natural, maximum-effort labor. Let me say, I've never witnessed a more awe-inspiring performance of any kind. I stood completely heart broken, watching my wife suffer and cry. But she did it, and she would have done it again for you without hesitation. That's where my fear began.

That last time I watched helpless from the sidelines as nurses scrambled around in a hurry. They thought Max might have gone blue sometime in the middle of that second hour. They got him out as quick as they could and carried him off to a specialized unit to run tests, to needle him, to poke him all throughout his very first night on earth.

It was terrifying, crippling even. It rocked our world in a very intense way. Carrying that emotion

CHRIS MOORE — BARBELL BUDDHA

down onto the shitty hospital fold-out sofa is a sure recipe for a bad night's sleep. Baby girl, you should know that fear is not as heavy as it looks. It's never an easy thing, never ever, but it doesn't have to be heavy. Max was just fine, which was the biggest possible relief. And you, my darling girl, you arrived in this world right on time. Perfect.

It only took six hours or so from the start to finish. The pace had us hopeful, but reserving our sense of caution. The memory of Max's labor was still fresh. It must have been what fueled the electrifying hormone rush that hit me right as the doctor said those words, "Oh goodness, she's got a head full of dark hair, Momma." I'll never forget that.

The energy in the room was crushing, it was euphoric, it was electrifying, it was everything all at once. But then it was gone just as quick, like a vapor, as soon as I cut your cord and realized that we might be in the clear.

It was alright. No, it was more than alright. It was mind-blowing! You are my daughter, my precious little daughter, and now you're chirping and panting away in your bed, upstairs, right above my head. You are here, you are real, and now I'm all wrapped up around your finger and in love. How could I ever say no to you, or scold you? How's it going to feel when we share Ben & Jerry's ice cream for the very first time, or when we first let each other down? What about all those times where I'm going to feel powerless, helpless, in way over my head? What am I to do then?

I can't wait for it, darling.

I can already see the hints of personality in the corners of your smile. I wonder what will interest you most. What you'll study. What you'll give your life over to. Where you'll find beauty and love. I can hear you crying right now, your voice high pitched and strong. I wonder what you'll use that voice for later on down the road. I wonder what you'll fight for, what you will cry over. Whatever the cause may be, I just hope you use that voice, Baby. In your own way, be loud.

And I can tell you've got the absolute best of whatever your mother and I have to offer. Even though you're so tiny, you've got these incredibly strong little arms and shoulders. I have to hold onto you real tight because you've already tried to jump out of my arms a few times.

It seems obvious. If I had just one guess, I'd say you're going to be a hell of an athlete, but I want you to know that it's perfectly alright with me if you choose to do something completely different with your time. You're the most unique thing in this universe, so please don't pretend to be something you're not. Be whatever you want to be, Mae. If that's all the advice you ever accept from me, it's alright.

I hope you get a chance to feel this. It's surreal. I don't know what I've done to be so lucky. It's a dream to hold you, to kiss your little dimpled cheek and to daydream of the future. I'm pinching myself. I cannot stop asking your mother the question, "Can you fucking believe that we've got two babies? How crazy is this? How great is this?"

I do realize the sort of challenge that I'm facing here. This is it, the real thing. This is where the new chapter starts picking up steam. The train is in motion, now. The ticket is punched. There's no getting off. As incredible and intense as it all might be, Mae, I want you to know that there's exactly one thing I'm sure of. One thing. I'm so happy to have the opportunity to be your Daddy. Baby girl, I will do my best to never let you down.

BE LOUD, BABY. USE THAT PRECIOUS VOICE.

COMING DOWN THE MOUNTAIN

The dream peaks right at the summit. The tippy top of the climb, the cathartic moment you've been waiting a giant chunk of your adult existence for, or so you think.

The never-ending, at times desperate, always grueling climb is done. Now, possibility flows out of the peak like an unstoppable waterfall, all the way down to that distant shore. If you truly want what you say you want, all you have to do now is walk. One foot after the other, close the distance between the summit and the ultimate goal, whatever it is. Call ahead, tell them you want your pitcher of margaritas ready. Fresh lime and salt. Be generous with the tequila.

Momentum will carry you there all on its own, or so you think.

The romanticized version of the dream included a triumphant descent, full of pomp and triumph, appropriately coupled with a soundtrack of righteous late-80s rock anthems straight out of my suburban origins. I can see it now as precisely as if it were this keyboard before me. I am grinning ear to ear, but with one eyebrow arched as if to communicate a warning to all those who would persist in trying to hold me down. This is no joke. I pack plenty black powder behind each word.

I smile because I can. The timely accompaniment of Jane's Addiction's "Mountain Song" does most of the moving for me. I turn the volume up to 11 and never once think of looking back until I hear the whispering start.

Every part of this dream seemed real. The long, hard climb does bring release. From now on, there is no limit for what you can achieve. There are no more large boulders to climb over or around. But now you have to deal with a new threat that is a master of resistance and fear, and entirely more real than your still coalescing dream. Here's a hint, you are now the prey.

I walk down the path, on fire with confidence and hope, renewed for the first time in years. And that's when I hear those words. Something is back over my shoulder, leaning against that tree just off the trail. It strikes a match and draws hot cigarette smoke. It whispers just loud enough for me to hear: "You sure you know what you're doin', kiddo?"

I hold the smile high, damming back the frown. The whisper shot right into my gut like an arrow. "Yeah, the hardest part is done now, right? All I need to do is keep moving. I'll just keep moving along."

I look back just enough to notice that devious look. The kind of expression that can only be fueled by experience, innumerable years of experience that spans the entire history of my hopeful species. Then comes the reply: "Is that right?" More smoke.

I stare and stare, but nothing else is said. I can't see it anymore, but nothing else is necessary. The arrow has done its work. The poison spreads. I can feel myself growing weak, hesitant, dizzy. I grab at whatever I can, any limb that's strong enough to hold up my weight. I feel heavier and heavier by the minute as the fever sets in.

I want to stop, if only for a moment. I look around for help, for an example of what to do, maybe a solution or some kind of serum that will magically remove the gripping fear. What I could not have imagined before is that this moment, right fucking there, is the real summit. The crossroads. The point where I might break.

Resistance has never had to work very hard for its meals. Most fall and die right here and I can see why. They were unprepared for it. They got frightened, turned back, or just got lost out here. But something else rings out at me, a simple truth: this force is a lying bitch. It cannot know what I know or see what I see. It only has this one trick, as effective as it might be for most hunts. With that realization, I find my relief. I remember that resistance whispers from within my own mind. I remember that a fear of the future is nothing more than a false projection. I only guess poorly, pessimistically at what might happen, drawing mostly from past wounds, failures, and blown opportunities. How could I not imagine the worst? How could it not be paralyzing? But that's just it. A simple change of perspective is enough to get me back on my feet, smiling, eyebrow cocked and loaded.

Jiddu Krishnamurti captured that moment perfectly: "What is needed, rather than running away or controlling or suppressing or any other resistance, is understanding fear. That means, watch it, learn about it, come directly into contact with it. We are to learn about fear, not how to escape from it." The fear I feel has nothing to do with the future. It's actually a very useful indicator. It's warning me of the gap between where I am, and where I'm trying to go. But the intention is not paralysis. Rather, it's a call to work harder, to face the trouble.

If I am to close this gap, if I am to remain outside the reach of that fucker with the cigarette, then I have to work harder than I ever did before. I have to close that gap with toil, learning all that I can at every moment. That effort is fortifying. It's the engine that keeps the momentum. It will drive me to where I need to be.

I feel better knowing what I have to do, but I'll be damned if I do it in silence. I dust off my boots, straighten my spine, then turn the volume back up to 11. I'm ready to do the work and hold my line. I'll keep up the walk.

Watch me cash it in, baby.

KEEP THE WHISPERS AT YOUR BACK.

WALK ON.

OVER PINTS

There are four seasonal corners in my heaven.

I begin with a bright white gulf shore with endless margarita pitchers and fresh shrimp cocktails all within my reach. There's nothing better than this. No other place can make me feel as light and carefree as I did when I was a kid.

For contrast, I move on to a late-autumn afternoon. I sip a perfect coffee at my favorite corner java spot well within view of the canal, the brilliant shifting leaves, and the endless procession of bicycles gliding down the city streets. There's just something about watching the fade set in, knowing that winter is right around the corner. It's hard not to be present for that sort of beauty. If I could, I'd watch every single leaf go bright orange.

Next come a few bitterly cold winter nights in front of a roaring fireplace. My only needs here consist of two good books and a bottle of scotch, the latter being a simple pleasure I've only recently learned to fully appreciate. Perhaps I'll also keep a notepad for capturing the Muse's faint mumbling, but maybe I won't. The quiet is welcome.

That quiet and pause are the real secret. It also doesn't hurt to shiver for a while. After all, you don't want your heaven to be eternally comfortable and perfect. As much as I like the idea of spending the afterlife shoveling down Chubby Hubby ice cream and listening to Led Zeppelin tunes, I know that the sweet taste only lasts for a limited number of bites. Balance will always matter. There will always be a need for some discomfort, as it's the only thing capable of giving rise to a real pleasure.

My last stop is the most stimulating by far. Here, a perfect spring get-together is my catalyst for new thought and insight, new action and understanding. I walk up to the pub door through a landscape of brilliant cherry blossoms and patches of green clover. I'm in top shape, ready for Thursday night conversation with close friends over one too many pints of Scottish Ale.

All in all, this is an absolutely perfect evening. I start to make my best points by about the fifth round of beers. By that time, all filters are off. You just say what you need to say. Although I must admit, it feels a lot like I'm just talking to myself at this point. This is a side effect of my now slightly pickled consciousness no doubt.

I take another big pull from that tall frosted glass, wipe my upper lip, then clumsily declare, "You know, I used to see all these options. I think that was my problem."

"And, that was a bad thing?" I hear in return.

"Yeah, it's a specific sort of paralysis. The most helpful thing in the world is to honestly acknowledge your limitations. There are countless things you would love to go out and do, to be sure, but the time might not be right. Maybe you just cannot choose now. Maybe you don't have the experience yet, as frustrating as that might be. Maybe the thing is really not for you at all, but you don't know that. There will always be a roadblock and this nagging feeling that the clock is ticking down, that there's somewhere you need to go right now. But that's not so. When the water's dirty, you have to sit down a while and wait for it to clear, as hard as that might be. Then the choice is obvious."

To my right, I hear the devil's advocate chime in. "That's one way of looking at it, I suppose, but why not take a longer view?"

"And that would be?"

"Well, everyone seems to think that progress is a linear sort of thing. You start out green and terrible, but you work hard and take your shots when you can. You hit the roadblocks and feel the pressure, but eventually you climb to the top of the hill and have a picnic in the sunshine! You wait for those perfect moments before you act. You get a sense that you're arriving someplace."

"I don't know, man, that sounds pretty good to me."

"Sure, it's enough for most. But others take advantage of the view. They notice that life is nothing more than a huge landscape dotted with countless hills and tall mountains off in the distance. Instead of getting comfortable and overly specialized, they take a shot at the next hill. Because, why not? To stick around would be safe and easy, but that's not all it's cracked up to be. Even if your little hill comes furnished with plenty of ice cream, how long do you expect that to keep you happy?"

"That's true, although, I really wouldn't mind having that problem!"

"No doubt. The key is knowing when you've had your fill. You can't let yourself get sick and grow roots, but that just makes the next move harder. At some point, you have to get up and walk back down into the valley. Most don't ever bother with that step. Instead of moving forward, it just feels like stepping backwards. They go static. They wear away until they can no longer move."

We all give it a proper think while our lovely waitress dishes out the final round. Like anything great, the chat must end. But before I go on to the next corner, the final point is raised.

"So, how long do you go on? One hill won't do, that much we agree on. Even if you're quite happy at your picnic, the ground will eventually retreat from beneath your ass. You'll be all the way back to the bottom whether you like it or not. But it also seems silly to go on looking forever, no?"

It's up to me to make the last point. I put down my glass, bottoms up, and say the only thing that seems relevant.

"You guys know how much I love quotes, right? We all do. Often, a few wise words are all you need to correct course. As drunk as I may be, one line in particular comes to mind now. It's from Laozi, everybody's favorite Chinese philosopher, right?"

"Yeah, yeah, the 'journey of a thousand miles begins with a single step' guy, right?"

"Right! And just like that line, which is also true act without expectation. You can't expect to be happy forever right where you are. How could you? You and the world are both shifting around and changing. But you also can't expect to always find what you're after at the top of the next hill. That's the problem with expectation. You don't really know what you want. So, you're better off just focusing on your behavior right now. That's the great agent of change. It's not the wanting, it's the stepping. The kind of person who walks for the sake of it alone becomes the kind of person who doesn't need the expectations. They simply do what matters most, right now, always. With that view, how could you not end up right where you need to be? That habit makes you into the kind of person you need to be."

A final cheers and I step back out into springtime with a crooked gait, but a clear goal. These next few steps are all that matter. Sweet and sour at times, for sure. I will get plenty tired from the walk. But I'm not worried. That's what makes the whole journey worth the fuss. I'll find myself on that gulf shore soon enough.

But please, if I may call ahead, someone get the pitchers ready.

SIT WHEN YOU MUST, BUT NOT FOR LONG.

THERE ARE TOO MANY HILLS.

PEP TALK

I love listening to chatter and hustle over morning coffee.

This café is filled with busy little bees. Everyone has their to-do lists, their missions to complete. It's amazing once you've learned to notice these things. If I could ask each one of these folks about their biggest challenges, regrets, opportunities, limitations, blessings and heartaches I doubt any two answers would be the same. We are all largely the same, yet so unique. That is a fascinating starting point.

Life isn't any different now than in years past. We're just keeping pace the best we can with the senses and abilities we're afforded by nature.

I sit quietly and sip, attentively scanning the room for interesting stories, novel perspectives, and maybe some pithy commentary regarding current news events. This is nothing more than practice, really. I'm working on being right here right now, not where I've just come from, and not where I'm about to rush off to once my latte runs dry. As you might guess, this is easier said than done. As Alan Watts reminds us about the present, this is what there is and all there is. Fuck, I forget that every day, right around the time I begin to worry over my wife's pregnant belly and the bright future that could be ahead.

Practice really is the perfect word. You have to work at it or your spark and uniqueness will just get lost in that endless chatter. Be warned, it's a deep, dark void. It will never fill up, so don't go tossing your candle down there. Instead, hold it up for the world to see.

Just as I arrive at my last few sips I notice

television commentary pouring out over everything from the top right corner of the room. It was a sports show, to be specific, which is not all that different from any other modern news program. This is entertaining if sports are your thing, I guess, but I have to work pretty damn hard to find anything of real substance there. Mostly it's just flapping heads with awesome hair, desperate to fill advertising hours, linking together and projecting disparate statistics and figures that don't mean a goddamn thing. I was more than ready to move along...until the TV talk turned personal.

The topic was a particular player who was getting a little too long in the tooth to play the game. American Football, to be specific, a sport that is as big and powerful in the States as any large corporation pushing preserved pastries and overpriced coffee-like beverages. "This guy has been hanging around for far too long! Can he still move like he used to? No way! Does he have what it takes to make it through another season, to lead this team to a championship? Come on, isn't thirty-three too old?"

"Thirty-three!," I reply with a pissy attitude and hot-coffee breath. "Man, here I was feeling pretty good about everything. Who knew I was so fucking old?"

Of course it's only brash sarcasm. I know where I stand, and it's pretty damn far away from the field. That's the way I see sport. You go into it to learn something, mostly about yourself. You train, refine, struggle, rise, and succeed. For me, that process took a little over twenty years! But, at what point do you move along? How many little medals and accomplishments are necessary? How much wear and tear are you willing to trade? It's a personal decision, of course. If it's important to you, then it's important to you. Pursue it.

For me, sport was the best possible way to cut my teeth, to shake off my overly cozy youth and toughen up, to learn how to work for once. It was essential, until it wasn't. I eventually got the message, so I hung up the phone and moved on. That said, what I lack in cartilage I make up for with new perspective. I fucked up plenty along the way, but I also worked really hard and ended up going a lot further in sport than anyone would have guessed, including my own parents. I've also eaten a lot of shit from more than a few really terrible coaches. Frankly, that experience inspires me to now do the opposite, to teach and share all that experience, not to bark aloud. Whatever light I have, I'm going to hold it up and shine it all around. So maybe I'll shine it back on that field.

I wouldn't mind coaching a team someday. Perhaps one of my kid's little league squads as a start. I think I'd do a damn good job. In fact, I already have some ideas about what I would say during my first big pep talk, maybe after our first really tough practice.

I respectively step up to the small group of kids who look like they just got their dicks violently kicked in. It's a tough scene, man. Trust me. I've been there. A kid on my left is gasping like a fat zombie. "Take a knee son, and have some water. You look like a fish with peanut butter in its mouth." The fat kid on my right looks train-wrecked and desperate for a snack and nap. I can relate. He feels way in over his head. Luckily, he'll be fine.

Everyone here will be fine. They just need time.

"Look, I'll be honest with you guys. You've got a lot of work to do. And it's going to be hard as hell, sure. But I can promise you two things (pause for dramatic effect). This is all going to be worth it, and regardless of how you feel, this is the best thing for you right now.

"I wish it weren't so, but the only way to know what you really want in this life is to spend some time right up close, cheek to cheek, with what you don't want, what you dread, what sucks. All feeling and emotion is temporary. Don't worry with that, trust me. You'll be glad you put in the work, because you'll be prepared for hard times down the line. Without it, you might never ripen.

"Do you guys know what it takes to master something, to really perfect it and reach your true potential? Martial arts, writing, cooking, strength, carpentry, business, any sort of thing? Turns out there's no secret to it. You just have to come back the next day, and the next, and the next, ready and open to the change that needs to happen. Always improving. Always moving the needle forward. You've got to learn to see the work as your greatest ally. In a world where the starting point is rarely fair and talent is often limited, saying yes to the work and to the possibility of becoming something else is how you move forward.

"A great athlete drills and drills to shape themselves, even when it sucks really bad. Even when it would be far easier to do just about anything else. They drill. The writer sits back down at the keyboard, even when they don't feel up to it, especially when they don't feel up to it. Because that's what they have to do. So too goes the work of a master carpenter, a true warrior, a great teacher, and shit, I suppose even the random sports commentator. Why? Because with time you'll become what you practice. You either come back to it the next day or you don't. It's your choice.

"There's no time for focusing on the downside. That much is obvious enough. But you have to work hard to remind yourself of the opportunities. The good stuff. The fact that, even though you are gasping now, you have this really awesome chance to decide exactly what you'll be. Right now you can choose to stand up and leave this field excited with the work you've got done here today. Eager to rise to the challenge and do better tomorrow. This is it and that is all there is. The decision is yours. Are you gonna come back tomorrow and do better or what?"

In the daydream, my little monologue is followed by the mighty roar of some ten or twenty little lions. But, I know reality would be much different. The dream is enough to keep me interested at least.

I dump my empty cup and make my way to the door. I pass through the chattering crowd, which is now made up of brand new faces and another twenty or so missions. I smile, but I've got my own to get back to. It starts now, with this next step. I've made my decision. The next thing has been waiting long enough.

DRILL, DRILL.

SHAPE YOURSELF.

JUST BE CAREFUL ABOUT WHAT YOU PRACTICE.

THE DEBAUCHERY DIARY

In mid-2009 I spent some 12 hours floating down a river with my Barbell Shrugged *brothers and some close buddies. We had about 200 beers with us that day, which is far too much. This is what came of the experience, the very first time I wrote to tell a story.*

The alarm sounded at 4:30 Saturday morning. Only bad thoughts exist this early in the day. I had fallen into bed just three hours before, simultaneously exhausted and elated. As my eyes clamped shut, I was certain that I had seen one of the best rock shows of my life. Now, as waves of sound from tiny speakers raced across my medium-rare left eardrum, self-pity and anger seemed like much more appropriate feelings.

Damn, this trip seemed like such a good idea yesterday.

By 7:00 we were ahead of schedule, half way to Buffalo City and feeling mostly human again. It's amazing what good company can do – that and a steady stream of 80s metal and a well-rounded breakfast consisting of barbecue pork grinds, beef jerky, salted cashew pieces, and the ever-present TaB cola. Lucas manned the wheel brilliantly, guiding the car as it sliced up and down that snaking Ozark highway. He was focused, like a space monkey just shot into orbit, only thinking about the job at hand, unconcerned and unsure of when and if he'd get home. I imagined the feeling to be some kind of trucker's high. A delirious, in-between state of consciousness induced by sleep deprivation, fatty food and dangerously fast speeds. If only we had some uppers to add to the mix...now that would have made for a fun ride!

We touched down at the cabin just before ten. The scene was gorgeous, a picturesque wooden lodge contrasting sharply with a rugged mountain backdrop. As we unpacked and approached the back porch, I swore I felt the building pulsing with energy. Like the scene of a meteor crash, there had been an impact here the night before. The area was still cooling down. Only, instead of a crater and scattered debris, all you could see were crumpled Miller Light cans and scattered Solo cups.

Andy came stumbling out of the back door, sleepy-eyed and hung over, giving me a great big hug, the kind that said, "I hope to Christ you're ready to party." Stepping into the cabin, I was struck by a perfume of cedar, roasting bacon, and stale beer. Gathered in communion around the kitchen were just about all the men I care to know. They were a little worse for wear but excited to be prepping for another day on the river. These men are lifelong friends, training partners, past roommates. When life allows for this sort of reunion, there is no delay or hesitation. No questions. You stock the cooler, grab a few bottles of ibuprofen and you get on board.

As we began to settle in, Bledsoe shouted out from the front doorway, "Hey, grab your shit! We're heading to the river in five minutes!" I hustled, quickly tucking my bag into an unoccupied corner of the cabin. After a quick change of clothes and a coating of sun block, I managed to stumble over to the stove to score the last few abandoned strips of bacon. It would

have to do for now. "Two minutes, assholes! Let's go!"
Right out front, there was a big passenger van pulling
a long rack of canoes and kayaks. Tucked alongside the
rented vessels were multiple coolers packed with 200
or so cans of beer. The atmosphere in the van reminded
me of a grade school field trip, us packed in like
prepubescent sardines. The topic of conversation quickly
turned to alcohol.

"Hey, do you think we have enough beer?"

"Yeah, there's no way we could ever drink all that."

"Bullshit! Did you see how much we went through
last night?"

"Did you guys see how shit-faced Jon was?

"I wasn't that shit faced..."

"Dude! You Thai-kicked me in the thigh then
spewed all over the porch!"

As I walked to the back door of the van, our guide
recommended I sit in the front. "Hey there, big feller. Ya
might oughtta get up here in front with me. More leg
room, you know." That seemed just fine, until I realized
Doug was sitting directly behind me. With each bump of
the road, I could hear him gargle and gasp a bit. Just the
week before in training, he somehow managed to wrench
a hip right out of the socket. I guess mixing prescription-
strength pain killers with copious amounts of beer makes
for a pretty brutal hangover. "Dude, are you alright?
You're looking pretty rough."

Resigned, Doug tilted his head up slightly, replying
"Yeah, I'll make it. No worries." I was prepared to take it
for the team. Plus even though getting hurled on would
suck, it would make for a hell of a funny story, and trips
like these are measured in stories.

We got organized at the launch point, laying out all the boats next to each other. Each was stocked with a portion of the beer, and all the food we could reasonably expect to consume. Our initial plan was simple. We would form a flotilla, drifting down the river in a tight pack. We would drink, then drink...then time permitting, we would drink. All until we washed up on shore unconscious some eight miles downriver.

In my boat, I was joined by Patrick and Pukin' Mike – a fortuitous team-up that would prove memorable. We placed the leading edges of our canoe in the water and set off, Mike heading up the front of the boat, Patrick tucked into the middle, lounging mostly, with me bringing up the rear. The first thing you realize in a boat like this is that teamwork is crucial. Obviously, you have to work together to paddle with any sort of efficiency. But also, with three knuckleheads dicking around in there, your chances of flipping over into the water are really friggin' high. It's shaky as hell. After those first few strokes, my eyes were drawn down to the river. There was an incredible contrast between the perfectly clear, ice-cold water and the mossy green and brown stones lodged below. This was the first time I had ever been in a canoe. I recognized it immediately as a special experience.

We began to move around the first bend of the river when we realized we were in a flotilla of two. "Where the hell is everybody?" I asked. All the sudden, you could hear a yell in the background. "HELP!... HELP!" Pointing behind, Patrick began to laugh, "Oh man, look at these jokers." The call was coming from

Andy. He and Doug's boat made it about ten feet into the water before capsizing.

It was probably the shock of the frigid water, and the fact that Doug was semiconscious with a bad leg, that generated the initial panic. Otherwise, I don't think they could have drowned in a few feet of water. But who the hell knows. All around them, the other boats were spread out across the horizon. The sound of raucous laughter drifted down the valley towards us. We all made brief eye contact before paddling on.

Man, things were already starting to get crazy. And we had still got 200 beers to drink.

When you're in a canoe with two other men, the most important thing is settling into a rhythm. Open a fresh, frosty beer with a smooth swipe of your index finger. Take a quick, powerful pull from the can, and then place the beer securely between your feet. Reach for your paddle, being very careful not to make any sudden or dramatic movements. Take a few long strokes on either side of the vessel. For Christsakes, only paddle with the minimal effort required to stay on course! This is not a race, got that? Now, put the paddle down. Repeat steps one through six until you're drunk enough to forget everything I just told you.

That's when the fun starts.

After about an hour on the river, all of our boats slowly began to coalesce into the floating tailgate party we had initially envisioned. Wind funneled down into the river valley, rapidly cooling as it rolled across the water. Still, the sun pressed down just enough to drive our thirst.

I asked Mike for another beer and he reached over

the side of the boat, retrieving an old sun-bleached plastic bag from the current. This was our ready-access stash kept perfectly chilled by the flowing river.

Without turning around Mike tossed the can overhead with a perfect trajectory, carrying the payload over an un-flinching Patrick and into my lap. Like I said, rhythm is everything.

"Hey, what do we have here?" Patrick asked. "I think... yeah...looks like some chicks, bro. River Chicks..."

We had previously established that while on the water, you could use river as an effective adjective. You didn't say that beef jerky was good. You said, "Damn, this is good river jerky!" Your beer wasn't cold...it was river cold. We were getting pretty drunk, but with time, we'd be river drunk!

Up ahead, those girls Patrick spotted were settled into the river bank fishing, listening to Elvis Presley, of all things. From a boat behind our own, I could hear a scowling Derek ask, "What the hell is that shit?"

"Dude, you don't know Elvis when you hear him?" I guess some folks just don't have an appreciation for The King.

The poor girls must have been terrified to see twenty inebriated, rowdy men floating down the river towards them. It's probably the same exact feeling Native Americans had when they saw white men coming up the Mississippi River for the first time – an initial curiosity, followed by the realization that this could only end in disaster. Of course, we were just passing by.

We thought what all dumb, deluded guys think in that sort of situation, "Man, did you see those chicks back there? Dude, they were totally into us. Whatever...You got any more of those river chips?"

Rocky beaches and small islands were scattered all along the length of the river. We spotted one particularly inviting stretch of land and decided to stop in order to shotgun beers and grab a bite to eat. All the guys lined up along the shore, cans in hand.

"Ready? 3, 2, 1...Go!"

With a quick jab, a small hole is ripped into the bottom of the can. The mouth is placed over the hole, then the can is opened from up top. A quick pressure change drives the beer down through the bottom of the can, into your alcohol trough of a stomach.

I crushed my empty can and tossed into the back of our canoe. By this time, the sun was hung directly over my head. I felt my body temperature climbing, so I popped open a fresh beer and began to wade slowly out into the river. There was a sharp contrast between my chilled shanks and the bubbling warmth of my upper body. I really wanted to dive deeper in and swim, but the water was just too damn cold. Perhaps later.

All at once, warning signals were going off in my mind. Behind me, there was a loud, repetitive splashing. Turning my head, I saw Andy charging straight towards me. Confusion quickly turned into the understanding that I was about to get creamed. Instinctively, I spread my feet out wide into the rocky riverbed. The impact was quick and forceful. Andy's body drove through my right shoulder, then whipped around my torso like lightning. My balance lost, I was driven head first into the river.

The shock was immediate and intense. Not only was I completely submerged, but I also gulped down a throat-full of water upon entry. Being quickly cooled from inside and out simultaneously is a hell of a sensation!

"Holy Fuck!!!"

Laughing, Andy taunted, "Cold isn't it? Not so funny when it's you, huh?

Andy would go on to "hunt" several other guys over the course of the day, instilling a certain measure of fear at every shotgun stop. He even tried his luck with other large mammals.

We were in the middle of a heated conversation – the kind that only drunk dudes can have. "Hey, hey. Here's a question for you. Who's the lamest superhero?" I asked.

"Lamest?"

"Yeah. Other than Thor or Green Lantern, of course. Who's the lamest?"

"Oh, dude, Aqua Man. No doubt. All he can do is talk to fish! Who cares about that shit? He's even gotta be close to the water to fight anybody. C'mon.."

"Okay, okay. What about this. Who's cooler? Iron Man, or Batman?" Bledsoe shouted out immediately, "BATMAN! That's easy."

"Really? I mean, they're both rich. And sure, they both kick a lot of ass. None of us are going to argue that. But come on, Bruce Wayne just takes all toys and inventions from his own company. Tony Stark actually has to invent all of his own shit!"

Bledsoe slipped into deep contemplation, his expression making him look like he had a bad ice cream headache. "Hmmm, you have a point. I never thought of it that way."

Cory was lazily paddling beside me in his kayak, his young black Labrador straddled sleepily across his lap. "Holy shit, what is that? Are those cows?" Initially, we thought it was just an hallucination. But these things were real! What looked like wild cows grazing on a grassy island, suspended out in the middle of the river.

"Hey Andy! If you like tackling so much, why don't you get your ass over there and tackle that fucking cow? I'll give you a hundred bucks."

Andy was quick to accept the challenge. "Oh yeah? You're on."

We disbanded in an instant, paddling violently towards the island. Startled, the cows retreated to the mainland. After embedding his canoe into the river bank, Andy hopped out and immediately assumed a predatory stance.

"Holy shit, he's actually going to do this!"

We took our positions high on the island to get a good vantage point, while not interfering with the hunt. Creeping out into the field, Andy was focused. It looked just like a scene out of *National Geographic* magazine. The brash young lion staring down the massive elephant, foolishly confident he can make the kill.

"God, we're so fucking paleo right now! Hunting a wild cow?"

"Hey, you know if he actually does this, you have to come up with a hundred dollars," Patrick reminded me.

"Oh, it's so worth it."

"But what if they charge him? Those fucking things are huge! Maybe we should tell him to forget it. He could get killed."

"Well...You're probably right."

It was too late. Sensing the time was ripe, Andy exploded out of his crouched position, accelerating towards the cows. For an instant, they were resigned to holding their ground and call his bluff. But soon after, they turned and high-tailed it as fast as possible up into the tree line.

To be perfectly honest, we did hope he would get his hands on one of those things. "Ah, dude, it wasn't meant to be. Maybe if you weren't so drunk?... Here, have another beer."

Some five hours or so after launch, we drifted towards the dock adjacent to our cabin. Just in time, too. All 200 of those beers were just about gone.

I should have known something wasn't right. Too much time had gone by with no attempts at shenanigans. It was eerie. Then, like a Hail Mary pass at the end of a football game, a large chunk of ice went soaring through the air, coming right towards us. One of the guys ahead was emptying out his cooler into the river. He thought it would be funny as hell to scare us into dumping our canoe. That's just what happened.

As the ice neared, Mike was spooked out of position, pitching the canoe quickly to the right. Patrick and I tried to counter the shift, but it was too late. We flipped right over, dead center in the middle of the river. Shooting back up to the surface, we gasped for air, then grabbed onto the canoe, and any cargo we could save.

"What the hell were you thinkin', ya River Dummy!?" Patrick asked.

"Dude, sorry. I thought it was going to hit us!" We fought to maintain control of the boat long enough to tread towards a shallow point in the river ahead. "Just a little further!"

We slid the front of the canoe up onto the rock, temporarily holding it in place while we climbed to dry land. Mike grasped the back of the boat and waited for me. As soon as I got a hand on the front, I stepped onto a slippery patch of algae, my feet coming out from underneath me. The boat was dislodged by the quick current, and was being pushed right towards my head. Mike gained control just in time, with the tip of the canoe only inches from my melon. I rolled to my left and beached myself on dry stone.

"Holy shit! Are you okay?"

"Yeah, I just slipped. No worries..."

"That could have been bad!"

After composing ourselves, we drained the water from the boat, repacked our gear and launched into the rapids. By that time, the rest of the guys were out of sight. I was exhausted, my beer buzz shaken off during that impromptu dip in the river. "Fuck me, let's get home."

When we finally made it to the cabin's dock, the guys were settled in and grilling food on the back porch. All the boats appeared to be on shore, aside from the one red canoe that seemed abandoned, drifting down the river. "Don't worry about that," Derek said, "Bledsoe and Cory are going after it."

We struggled to drag our boat up to dry land. I immediately dropped all of my gear and headed up to the cabin, each step of the way peeling off pieces of wet clothing. My skin was saturated with water, wavy and wrinkled.

Slipping past the grill and into the kitchen, I swiped a few chunks of red meat, a few cookies, then collapsed onto the floor. My last memory before passing out was that of Mike storming around the cabin, shouting, "You fuckers better not get sleepy on me. We've still got the whole night ahead of us. I'm just warming up!"

Man, a hard wooden floor never felt so comfortable.

I was jarred awake by a sudden scream, "HEY EVERYBODY! HERE COMES THE CHOO CHOO!" I manually peeled open my left eye, and noticed a growing swarm of activity around the kitchen. In the center, Mike was vigorously pumping and priming the half-full keg of Turbo Dog. Rest time was over. I'd better get up. If these guys found me asleep, it would be hell.

Feeling crippled and lame, I pressed my forehead down into my makeshift mattress, creating a tiny crack of clearance between body and floor. I wedged my hands into pushup position, and with a quick shove, popped my lifeless stone torso upright. A sharp pressure in my lower back surged, forcing air from my lungs with an audible grunt. I placed one foot out in front of my body, pitching forward in a controlled fall. Just a quick shuffle later and I was on my feet.

The boys seemed glad to see me conscious. "Dude, you look like shit! Here, you better have a drink." Let me tell you, if I was ever capable of drinking twelve beers as a warm-up to the main event, those days were long gone. "God," I thought to myself, "I could kill for a Diet Coke right now."

To my right, a small group of the guys were setting up for poker at the kitchen table. In the center of that table, a teetering pile of small coins formed as everyone bought into the game. Chips were scattered all around the periphery, along with fresh cans of beer and plates of food. To my left, another group was bringing grass-fed beef burgers and steaks in from the grill. I slipped in around them, grabbing bits from each tray. In the center of the hustle, huddled around the keg, Mike and Derek were performing a unique, seemingly complicated maneuver.

Warning: before attempting the Gargoyle, make sure to see your physician. If you have any orthopedic injuries, balance problems, hernias, etc., you should not attempt the Gargoyle. If you see yourself ever wanting to have children, then please consider some other means of inebriation. The chances of severe scrotal snagging are relatively high.

Proper execution is as follows:

1. Approach the keg, firmly grasping the top handles of the vessel.

2. Place one foot on top of the keg, clinching the rim firmly with the toes for stability.

3. Use the down leg to jump, quickly placing the other foot adjacent to the first (this is the trickiest bit of the procedure).

4. Release the hands.

5. Grasp the keg pump with one hand, and pick up the spout with the other.

6. Vigorously pump the keg whilst sucking foamy

beer from the spout. Your friends will laugh because it will look as though you're pleasuring yourself. This is how you know you're doing it right!

7. Once you become light headed and fall off the keg, or you violently spew beer from the mouth, you'll know you've completed the Gargoyle. Congratulations. You might want to sit down now.

By 1:00 a.m., I was ready to be put down. The wicked combination of sleep deprivation, alcohol, and excessive red-meat ingestion was more than any man should expect to tolerate.

At the first opportune moment, I slipped off to the back corner of the nearest bedroom, constructing a sleeping nest by stacking random blankets. As I settled in, I could hear someone shouting from upstairs, "Dude, how many Smirnoff Ice's did you stash around here? No, I ain't no more! I don't care about the rules."

Back in the kitchen, the conversation turned to cooking. "Hey, does anyone know how to cook a cow heart? Can you grill it? Bake it?" Mike asked. "What does the Internet say? Jason, Google, 'How to cook cow heart.'"

"No, no, no," Derek interrupted, "I think you gotta braise it. Or maybe stew that shit!" It was like an episode of Iron Chef, only instead of Asian chefs preparing meals with wild ingredients, this version featured drunken CrossFitters with knives. Slipping away, I thought, "I'd watch that show."

The next few hours were an ethereal mix of dream and reality. Unrelenting noises echoed through the cabin, mixing with fresh memories in my mind to form something in-between.

Then at 4:30 a.m., the party died.

Breakfast that morning was no different than the previous two. Organic eggs were scrambled by the dozen on the stove top. Thick cut, peppered bacon was roasting away under the broiler, filling the room with sweet pork perfume. Strawberries, blueberries, and halved avocados lined the kitchen counter. Everything looked the same as the night before, but the energy that had carried the weekend was gone. Even the biggest party animals among us were worn and ready for home.

All thoughts turned to what needed to be done before we could leave. We started by finishing off or storing all of the remaining food. We cleaned every beer-soaked, greasy corner of the cabin. We packed and said our goodbyes. Dawning alongside the morning light was the realization that, while we're not old, none of us are young anymore. With each year, we settle deeper into our lives, our careers, our families. We have ever-growing responsibility. We all understood that weekends like this were rare, but also that we would do it again.

Our goodbyes were short.

I caught a ride back to Memphis with Bledsoe, Doug, and Jon. We took the narrow 126 state highway out of Buffalo City, rolling out of the hills and into the closest thing to civilization northern Arkansas could offer.

"Mike, I gotta have a decent cup of coffee." I asked from the back seat. "It's been two days, dude. I need it. What are our options?"

"Me too. I don't really see anything like Starbucks around here. That's for sure. Maybe we can hit up McDonald's?"

In the passenger seat, Doug was oblivious to all conversation. With crutches stretched over the armrest next to his left leg, he smiled and stared across the dashboard into the horizon ahead. Jon was sitting next to me in the back. His aviator shades hid red and irritated eyes as he texted away.

We drove for twenty minutes or so before turning off into the tiny town of Mountain Home and finding a McDonald's tucked inside the local Wal-Mart, the weekend place to see and be seen in this sunny, remote outpost. Walking through the front door, I felt like we got an accurate sample of the entire local population. There were obese men driving around in motorized Rascals, eating Funyuns, ass-cracks hanging out. Angry grandmas with purple hair, drawn-on eyebrows, and makeup-encrusted mustaches. Little kids running around in their underwear, violently waving rebel flags...or not. That could have just been something I saw on PeopleofWalmart.com.

Mike approached the young girl behind the McDonald's counter, "Uh, yeah. I'll have the fried apple pie, coffee...and that'll be it."

Bless her little backwoods heart. The girl responded, "I'm sorry sir, but we don't carry fried apple pie coffee."

"What? No, no, I want the pie, then a cup of coffee to go along with it."

The girls stared blankly back at him, responding, "That'll be $2.20, please."

I'd forgotten how cheap shitty food could be. "You can get two fried apple pies and a large coffee for a few bucks! Holy shit, I'll have what he's having."

I finished off both pies and half of the coffee before we even got back to the car. Just as we pulled out of the parking lot and began merging back onto the highway, we were cut off by a speeding Dodge Caravan. It was yellow with a thin black pinstripe running down its length. Patches of bright-red rust surrounded the rear left wheel-well. Pulling ahead, the women driving the van looked at us in her mirror and flipped us the bird.

"Oh yeah! Well, fuuuck you, too!" Mike shouted. "Ah...who cares. She'll probably run herself off the road anyhow. Serves her right." He took another long sip of coffee to settle his nerves, then consulted the GPS for directions.

After the initial rush, my pie-fueled energy jolt had resulted in a mean backlash. All that caffeine was powerless to counter the effects. I was knocked out cold before we even got back to the highway.

We were just outside of Jonesboro when the sugar began to lose its grip on my mind. Snapping awake, I found the guys staring at a semi-truck ahead of us. Doug had his phone in hand, videotaping every moment.

"Uh....uuuuuhhhhhh.......Aaaaawwwwwwww! He came so close that time."

Looking forward, I could see that truck swaying wildly back and forth down the highway. Starting in the right lane, the vehicle would gently pull towards the middle line, then whip back towards the right-hand barrier. Just before impact, the driver jerked the wheel straight. We must have watched this cycle repeat itself twenty times before deciding to call the cops. Doug did the honors.

"Yeah, hello? Yes, we're driving through Jonesboro towards Memphis. There's this big yellow truck just swerving all over the fucking place...Oh, you're on your way already? Okay....Yeah, sure thing. Bye."

"They already know?"

"Yeah, she said they already received a bunch of calls about this guy."

Jon added, "Or maybe they just thought you were a douche for cursing at them."

"Whatever. I feel better about it." Doug turned the phone back on its side and resumed recording. "God, this is like *Final Destination 5*."

There is an obvious, undeniable beauty in watching an impending disaster. We found ourselves actively wishing for this guy to crash and burn, simply for our brief amusement. After all, if he wanted to drive reckless, then he deserved it. This wouldn't rest heavy on our hearts, not for one second.

Where are you when we need you, Batman or Iron Man?

Just as we entered a construction zone, Mike needed to stop. "Man, I gotta pee really bad. I'm going to have to pull over."

"What!? You can't do that now! Look at all these barrels, the narrowed lanes and construction equipment...He's gonna wreck now for sure!" We waited ten more minutes, but no luck. That driver pushed the semi back and forth between the right and left barriers, coming within mere feet of making contact, but he never did.

"Son of a bitch."

"Alright guys, there's a Stucky's. I have to stop. Sorry." Jon was disappointed. "Mike, I'm blaming you if we get up there and there's a bloody crash. There's no excuse for missing that kind of magic." Doug actually chimed in with a very sensible comment. "Can you guys believe those cops never showed? That's so irresponsible."

With freshly stretched legs and voided bladders, we got back on the road, bypassing the exit to Blytheville with Memphis dead ahead. The vehicle was silent and still right up until we got to West Memphis.

Just ahead near the median, we began to see a pillar of smoke climbing towards the sky. Cars began to coalesce to form a barrier around the scene. We slowed down to 20 mph. "What's going on? Looks like a wreck."

"No fucking way. It's the truck!"

As if the air was instantly sucked from the cabin, our voices fell flat – an eerie silence. That same semi-truck had embedded itself into the central concrete barrier, cargo trailers badly twisted and bowed. The stunned truck driver sat on the entry step below the open passenger side door. An early responder stood beside him holding a towel to his head. A likely laceration.

As we slowly pulled ahead of the wreck, I quickly pivoted in my seat, looking over my left shoulder and through the back window. Fused between the front of the truck and what remained of the barrier, I could just make out the shape of a van. Yellow.

No way. Co*uld it be the same van?* I thought.

Through wisps of smoke, I could see a fractured

windshield. Beams of sunlight shined through the gutted rear of the van but were obscured by dark red patches on the driver's side. We all turned back towards the road ahead and resumed our breathing.

PART 2

SAVED TIME

Alan Watts was one of the most engaging and thought-provoking public figures of the twentieth century. His fame was inevitable, I suppose. As one of the first great popularizers of Eastern philosophy in the West, he had nothing but interesting, bizarre, brand-new ideas to offer. A perfect niche, coupled with an attention-grabbing persona and British accent. His would-be pupils flocked in droves.

You could spend years digging into all of his lectures and books, but one of his most powerful lessons was also one of the easiest with which to connect. It's something we face every single day: the challenge of creating and chasing goals. As the lesson goes, imagine a musician is playing a song in concert. There is a start, middle, and a final note. It's a temporal thing, moving from its beginning to its end, but the end itself is never the goal, right? Nothing would suck more than if the band just came right out to the front of the stage and played the final grand crash of notes right at the start.

"We've enjoyed rocking your tits off tonight, Cleveland!...That's right! We'll see you again real soon, baby. Good night, good night. See you next time."

No one in the audience is looking for the end. They want everything that comes in between. They want to enjoy themselves and sing along to the tune, because it makes everything in their lives make sense, because it exhilarates, cleanses, and empowers. It sets the worried mind at ease. But there is never an attempt to compare the tune with anything else. You're never asked to hold this particular arrangement of notes higher than any other. You just make the most out of the experience, and you depart humming along to the melody.

It seems like anything that's really worth doing would function the same exact way. Work, training, love, it all has to add more to your life than it takes away. That's the key metric.

Alan's lecture comes to a fine point as he draws attention to society and the powerful, burdensome expectations placed by and upon it. We are led by a carrot and stick from the onset. We pass from grade to grade, from high school to graduate work, to the corner office, to the promise of a well-deserved beach retirement, or perhaps a post-mortem celestial payday. That's a troubling pattern, isn't it? Do you think for one second that enduring happiness will be waiting for you around the next corner? Does it make sense to look for it here first?

That dangling promise leads us all the way down the road, but to what? Was there ever a human that got just what they wanted and were then forever content? It's exceedingly doubtful. This is just not a core primate behavioral trait, I'm afraid. "There, I did what I set out to do. Now it's time to fly off to Kyoto and sit quietly in meditation for the next 50 years of my life. Just me, a pot of frothy green tea, and my little sand garden that I painstakingly construct and then destroy daily. I'm Zen as fuck right now."

That's a romantic notion for sure, but it's fundamentally counter to how the Western mind is constructed. And that's not a bad thing, necessarily. In a bat-shit crazy and highly contrary world, the West is the Ying to the Eastern Yang, so to speak. You get the point. The hurried Western masses are here to hustle and push the needle forward, to test limits, to spill a righteous rock and roll vibe all over everything. But like anything, it gets old quickly without balance.

It's good to be reminded about the other side, where folks recognize the necessity of sitting down a couple times a day and considering all the outcomes we are chasing. To consider our pace, the cost, the expectations and pressures, our true selves, and our honest desires. The what, how, and why of everything (Hint: we're all paying too high of a price for something right now. That's certain).

I think my true-self blooms and comes into focus in the gym, especially during the springtime. The cold gets harder and harder.

I feel heavier and slower during darker winter months. I'm always guilty of getting a late start, which carves a large chunk of light off my shortened day. By the time I catch back up, there's this sense that time is running out. That I should hurry up and get this warm-up, this training, this conditioning done so that I can get back to the real work. If I can get all that done, then I have a better shot getting to that next level. I'll get the fucking carrot!

The shame is that these behaviors chip away at all of the pleasure and value. Just like the band that starts with the final clash of notes, you find yourself rushing off towards some ending, right past everything that matters the most. All the habits, rituals and daily decisions that actually get you the change you want. But in the spring there's still plenty of daylight in the later hours when I train and grow more active. I'm reminded that I've actually got all the time I need. That what matters most is what's happening right now. Everything else can wait its turn. It will all come in due time.

The immediate goal is to search for limitations and boundaries, and then gently push them outward to new ground. I take my time and enjoy myself. I don't watch any clocks or fixate on my shortcomings, although they are many. Whatever, it's fine. I just keep doing, like a fish that swims along without worrying too much about all that water out ahead (How's that for some hippy guru talk?). When I train with that sort of perspective, every movement feels way more productive and rewarding. Inevitably I don't rush. I lift more, with better form. I work harder.

Creativity happens organically. I do what I love most of all more often, and I start to get really fucking good at it. I smile wider. I recover in less time. In time, I begin to believe that I can achieve absolutely anything that's worth planning for, without much fuss or worry. This is the path to mastery.

We need to know what direction we're heading in, but maybe we should abandon goal setting as we typically think of it. Not out of some passive, idealistic, flower-power-inspired mumbo jumbo bullshit motive. No, we want to do and achieve great things for as long as we can because it's the best and most joyful way to spend this time. It yields the best results. It makes the ride more rewarding. And yes, it just makes for the best sort of music.

IT'S ALL AROUND THE NEXT CORNER.

YOUR LIFE STARTS RIGHT HERE.

GET IN

It's so easy to complicate the start by looking around for a great example, or the best way to do the thing that we want to do. To create what we want to create. To be whatever it is that we'd like to be. Our best thinking sometimes, oftentimes, gets in the way. It binds and constricts when it overgrows. We tightly hold onto a long list of assumptions while painting ourselves into a corner, where only a limited number of options remain in view. It stops the thing from happening and unfolding as it could, as it should.

The trick is finding a way around the overthinking. A hack. A simple go-to jump-start strategy that applies equally well to any situation: the tough conversation, the risky start-up venture, the dreaded training session that you know's going to be brutal. You name it.

I loved a recent *Rolling Stone* piece on Jack White, from The White Stripes, The Raconteurs, and The Dead Weather, not to mention an increasing body of excellent solo work, countless production gigs, and guest appearances. Some call him the Willy Wonka of rock-and-roll, a dead-on nickname for this impressively eclectic and accomplished, forceful and raw musician.

That raw quality is the best aspect because it doesn't guarantee a predictable result. Never, ever count on it. But for me, I enjoy the unexpected most of all. That's the fun and true value of really great music. With Jack, half of the work I love, and the other half I don't feel ready for yet. That's alright. It just leaves something for me to discover later down the road. It gives balance to the tunes I'm already comfortable with and love. Speaking of which, the thunderous and reverberating track, "Ball and Biscuit," remains my favorite training tune of all time. Cue up that track, turn the volume to 11, then watch the room shake and thump with raw sound.

Every line of the article was worth a read, but it was the bit on Jack's work style that sprang off the page. His ex-wife, Karen, was recalling the no-nonsense production style that she experienced when they worked on one of her albums together. His timely, no bullshit advice was simply to, "Get in there, pick up your guitar and sing." There's no time for feeling insecure, quiet, timid, tone-deaf, whatever. There's only the moment. The iron is hot. If you think too much, you might let the moment cool, and that's a sure path towards boring, shitty, soulless music.

No-nonsense, baby. That's the way to go. That is the only truth the creative mind requires. It's the only coaching point, hack, or tool that you really need, spread out in eight little words. It breaks what binds. It forces the flow to begin and quicken.

Remember that these intense feelings of insecurity are quite common, possibly universal, with the exception of a few souls who were born with righteous confidence. But the rest of us don't have to hold back. We can let our best spill out, it just takes some practice. A little voice in the ear, shouting, "Get in there!"

I know, easier said than done. This is a better, simpler way, but it takes courage and practice. The quick, decisive action triggers a massive amount of discomfort, which is exactly why most people will avoid it. They will try anything else instead, even if the results are shitty. Even if nothing at all happens. But I can promise you, this gets easier with time. With the first step and some repetition, you will discover for yourself that jumping in feet first is the most-powerful thing you can do. It leverages the present, which is all you really have. It's magic, a sort of opportunity alchemy. It reveals, perfectly, honestly and without pretense.

And it's nothing new, by the way. This is not a hot discovery. Consider the fitting quote attributed to Thomas Jefferson: "Do you want to know what you are? Don't ask. Act! Action will delineate and define you."

Change, effect, strength, success, art, passion, enlightenment, comfort, healing, all the good stuff in life, anything at all that's worthwhile, none of it can come from planning and pondering alone. You will never find a starting point that feels perfectly right, because there's no such thing.

There is no way but this way. Move and act so quickly, so forcefully, so honestly, that you cannot help but express what you could be, what you should be.

DO YOU WANT TO KNOW WHAT YOU REALLY ARE?

ACT.

DOUBLE STRENGTH

The basic story arc has three parts.

First, there's the big opening number. The would-be champion and emerging hero decides to hand over everything in pursuit of mastery, the higher quality life, the next level of awareness. The effort is far from perfect, but perfect doesn't matter. It's not even a possible thing, so there's no point in fussing over it.

The only thing that does matter is whether or not the offering is absolute. All there is to give, whatever that might be, that's what you lay down on the altar.

Mastery is no low-budget item. It's not a matter of good fortune or gifts. You don't scoop it up in a two-for-one bargain bundle at the local department store. You really do have to dig for it, baby. You have to search out the supply and pay full price. The absolute premium.

Here's your lesson in value for value. Becoming the strongest, fittest, smartest, bravest, sexiest, more decisive, more ass-kicking version of yourself takes time. It requires a brutal workload, sweat, patience, sacrifice, an open mind, some heartache, frustration, intensity, a splash of fear and blood, a steady caffeine drip, daily recommitment and calibration, some recurrent joint pain and countless late nights, you name it. It's not all fun. The pursuit has to be placed at life's center stage, or pretty damn close to it. Anything less than that is just delusion and wishful thinking.

Catch yourself wishing. Never make excuses. Commit fully and do whatever is required if you really want to do something special. Buy in. Just don't pretend, there's no time for that shit.

The big twist and story tension comes along during the second act. What do you do when there's nothing left to give? Maybe you've been there. You've almost burned out completely. You're no longer into it. Right there the inspired and sharp protagonist will choose to seek out something brand new and sharply challenging. Something that is awkward and scary, but with a big potential upside. Something well beyond the expected, comfortable and the safe.

The twist is that you might not get anywhere close to mastery by pushing in the same direction forever, expecting more and more and more. You will not get there by holding on tightly to what you have. So maybe let go of some of the rules. Do something else for a while, learn new lessons, let your tank refill with something else. I think from there the best thing you can do is just expand and build upon your previous experiences.

That third act is the dramatic return, but don't call it a comeback. That's not really what's going on. The new hero doesn't "come back" to the same thing, as the same person. It's more of a rediscovery. The departure, the letting go, is actually the very best way to gain new insights. You see the thing in a brand new light, from a higher perspective. The space provides context and insight into past missteps. You notice opportunities that were left on the vine. Better still, you will get a very clear view of your true strengths, your unique genius. That's when the real productivity and impact will begin.

As Baltasar Gracian wrote over three hundred years ago, the key is to, "Identify your king of attributes and apply it in double strength."

Work relentlessly, passionately, openly to combine all your experience with a new appreciation of your uniqueness. Do that and nothing will stop your flow.

IDENTIFY YOUR KING OF ATTRIBUTES AND APPLY IT IN DOUBLE STRENGTH.

THE BIG THINGS

I don't have much room in my life any longer for regret. Maybe I've outgrown the emotion. Or, it might be fair to say that I've had my fill of it.

This is not the sort of thing you can avoid. Call it a consequence of living. Everyone starts off in a similar spot, feeling a little bit on the small side, a few steps behind. You don't know any better. There's no sense of boundaries, only a roughly sketched out map covering everything between you, your school, and perhaps your best friend's house down the street. What else is there to do, other than venturing out in search of new fence lines and fresh stomping grounds? We all feel the need to make our world bigger.

We rush out looking for big things to climb over and conquer, like little conquistadors armed with plastic cocktail swords and raw ambition. We rapidly expand our little maps. We move on and on to bigger and brighter things. We spend a lot of time learning in the most effective and hardest possible way, by running face-first into more than a few of those really big things. That particular pain is really common and very necessary.

The coach John Wooden said that it's the little things that make the big things happen. The big things are of course the goals. The end game is getting all the way to graduation and beyond. To the passion-filled career, and all the weight that comes with that search. To the setting of endless personal records in the gym. The earning of the perfectly shaped, hard ass that any sane man would be thrilled to bounce a quarter off of. You name it, we're after it. And on we go, until we get that thing, or until we don't. In every last case the optimal result hides in the little habits and rituals, the tiny details, a positive perspective you water and nurture every morning over coffee and quiet time.

This doesn't come naturally. It's not easy. The really easy thing would be to slip back into the old grooves. The old behaviors and habits that have kept you right where you are. It's not an easy thing to do, but it's a habit that can be broken down and repurposed like any other.

Get motivated. Take swift, bold action. Bolder than bold, make it immediate and pronounced. Step well outside of your comfort zone. Do the opposite thing. Demonstrate to yourself that this thing is possible and that there's really nothing stopping you once the threshold is crossed. Once the fear is defanged.

Once the momentum starts building. This is how you make the desired outcome possible, probable, inevitable. Some changes cannot be stopped once the fuse is lit. In that way you make the desired outcome inevitable. Also, if you're like me, it doesn't hurt to follow all that up with a few Clash or Queens of the Stone Age tunes. That rhythm, impulse and attitude goes a long way when resistance and doubt come knocking. Music for me will always be an energy source that never runs dry. It's all a beautiful reminder that there's actually nothing to chase down and climb over. Nothing needs to be forced. There are no walls to run face first into, no more bloody noses, no more unfounded feelings of missing out on something.

That fucking regret vibe only seems to come around during the times I find myself looking out at someone else's big thing. Their version of happiness, art, work, worth, progress, contentment, and everything in between. I ask myself, "What could I have done differently? That looks so good, how can I get over there, to that thing, to that place? How could I have that for myself?" But all that emotion passes instantly, like a vapor, as soon as I realize that most of the big, obvious things within my view aren't mine for the chasing, precisely because they are someone else's big thing. It's not for me. It never was. It shouldn't be. And if I do try and chase after someone else's stuff, it should be no fucking surprise if my days turn out to be less than fulfilling.

One little shift in perspective is all it takes, and suddenly everything makes a lot more sense. I need no one else's map. There's nothing out there for me to conquer. The only big things in this world that matter at all are those things I choose to build for myself.

Selfishness is this dirty word. "Do as you should. Follow this plan. Make your parents happy. Gain the acceptance of every neighbor, every colleague, the boss, the gatekeepers." But this is all folly. If you want to break the pattern, you have to accept the fact that selfishness is the most important thing in this world. The selfish you is not concerned with the status quo, chasing, mimicry, desperation, what have you. No, being selfish is more of a healthy focus. Ask yourself, "What do I need to do right now to be happy? What is it? What do I require? When was the last time that I said 'no' so that I could instead train as I should...eat as I should, when I should...work as

I should, when and where it's organic and painless to do so?" And what of the most essential question you could ever ask yourself? "What's the most important thing I could do with my time right now, in this instant?"

There's no room for regret. There's no time for climbing up and over someone else's big thing. Find yours, then give it everything you have, honestly, openly, with no expectation. Get that, hold it tight, then look back one day and realize that this was the moment when everything changed.

FIND YOUR OBSTACLE.

CLIMB FOR YOURSELF.

TRAPPED

Have you ever seen a monkey trap in action? It's fascinating. You just place a little chunk of fruit or some other tasty, desirable morsel down into the very bottom of an anchored container, then you wait. That's it. Assuming that there are actual monkeys around for the catching, it's inevitable that one will traipse along and make a play at the bait.

There's no hook, no snare, no jagged metal teeth to bite down into soft flesh, because it's not necessary. There's only the internal craving and that tiny little hole that's not quite big enough for a clenched fist to fit back through. The monkey wants what it wants. It will never let go, not even when a hunter with a giant spiked club comes along with vicious intent. At that point, fate will take over. It's the only way out.

Curiously enough, the trap works to perfection on "higher" primates as well. You just need something a little bit fancier and more alluring than a heavy pot and a few banana bits. Maybe a no-money-down, risk-free guarantee would do the job, or perhaps the promise of a sure and safe thing? Even better, how about a good old-fashioned plan? An area of study, career, a dream? It has to be something that you've worked really hard for, at great personal expense, for a really long time. This "thing" is something that you would rather not let go of, no matter how miserable it's making you. Does that sound familiar?

Joseph Campbell has a view on situations like these. It's a warning, really. If I may paraphrase, if you

want a higher-quality life, then you have to let go of
the one you planned on all along. The lives that have
been heavily shaped and warped by outside influence
and expectation. I think everyone has experienced
that effect, and we all recognize that the decision of
letting go is much easier said than done. As soon as
you get your hand wrapped around something mostly
comfortable, the surest thing you have access to, the
tastiest morsel, then you're effectively doomed. From
that point on you will sit still right there, next to your
pot, fist clenched, and you will wait on fate to make
the final move.

If it's any consolation, this classic human
trap usually doesn't come with a hunter wielding
a gigantic, spiked club. It's more of a probability
thing. Sure, the old plan makes it feel as though a
magnificent bird could come flying out of the bush
at any moment. If you would just stay here and keep
waiting, then you might end up with two birds, right?
But no, the odds just go down and down and down the
longer you sit there.

We're all being hunted by something, and
regardless of what it is the fucking thing is hoping that
we do not let go and walk away. If we want change,
an impulse to shake us loose, then we have to do
something. Reaction for action. Effect always follows
cause, so maybe we must simply initiate a cause. A
strong action. That must be the kind of decision that
points you towards bliss, right? I choose to believe
that.

As Campbell also said, you can only take a step
towards your happy place after you let go of the old
thing. The act alone sends you along a path towards

kind souls that only want to open the doors for you. Don't be afraid. There's no sense in backing away, not even an inch from the leading edge, the source, that one thing that fuels your highest-quality effort, that helps you to make sense of it all, that makes you happy. This is the sort of music that always sounds right to your ear.

I'm inclined to believe Campbell. There's no sense in being afraid, especially if you're in pursuit of what sounds best. All we need here is a little bit of trust. Always keep stepping towards the people that you need to be around. Get right up close to the stimuli that will keep pushing you forward, provoking change. Step towards the energy, the source, wherever it's coming from, and you are sure to change in the best-possible way. It's what I have to believe now, because it's working in my life.

Will you try the same? Go on, get up close. Give it a try. Let go of the old, and go find something worth holding onto tightly.

WHAT ARE YOU HOLDING ONTO TOO TIGHTLY?

THE CROSSROADS

The morning the big change became real was so strange, but not in any of the ways I had imagined.

I braced for this seismic, existential shakedown. Maybe there would be a clear and ominous rumbling from someplace really dark and just out of sight. Or at least there would be that really unpleasant free-falling tummy sensation that we all get during a wild and turbulent airplane ride. But no, there was nothing to feel. The moment was defined more by what wasn't.

The other side of the crossroads was its own unique thing. I didn't fall down to my knees under the weight of the moment. I asked no one and nothing for mercy. Of course, it wasn't what I expected. It couldn't be.

Tell me, when was the last time you noticed some brand-new version of reality matching up in any way against your fevered, nervous projections? Never is the correct answer, but that doesn't stop the caffeine-enabled and overly anxious chimp mind within from giving it a go. This is its own lesson.

The current breakthrough is just another sort of illusion. The shift will come again and again, and you will be reminded that you cannot totally outrun the indelible mark of your lowly origin, your long and less than ideal personal history, what you've been fed your entire life, what you always thought was normal and possible and reasonable and right in life.

Here's a pro tip: assume that nothing is as it seems. But, you can learn from all of this. Right now.

It's quite true. You can carry this new experience along with you and fortify that new baby perspective of yours. The struggle, a fight, the war will come to you again and again, and you'll be a little more prepared to hold the line and move forward the next time through.

The only obligation I felt that first morning was to just buy the flowers. It was a small and understated arrangement of spring lilies and daisies that I was sure Dad would really enjoy. "At least he would have...Not now, Chris. Not here in the Kroger self-checkout line. This is surely less than ideal. Hold it together for a while longer. Go on about your business. Chin up, keep moving."

I made the quiet thirty-minute drive straight south, parked along the longest driveway path I've ever known, and slowly made my way up the bare hill to say hello. The strangest part of the visit was the sensation of being really nervous, despite everything, as if I was apologizing for something. I felt like I was still a clueless teenager desperate to find my path and to feel reassured. I needed my Dad right then, just as I need him some thirteen years prior when I first decided to leave the sport that had consumed my life for over a decade.

"Dad, I don't think I want to play football anymore. I don't want to be a football player." Nothing had ever hurt as bad as those words. Sure, this had always been a goal of mine, but for Dad it was a special point of pride. I had played for his absolute favorite team in the whole fucking world, for Cristsakes! I was a "Tiger." Until I wasn't.

The moment was so heavy for me, and the inner chimp really did his thing. How could I do this to him? How could I leave here knowing that he would now refer back to good times in the past tense? What was he going to see me as now? Worse still, what would I see and what would I do? Who would I be?

Of course, the projections didn't fit the reality. I was tired. I was injured. I wasn't fulfilled by this any longer and he saw that perfectly well for himself. "It's alright, son. If you believe that it's the right thing to do, then it's alright. Everything will be alright."

I climbed the hill as slowly as I could. I laid the flowers down softly and took a seat on the freshly laid sod. The very first thing I noticed were these little green grass tendrils stretching and reaching out for something new to grab onto, fed and encouraged by the earliest rays of spring sunlight. A long oak tree branch was hung overhead, dotted with countless little brown leaf buds. This was balance. It was a reminder that the moment couldn't be all that sad. My underlying optimism wasn't out of place. I asked for help.

"Here I go again, Dad. I can only imagine what you would be thinking right now, and how you would worry over me. I know. I find myself getting overwhelmed by the very same emotion every single time I look at Max as he runs round the house like mad, blissfully unaware of any danger. I feel it all over when I think of Mae and all that she could be. As if this latest decision wasn't enough, my world will once again change in the biggest possible way in just a few weeks. I don't feel ready, Dad, how could I? But I know, I know, there is no such thing as the right and perfect time. It'll be alright."

I paused, then spoke again: "I have to give you credit. I have no idea how you held it together all those years. How did you survive our missteps, our searching, our decisions? You were so tough, and patient, and so much wiser than I was prepared to accept at the time. I'm sorry I never quite got it before, but you knew I would eventually, didn't you?

I don't know how all of this is going to turn out. It's the biggest risk I've ever taken. There's so much on the line, but so much out there to achieve and experience. I know it's the right thing to do. I'm taking my leap of faith. I know you would be proud of this. Scared just as shitless as me, but I know you would be proud."

I stood up, stretched my legs, then looked out over and around this vast grid dotted with flowers. So many stories, lives spanning centuries, some stopped tragically short. What a powerful place. It's a reminder that there's no such thing as fair and unfair, there is only a singular reality. The clock is ticking and while we are alive there is an ever-present choice to make. We can sit here at these crossroads, floored by the moment and all the emotion still swirling around, or we can walk forward. We can take action. We can trust this. We can push with everything we've got. Act, act, act. Give the change a chance to take hold.

This was a powerful moment of clarity, and then it was done and gone.

I've never left a visit with Dad without making some kind of joke. It really helped to lighten the mood in the later years as he fought so hard to stretch his time, as I fought so hard to accept the truth of the situation. "Hey, I know you can't be all that busy, Pops. Do you think you could call in a favor for me? All things considered, I figured maybe you could go talk to management and put in a good word for your boy. I could use all the help I can get, you know?"

He knew, he always knew. So I'll hold up my end of the bargain. From here on I'm pushing forward. From here on there's no time for fear and worry and false projection. The only thing that matters is what I could become. This is the real breakthrough moment.

SIT DOWN. REST. DON'T RUSH THROUGH. TRUST IN WHAT YOU ARE. GIVE CHANGE A CHANCE.

COFFEE SHOP QUIRK

Stillness is equal parts upside and downside, light and dark, which is true of anything.

Let's shed some light on the upside of sitting down for a while. It brings your world into sharp focus. It reduces the noise that constantly hums and distracts. It works to peel back the social imprints and burdensome expectations. It redirects the attention towards what is personally important, real, and valued above everything else. If you don't have a clear idea of what you truly value, stop, stop right now.

If you have pushed and chased and struggled for anything external then you can identify with the problem. You might know the feeling that follows when you've been moving along in one direction for far too long. You might intimately know the symptoms, like forgetting just where you started and why. All that energy at the start, you might lose it and fall into some kind of strong gravity. Maybe a gig that you really don't like at all, more of the same kind of goal, the same old outcome, the same old behaviors and habits, because that's what you expect, that's what you're prepared to accept.

This is a lesson I've had to learn firsthand this year, in the hardest possible way. Don't wait around. Get back to what's important to you as soon as you can. There's no sense in waiting around, is there? Time can only make it harder.

Waiting around on the long straight line, that's a scary fate to consider. It's a path towards a safe and unremarkable story. A bad ending to a boring movie, one where the lead allows it all to happen, head first, bang! But that's not going to be our fate. So let this be our daily sacrament. Yes, be still for a moment, preferably over a beautiful dark roast and a big chunk of 88% dark chocolate. Carefully consider what is important to you. Be brutally honest because this is your life. Your current trajectory. Assess the future target and whether it has changed or should change. It just might.

You should be still more often, even if it's just for the chocolate and coffee. Of course, that little coffee habit/addiction has its own benefits. Actually, it was the thought of pour-over brew that set me back in motion on a slow, rainy Tuesday afternoon. I decided that I had been sitting around for too long, no motion, out of balance. There was no lack of effort, just a shortage of input and stimulation, and as you would expect, there were no bold ideas for what key to strike next. The input and the motion are so important.

That's actually the dark and hairy underbelly of stillness. If you get too comfortable, you'll get further and further away from your edge, your bite, your primal self that just wants to punch the world right in the fucking teeth with zero hesitation. Your piss and vinegar will be slowly drained and replaced with Hershey's chocolate syrup and empty bags of Funyuns. Good luck making your changes then.

"Not today. Why ever let this process start? Why not force some motion?"

My Tuesday got going full speed when I decided to hop over to the coffee shop for a decent espresso, maybe with a bit of steamed whole milk poured over the top.

You can get a fairly decent cup of coffee just about any place nowadays, thank God, but sometimes you need something more than just the caffeine alone. What you really want are the novel and stimulating surroundings. That enhances the drug-kick, certainly, but it's also the best hunting ground for fresh ideas. I like someplace unique and permanently infused with the smell of freshly ground, choice Arabica beans. The typical chain cafe often won't do, so I tend to pick the quirkiest option, the kind that might sell patchouli incense and vegan coconut cream cupcakes from behind the front counter. What can I say, I'm really nothing more than a closeted bohemian. I love the people here and the counter-cultural points of view, even if the irony comes painted on a little thick.

Oh, how I love the coffee shop.

The urge takes hold right on the other side of the front door, to pick the perfect seat right next to an operational power outlet, to boot-up as quickly as possible, to get back to the business of "Arting" as hard as possible.

"Hello, there. Could I have a big-ass latte, please?"

"Sure," the lovely lady behind the counter replied. "I assume that by "big-ass" latte, what you require is a drink with four shots? For here or to go?"

"Wow, that would actually be perfect. It's for here, thanks... Hey, could you serve it in that giant coffee mug over there? The one that says, 'I drank my coffee before it was cool.'"

"Alright, you got it. And perfect timing. You just made it in time for happy hour! Every cup is half off."

"You don't say. Coffee happy hour? That's brilliant."

I considered buying a big pack of the incense.

Maybe a few of those stirring, historic, pop-culture black and white postcards that I was sure would look great pinned to my office doorframe. But better judgment prevailed. My space needs no additional sentimental clutter, and as much as I love a really smoky and pungent room, burning incense in the house is the quickest way to provoke conflict with the domestic authorities. I took my half-priced, big-ass latte and made my way to the art spot.

The key strokes take time. There's no rushing it. All you can do is get your hands back to the keyboard. Reconsider what's important today. Wait for the whispers, listen for the little sparks that string together the thoughts. Sip the latte. Stroke away. Sip, sip, stroke, stroke, finish the job. Get moving again. Go pee, that really was a bunch of caffeinated fluid. You must be absolutely bursting. But hurry back, the ideas will not shape themselves.

I wandered back towards the front counter. "Oh, the restroom is just there," replied the lovely lady. "Down that hall and to the left."

"Great, thanks again."

I passed along the art-lined walls, top to bottom. You know how it goes. Local artists lay down their vision and heart. Then they put it up for sale, hopeful that someone will connect with their point of view and pay the hundred and fifty bucks to take that view home and hang it right over their vintage turntable.

I absolutely adore the effort, but my inner bohemian gawks at the commoditization. I snap a pic with my phone instead, which I'm sure displeases the

Muse. It's at least a small sin against the Art, I know. I'll pay that bill later.

I pee, wash and dry my hands, and reach for the knob before noticing random chalk graffiti on the back of the door. It provides exactly the sort of quirky stimulus I was after. Right there scribbled in bright pink across pitch-black chalkboard paint, "You have to be flexible to blow your own mind." I love that line, yes, because it is funny as hell, but also because I agree.

I've squeezed some artful meaning out of it, even if it's just the hasty scribblings of some hipster, or something I could have easily ignored altogether. The interpretation a quick chunk of coffee-inspired wisdom – is to move around when in doubt; it'll calm the worried mind. Change your perspective, seek out stimulus in interesting places, let yourself change, let go of it, and do more of what you value. But the most critical part is to not take things too seriously. If you can laugh then you can be creative. You can find a voice. Keep at this for long enough and you very well might do something extraordinary. You might just blow your mind.

THE VERY BEST IDEAS POP UP IN THE QUIRKIEST OF PLACES.

FALLING DOWN

It was great having an older brother growing up. Sure, the nine-year age gap caused some separation and connection issues, but it wasn't all that bad. It also gave me a kind of head start, an incentive for growth. I always had someone around to look up to. I rushed the aging where I could.

I have all these memories of sneaking into his room and screwing around. I know, it's lame, but you can hardly give your little brother shit for this kind of stuff. Sneaking around that space was always the coolest thing to do on an average Friday night. He would go off to do whatever it was that high school kids did back in 1989. What was I up to? Well, mostly breaking out his fresh copies of *Mother's Milk* and *Sonic Temple*, playing them on repeat, hoping he wouldn't come home early and break up my party. It took time to put everything back in its place, and to get those damn stereo settings just the way he had it.

The only thing better was hanging out in the backyard as his whole crew of friends skated together. This was your average 1980s, middle-class suburban housing development. Very flat. Very plain. Very affordable and comfortable, all things considered. Every day some beautiful stretch of woods got wiped clean to make space for more cookie-cutter concrete slabs. The upside to the development was the abundance of free lumber. Well, "free" by the standards of young skateboard punks. They stole that shit and built a sky-high half pipe, at least that's about how high it seemed from my nine-year-old self's point of view.

I would stand far back from the action, swinging around my He-Man sword, pretending to do the sort of stuff that a young snot-nosed kid would do. The memories keep flashing on now in my brain. The half-pipe fashion was all tacky tank tops, frosted hair tips and giant elbow pads. Bright and bold skeletons decorated the bottom surfaces of spinning boards.

Best of all, the falls were epic. I loved seeing these guys eat it time and time again, if only because it made it all the more epic when they actually stuck the trick. That's really the core lesson. My brother and his friends were pretty damn good, but everyone took their fair share of dives off the back of that ramp. Rushed emergency room trips were par for the course, the price you paid for learning that new trick. The glory of sticking the landing never came free of charge. If you wanted to do something rad then you had to take on the risk. You had to get out on the edge and be ready to fall down hard. You had to hurt. That was all there was to it.

I feel fortunate for all of these experiences and memories. For one, I still love those all those old Red Hot Chili Pepper and Cult albums, the crest of my 80s music interests I'm afraid. They set a unique tone for my childhood. But I'm also glad to have witnessed all that falling down. The edginess and risk, it's a great lesson to look back on now. It is damn good to be reminded that falling down is not really a bad thing at all. This is how you build skill. It's how you learn to stay on balance and on top of the board, so to speak.

It's twenty-five years on now. Every moment of life

seems to bring something new, something just a little bit more challenging than before. For better or worse, there's an escalation of responsibility, possibility, pain, joy, loss, and love. There's that humbling and ever-present anchor point between the novel experiences and my stiffening joints. It's fine. That's the trade-off. And it sure as hell beats the alternative of standing still. I'm sure my nine-year-old self would agree.

Life is no slow trickle. It bursts out from odd angles, sometimes all at once and with the worst-possible timing. So why would we ever expect smooth sailing? Why would we assume that progress is always this linear and continuous thing and that falling down and fucking up is all that bad?

If the whole trick to life is keeping the balance while you learn your tricks, then baby, get ready to fall off your board from time to time. Okay, maybe expect to fall down a lot of the time, most of the time even, at least for the first few years. Remember that the ability to fall off this ramp is a pleasure, an opportunity. It's the only way you're going to learn the trick, the key calibrating step, the greatest reminder you could ever ask for. Hey, do you want to do something radical or not? Yes, I thought so. Fall down smiling.

Author's note: Rad is just as cool as it's ever been. Use the slang like it was 1989, baby.

FALLING DOWN IS A PLEASURE. AN OPPORTUNITY.

FEEL GOOD TENSION

My hometown seems like a decent place to start.

I know it doesn't matter all that much. It's just a relatively small historical footnote. Age allows you to extend your view outwards. You start to think beyond the random point of your physical origin. You start to recognize how everything ties together, so you move on to more elegant ideas. You find a path or approach that feels righteous, rocking and fulfilling, and you let it take you anyplace you want to go. You grow.

I know finding the path is tricky as hell, but it's also where you'll find your pair of ruby red slippers, baby. Knock them together. Do so often. The starting point and time hardly matters, so worry less about that bit.

There are the slippers, then there's the music. I love that as much as anything. Yes, this particular ego. Me. I hardly ever shower, drive, feed, work, train, or go about my leisure without good tunes playing. It's like spending time in my own little temple. There's nothing better.

Consider the peak concert experience, that intermission when things quiet down just enough for you to notice the other fans in the audience. There you'll see the same intense love and emotion expressed on countless other faces. Yes, that's about the time you start really feeling connected to something larger and grander than yourself. It's no wonder that hippie dreams of utopia find their apex at concert festivals, because that's exactly where it seems most in reach.

We're all experiencing the journey together,

making similar decisions, facing the same sort of bullshit, trying our best to create good things, ask questions, seek a better path. We share the same awesome gift of consciousness, although it can be a bit of a burden at times. You have to appreciate that force more when you consider it for what it really is – a divine and ultimately powerful gift. That's enough to give pause to any ego.

Ok, but I must admit that my ego presses forward. It acknowledges that I am a unique thing, perhaps for the worse, from Memphis, Tennessee. The "I" happened, coincidently enough, about fifteen minutes from my current location. Little Chris, the product of a highly introspective and overly thoughtful mother and, of course, an eccentric know-it-all father who could bullshit and yap with the best of them (He'd be the first to admit as much if he were here).

Drive a half-hour east from my humble birth spot and you'll find ground zero of rock and roll. There, in a tiny, unassuming studio Jerry Lee Lewis, Johnny Cash and Elvis Presley all sat together, young and hungry, some sixty years ago. To think that rock's epicenter was right here. What a fucking trip. This place still hums with the background radiation. You can feel it. The residual heat and faint aftershock rumbling. From this place, a pressure wave shot out in all directions and changed our culture forever.

Unfortunately, a similar but far-more painful shot rang out just a few more minutes down the road, right up on the balcony of the Lorraine Motel. Make no mistake, this community is still paying the bill for

CHRIS MOORE — BARBELL BUDDHA

that. The heaviest and most-powerful sort of moment. Put your ear to the ground and you can still hear the echo of it. To think that my parents experienced both of those events firsthand. That is truly extraordinary. And to think that I have lived to see a time where my phone will play any song I can think of instantly, on demand, whenever I want. What a contrast. What growth. What change, indeed.

As interesting as my hometown may be I consider the question often. "When are you going to leave this place? If you could do it, why wouldn't you?" I get it. I see it scribbled all over Mike's face. He's got a baked-in West Coast sunset behind his eyes. And I must admit, it's alluring as hell. I could see myself spending late afternoons on the beach, a small table set with a pitcher of corvette summers. That still excellent Daft Punk album would be the soundtrack of my afternoon. There I'd be, pretty damn comfortable.

Here I am, looking out on emerald green again. It can't be all that great, can it? Surely the shine wears off in time? It would be terrible to take the beach for granted, and I would hate to get too comfortable. But I wonder if I wouldn't miss this southern town's madness. A touch of its corruption. The strange beat. The tension that is fed by all the history and pain. If nothing else, shouldn't I be thankful for the influence?

At the very least, I can utilize that tension. I already knew as much in the gym. You can boil every strength training program in the world down to one idea: you need the tension. Just a bit to start, then more. A slightly elevated mechanical distress spread across the soft-tissue and skeletal structure of your body is what you need to trigger a response. A fortification of muscle and bone. An up-regulation of metabolic and hormonal activity. Stop or mute that tension and you stop the reaction. However, add a bit more in careful, progressive doses and you can foster an incredible shift. That's why nothing can ever beat a simple, heavy barbell. It's a divine instrument of tension and change. What could be more powerful?

Remember, everything is connected. So how could we not view all kinds of tension as something good? How could we not be at least a little skeptical when we stumble across a smooth and overly quiet path? When things seems a little too cozy, sure, and laid back? Isn't that really bad for progress?

Fuck man, who am I kidding? If I get a shot at the beach and a few of those tequila cocktail pitchers, I'm going to take it. This much is likely. But that said, I'll make sure to fill my ears with Johnny Cash and Jerry Lee Lewis tunes. Maybe that'll be enough to remind me of the rhythm and tensions still wafting around my hometown. It's just another sort of barbell I can carry around with me to create that useful dose of tension.

NEVER FORGET: YOU NEED THE TENSION.

FOG IN, FOG OUT

There is a time and place for quick thrills. A good, old-fashioned sugar rush. Any higher primate knows how to scratch that itch when necessary. And most of us understand that it's probably not a good idea to turn the scratching into a daily habit. The sugar rush can never be all that filling. It doesn't renew itself beyond the initial dopamine hit. It's a fun way to spend your Friday night, to be sure, but not beyond.

On the flip-side, I think the greatest real return and bang for our buck usually follows construction of some kind, as often as we can manage it. Consider the full-body quiver that follows a really tough workout. It's empowering, confirming, invigorating. It's a sign that you've done the work and will soon be elevated, upgraded to something a little better than you were before. That's a different sort of hit, the crystal clear and blissful feeling that follows a job well done. The very real and enduring rush of having built something amazing. And for the artist types, consider that perfect moment where a rich vein of inspiration is struck and raw ideas gush out into the world as something real and quite divine. That's incredibly renewing, but hell, it's one of the hardest things to keep up. It's hard to remain faithful in the process.

I tend to identify with Dorothy Parker, who said, "I hate writing, but I love having written." For me, this is a perfect quote because it tells the absolute truth. That thing you've built, the passion you've tapped into, and the inspiration you've poured out. It doesn't come easy or for free. It can hurt more than you would ever expect. It can be damn frustrating, but nothing really great comes without that cost.

Resistance is at work, but sometimes I feel like we need a stronger word for it. Maybe you've noticed, but the process of building and creating anything – especially a better version of yourself – can sometimes feel like running face-first into a giant brick wall. It resists, and it can knock you down flat on your ass. It pulls your plug, then it throws out a smoke screen and hides itself away.

If you've ever been to San Francisco, I will bet you've noticed the intense fog. One moment you're enjoying a nice cup of seafood stew down along the pier, practically bathing in the perfect breezy weather and bright sunshine. Then just a few spoonfuls later the thick clouds roll in and you can hardly see past your table.

Constructive and creative fog can roll over us just as quickly. One moment you're excited to build and express your passion. You make progress, you thrive, then you reach a roadblock. You just can't get back into it. You don't feel the same energy or pulsing motive. You lose the scent. You don't quite know where to pick back up.

There are two strategies. First things first, come back to it. The thing about those walls, barriers and roadblocks are that they are not warnings or ominous incidents. They are guaranteed. You can be sure that your free-flow ascension and creative spirit will run up against the wall sooner or later. So you cannot roll over. You have to step back up and resume what you were doing. That means dragging your body back for more. It means picking your tools up. It means sitting back down and making that honest effort, no matter what.

I don't know about you, but I live for the insights. They outweigh any of the frustration. The work can be done, so sit down. Go back. This is how you deal with that resistance initially. But it is fair to say that some walls are bigger than others. You have to be prepared for those days when the resistance is at its strongest and the barriers seem a little too big.

A second strategy is helpful here. Rest as you know you should, just for a moment. Coarsely grind some freshly roasted Blue Mountain coffee beans. Pour some hot water over. Wait. Be patient, this should take at least four minutes. Think the whole thing over, or maybe don't. It might not matter at all in the end. The truly divine, stimulating, psychoactive alkaloid that lies within the beans will help you to tune back in. While you wait for the brew to take effect, go ahead and play a Led Zeppelin or Al Green record, the louder the better. Step back a bit further still. There's no need to jump back in yet. Trust me, the wall and your goal are not going anywhere. Just put down the tools. Go dig in the garden. Go for a long walk. Get on the couch for a while and have your mind blown by that latest episode of *Cosmos* that's waiting for you on the DVR. I know it might feel like a guilty pleasure when there's so much left to build and to do, but it's anything but. It's a must. It allows that struck vein to replenish and to run-over again. It brings back the lift.

That's the thing about progress. We sometimes assume it should be infinite and linear. It has to keep pace with how much we care and how much effort we put in. But that's just not reality. When the thick fog rolls in be sure to remember that it will roll on by just as quickly. The fog will clear, friend. I promise you.

YOUR FOG WILL CLEAR.

GOING SPARTAN

It's pretty common, really.

I tend to get all excited and lathered up at the prospect of a big day with its promises of something novel, up-tempo and challenging. If I'm fortunate, a new and vital perspective can be found waiting for me on the other side. So, with a big, wide smile on my face, I set my alarm to pre-dawn stun.

That's the easiest time to be excited. Something much closer to the truth emerges once alarm chime ricochets around your pitch-dark bedroom, ripping you from that deep sleep cycle and wiping away whatever remains of that easy shit-eating grin. This is the real buy-in. This is the moment where you decide whether you really want something, right?

I rise when necessary, of course, but the truth is that I've usually got little more than blurry eyes to offer this world before that second cup of coffee kicks in. And sure, it helps to play some Clash tunes at high volume to stir the pot up. But this time was different, very different. I set my phone down on the foot of the bed just shy of midnight. The alarm setting was stark, practically fluorescent. "Shit, 4:15 a.m. Now that's fucking early."

There was no lather, I can assure you. That's because I knew that something incredibly novel and humbling was waiting for me just up the hill. Usually, I can project at least a false sense of preparedness, but no luck this time. Fortunately, this was probably what I needed most in life right now. I needed to have my bell rung. "Brace yourself for stun, Chris. Try to think of this as medicine. As a potent green super-juice nutrient shot right into your heart."

The next bit I expected. You know how it goes. Just about as soon as you close your eyes and lay your head down the crack rings out. Luckily I went to bed already dressed for the morning "festivities." I rolled right out of the rack, grabbed my shit and dragged my carcass down that long cold hallway to the lodge lobby. My eyes were dull as old soup spoons. There was no visible bushy tail, but somehow there was a glimmer of energy. There's always at least some energy, especially when someone like Zach Even-Esh is around. He can't help but pour out infectious, honest energy.

"Rise and shine, baby. You ready for this thing, Big Buddha?"

"Shit, I'm not sure dude!" I replied, which was the only honest answer. "But it's going to be a great time...I think."

"Hell yeah, it's going to be killer, bro."

That's just what I was afraid of. Cue the smiles. If nothing else, it would serve to drain away some of the nervous energy.

Into the van and up the dark wet road we drove, just in time to meet up in Joe De Sena's driveway at 5:00 a.m., sharp. He was already there, waiting outside, ready. This is his morning routine, after all. Every...single...morning, without fail. I might have thought that was bullshit the night before, but the truth usually makes itself obvious. With hardly more than a quick, "Hey, how you guys doin'?," we were on that hill for a brisk, early morning warm-up jog, from Joe's perspective at least. From my point of view it was a little more intense. Doug came up alongside me with a smile.

"Done any one-mile warm-up jogs lately, dude?"

"Absolutely not, and especially not at 5:00 a.m. in cold rain." The same was true for the real workout that followed in that exquisite barn off to the side. This was a gnarly, calibrating medley of simple exercises, all performed for 100 repetitions – kettlebell swings, pull-ups, one-legged pistol squats, burpees, double-unders with a jump rope, rope climbs, and the finale, a few med-ball tosses against the wall for good measure. And we weren't alone. Joe's young children joined the fun at 6:00 a.m., right on the button, for their daily regimen of wrestling drills and Kung Fu practice. Yes, indeed, I kid you not.

At one point, right around the seventh circle of my own hell, I noticed a five-year-old little girl doing free-standing pistol squats and splits along a vertical beam, all the while counting out her repetitions in Chinese. I can assure you, this was all far outside of my comfort zone, far outside of all of my zones, really. An entirely new standard that couldn't help but be completely humbling and calibrating. And as I hoped, as novel, up-tempo and challenging as anything I can recall experiencing. And to think, this doesn't even include the one-mile, mountainside obstacle course climb that followed later that same afternoon.

If I had to choose I would say the peak learning experience came around during breakfast at the local general store, just after that brutal and eye-opening morning training session. We all took the time to relax and down a few glasses of fine green super-juice as we waited on our farm-fresh egg plates.

"I tell you, training in the morning is just the best," Joe said. "You get up, you get your shit done, and you've got the entire day ahead of you to do whatever you need to do."

"Oh, yeah, it's the best alright." I was so full of shit. I hadn't so much as broken a pre-dawn sweat in years, which is something I was going to have to change now. I simply couldn't measure up to this level of discipline, so I just sat there, sipped my juice and smiled. I did my best to ignore the less-than-pleasant cramping sensation pulsing away in both ass cheeks. "This was just the sort of stun you needed, Chris. You know it's true."

We chatted over runny egg-yolks and home fries. We met some members of the team, all of whom seemed to share this same pure, honest dawn-to-dusk work ethic. I felt painted with inspiration and shame all at the same time. I had to ask that last question, if only for my own reference for the next morning.

"So Joe, I imagine that even for you, some days are just harder than others. What do you tell yourself? When things just don't come easy, when the morning is extra harsh?" I didn't expect such a powerful answer.

"That's easy. It's a pleasure to suffer. To feel pain. Tell me, what's the alternative? Death...Death is the price we have to pay in exchange for this right to be alive, if only for a little while. So, we have to make it worth it. There's no time for anything else."

I finished my juice. I pushed away my empty plate. I grabbed my coffee on the go. It's hard to say just how impactful these moments were. My words don't seem sufficient. But the feeling is enough.

That old standard? It just won't do any longer, because now I know better. I've seen it for myself. That's the power of experience and perspective. Once you know you can't turn back. And if you do, you just don't deserve the pleasure of being stunned.

IT'S A PLEASURE TO SUFFER FOR A WHILE.

WHAT'S THE ALTERNATIVE?

THE CROWDED IN-BETWEEN

I'd love to have a tidy and organized work space. The
type of slate that is always wiped clean by five o'clock
sharp, everyday. But hell, who am I kidding? This
is fantasy talk, a romantic ideal that pops up in my
consciousness whenever I cross paths with someone
who, for lack of a better phrase, has their shit together.

You know the type, or at least the unrealistic
archetype that we so often hold ourselves to. For
these folks every action item gets done. Every detail
and calendar item is checked off right on time and
accounted for. Their life is one big bookshelf neatly
sorted by author, subject, color, and publication year.
Fuck, to be that organized, on point and productive,
that is some ideal indeed.

My life is a different story. Looking at my work
area now, loose sheets of paper stretch out in all
directions across my desk, each and every one marked
up with wild chicken scratch, sketched brain maps,
and random whispers from my Muse.

There's a small latched box in the top left
corner of my desk for keeping things, anything, those
random odds and ends. There's a stack of five books
waiting to be read. Every single inch in between
is occupied with stuff. A few musky candles, some
precious family pictures, some empty scotch tumblers
from the late night before, small figurines and
tchotchkes of all sorts dot the remaining real estate.
Behind me bookshelves are randomly stuffed with
volumes stuck here, there, or just about any place

with enough room to spare.

It's a sloppy scene, I admit, but that's hardly a bad thing. Not that I need to reach for ad hominem justification for my messiness, but didn't Albert Einstein himself promote a cluttered desk and mind over the empty alternatives? Yes, he did, you may look it up. So, this seems reason enough to let this work space be. I don't feel pressured to force myself into an unsuitable archetypal shape. It's perfectly alright if my slate is less than clean most of the time. It will empty bit by bit as it should, right on time, then it will run wild and overflow as new ideas come rolling in at random. It will serve as a reflection of my creative state, a status report of who I am right now and where I'm heading. Is clutter a pain in the ass? Yes. But I don't need my life to be neat. Those little figurines and tchotchkes have no practical utility, but they do remind me of who I am, what I love, and what I crave in life. So, they will stay. It all has a place.

I'd like to say my life overall was closer to the highly organized and productive ideal, but hell, it's just as cluttered as this work space. It might be worse. The random elements pile up and overflow. The whole scene gets real messy from time to time; frantic, anxious, overly self-critical, but that's alright. Somehow it still unfolds bit by bit, right on time, just as it should. Go figure.

The random elements mix and cross over, making for new and interesting points of view, possibilities, paths that really cannot otherwise be planned. It works, really well, so long as I don't try and pretend to be something that I am not. I should never again make the mistake of trying to force myself into any shape. The whole trick is to let my crowded in-between spaces be, even when they don't seem very useful. Nothing could be farther from the truth, of course. They are my everything. They are who I am, what I love, and where I should go. This is my reflection and my future, all the roadmap I will ever need. This is me.

NEVER FORCE YOURSELF INTO A MOLD. KEEP YOUR SHAPE.

FULL BELLY PAT-DOWN

Going to the airport is such a *Groundhog Day* experience. The same situation is presented to you over and again, a fact that begins to drill into you once you've been on the road a while.

Here, in this hyper-regulated and procedural space, you know exactly what to expect. First things first, you will probably be stressed over time. Either you are super late for your early morning Orlando flight to the National Deli Meat Association's annual convention, or you are all punctual and shit. You've put a lot of work into planning your travels beforehand, which is smart. Get the stress out ahead of schedule while you still have the time for drinking on the cheap in your own home. It's so expensive to get toasted in the airport. So yes, be a planner.

We planned this leg of the trip. We arrived right on time, breezed straight through the ticketing counter and the *1984*-style body-scanning interrogation zone. It was far better than I had expected. I popped off my shoes and slid my laptop out of its enclosure with magic fingers. My pockets empty, my attitude chill, I pranced up to the yellow line and right inside the full body scanner. I must say, I had never felt so safe and protected (Cough).

On the other side of my scan, I paused with a smile on my face because, shit, I am a gentlemen. Also, if nothing else, I know that a grin only improves my chances of getting out of this shithole without incident, so I kept up the projection. The very tall, very serious TSA agent was still there to flag me down, however. "Sir,

I'm going to have to pat down your belly. Is that okay?"

I thought that was quite odd, but with nothing to hide I had no objection. "Whatever you need to do, dude. I abide."

He swept down each side of my perfectly sculpted and toned abdominal musculature (Cough times two), then took one pass straight down the middle of my torso for good measure. He seemed to be experienced and pretty damn professional. He also didn't seem to absolutely despise his gig, which was refreshing.

I couldn't help but suppose and let my imagination loose. "This guy probably used to show off pigs or something at the local state fair. I feel a bit violated, but properly assessed."

In the end, I guess my stomach was so rock hard and impervious to X-ray that, surely, it must have been an explosive-containing steel structure...until the full-body strokes proved otherwise. I'd say, at best, my gut is a beer-containing padded keg. I am the faithful stuffed bear who just keeps up the grin.

This time around was a stark improvement on the day before, when we waited in the ticketing counter line for over an hour, only to be told in the end, "Ah, sorry, sir. You know, there's just nothing else going out today. Looks like you can get to Salt Lake around 6:30 p.m. tomorrow. Is that okay? Yeah, sorry."

This is part of the *Groundhog Day* test, I guess. In this environment, where the very last thing to expect is a good time, will you once again lose your shit and throw a fit that things didn't go exactly as you'd planned? The universe is watching. Don't blow up. "Hey, I booked a goddamn flight, alright? Everything was all planned out, perfectly I might add, I was right on time until I got to your counter. And what, you're telling me to just go home now? This is really putting a damper on my pre-flight high. Fuck me, this sucks. Thanks anyway, Miss, I guess. How do you live doing this shit job, anyhow?"

At least this is what my inflamed and chaffed inner chimp would love to shout. It's also what that poor lady behind the counter was expecting of me, as every other mouth-breather before had let loose in some way. "Hey, what do you mean 'nothing'?" There's only so much anyone can take.

The state is disgruntled. Unmindful. Hurried. Frazzled. In such situations, it's easy to miss the chance to smile and breathe deeply. There's no need to hurry. There's a Starbucks in the terminal ahead. There's *always* a Starbucks in the terminal ahead. This kind of thing is bound to happen, so I figure the best strategy is to simply assume it's part of the plan, or at least it's just the next level of the test. Smiling should come easy in that light.

It's worth pointing out that it's taken many years to accept this point of view. From my teenage years all the way up until the present moment I've been trying out all of the alternatives. I forced my own plan through a time or two. I've stressed over the future like mad. I've regretted segments of my past intensely. I've deferred love and personal freedom until some future date, out of fear, in exchange for money.

Of course, the alternatives were all wrong. Imagine that you're caught in the middle of a rapidly flowing river. You are scared and clutching a rock with white knuckles. You are holding on tight to prevent your own destruction.

When the flow seems to slow down, you reach out towards the riverbank, towards stability and safety, but all you get is powerful resistance. You're moving against the water now. The further you reach out, the more intensely you will be resisted, until you lose your grip altogether and get dragged off someplace you never wanted to go.

It seems wise, but it's just not so. It has taken time and countless rounds of groundhogging for me to finally grasp that this life, my little river, is not to be resisted. Instead the proper procedure is as follows: turn away from the resistance; point towards the flow; spot those rocks ahead, not out of fear, but as a way to simply pass them by; take a few deep breaths; let go of your rock; let the river take you wherever the hell it wants.

Basically, let your inflamed inner chimp go all Zen for once. Also, make sure to have a few plastic tumblers of Dewar's and ginger ale. It really does help.

TURN TOWARD THE FLOW. LET GO OF WHAT YOU'RE CLENCHING.

MIDNIGHT WATERMELON

I took a moment to catch my breath and zone out.

The previous hour had been burned away under a hot June sun, the typical errand running hustle and bustle. "Return this. Pick up that. Make sure to get home in time for the thing we've got planned at 2:30." Typical, but this is exactly why I don't mind waiting in lines anymore.

See for yourself. Just look around the next time you're in the queue. Note the pained and hurried faces. These are essentially flashing billboard signs for the agitated, inner higher primate. Listen for the audio cues, the gasps and grunts, the calls for a swift resolution from frayed and superficially affixed minds. You know the talk. We're all guilty of it from time to time.

"Why don't they just open up another line already? For Christsakes, I've got to get out of here. I have things to do! All sorts of...stuff. The lawn is not going to water itself. The game starts in an hour. Great, the iPad is down to 10% power. The kids will surely lose their shit now. That should make for a pleasant drive home. I don't know why I'm even buying that new Rascal Flatts CD. Like I'm even going to be able to listen to it. And this weather is just my luck. I bet that half-gallon of Breyers frozen dessert-like substance will be mostly melted by the time I pull the mini-van out of the parking lot."

Author's note: First, there is little reason to actually buy a Rascal Flatts album. If you dig that kind of thing, just go out into the world. Any dental office will do. You'll find it playing 100% of the time on bullshit terrestrial radio. Second, don't knock mini-vans. You simply haven't traveled until you've hit the road in a new, loaded Town & Country. Trust me. Finally, there should be no room in your life for cheap ice cream. As with tattoos and training equipment, money shouldn't factor into it. If you're going to go to the trouble, get the best your money can buy.

This is an easy behavioral rut to fall into. Fortunately, it's also an easy one to climb out of. I just remind the inner agitated primate that these moments of waiting are really nothing more than opportunities. So much of this life is about rushing around according to timelines. So much of it is typical. The queue is just a reminder to stop being so silly, to not treat these highly valuable moments of stillness as some sort of burden.

Yes, I was smiling in line...mostly. The cargo goods were a bit heavy for comfort's sake. My left hand was firmly hooked into a two-hundred-and-ten-count package of newborn diapers. That was the necessity I was after, you see. You'd be surprised just how quickly an eight-week-old can shit their way right through a huge pile of diapers. Under my right arm I clutched the surprisingly heavy impulse purchase: a peak, seedless Mississippi watermelon.

Aside from finding peace while you wait in line, consider these to be lessons two and three: remember that picking fresh fruit is no different from choosing a great woman. Their skin should be aglow, and they should feel much heavier than they look. Also, when a little voice whispers suggestions in your ear, you should take action, even if the whisper is quite mild.

"Buy that watermelon. Trust me. It'll be worth it."

The hustle and bustle begins again soon enough. Hours bleed together and the daylight is all but burned away. Midnight comes really quickly, but fortunately there are plenty more lessons to be learned in the wee small hours of the morning. They are no less obvious and useful, no less beautiful.

I seek redemption and spiritual renewal on Sunday mornings, just like most folks do. Of course, many will look for it around ten o'clock, but I see no point in waiting around that long. My home study can become a de facto cathedral by half-past midnight. The walls are bathed in a vivid spectrum of deep red, orange, and purple light. The air carries waves of ripping lyrics and melody right to my ears. My brain hums and dances with convivial compounds that convert every tiny detail into something ethereal and precious. Sure, this also requires a fair amount of calories, which is exactly why I usually find myself right back in the grocery checkout line the following day.

I began my last pantry raid by taking stock. I checked the cabinets for the typical cheat choices: salt- and dark-chocolate-coated almonds, anything crispy and crunchy, what have you. But nothing really hit the spot, until I realized there was that ten-pound perfectly chilled watermelon waiting for me in the mud-room fridge.

Let me assure you, I've likely never smiled so wide in my life.

I sharpened my trusty chef's knife and scored a shallow line from pole to pole. From there, you need only settle the knife right into that groove, then pop your hand firmly down on the back part of the blade near the handle. The tight rind will pop right open, revealing deep red and perfectly sweet flesh. Split your halves into fourths, cut into thin slices, leave that rind on. This will help the flesh stay at its peak. Sprinkle on a fine layer of Himalayan salt across the wedge, bite down, then you will know bliss.

I was just about done with the first quarter when the emotion started to come on with the shockingly obvious detail I had missed during the day's hustle and bustle: it was Father's Day. In fact, it was my very first since becoming a dad for the second time. It was also the first since losing my own father some seven months prior on Thanksgiving morning. That's the sort of moment worth getting emotional over. It packs a vicious initial bite, but thankfully that was a temporary sensation. I was more blown away by the melon itself.

Dad loved this very same late-night ritual. He would burn away his summer days and early evenings working his fingers down to dust at the local electrical plant. I would spend those same hours waiting for his return at home. I would shoot hoops, play video games, and watch way more TV than I should have. But I wanted that time to pass quickly. Dad would be home around 10:30 at night, at which point we would jump into his Toyota hatch-back and drive up to the grocery store. There we would buy two cans of boiled peanuts, a giant jar of hot tamales, and of course, the heaviest watermelon we could find. At home, the same process would unfold. Split that sucker from pole to pole, then carve and salt the slices. Eat your fill and pass out on the couch in front of some science-fiction movie rerun. These are some of the happiest moments of my life.

I didn't cry over the melon, thankfully. There was plenty of that back in the winter. No, I just ate and was happy, content with the notion that all we have in this life are the tiny moments. In the queue. At home during quiet hours. With family. The massive value of life is right here, bright red and juicy.

I miss my dad, but it's okay. I have this little ritual to share with him. I have my precious babies. It's too early to know what my little girl's tastes and habits will be. She's still mostly busy with filling those diapers and crying out for Momma's milk. She is stunning with that stern look, the one that suggests deep thought. Already I'm so proud of her, and I'm scared shitless! She will only get more beautiful from here.

The little boy is less of a mystery. They all are. He cries, he shouts, he giggles out loud as he runs around the house like a tiny caveman. He falls down hard, face first, often. But he gets back up. He laughs again. I kiss his head and tell him I love him so. He grins and replies, "I love you, Daddy." My heart melts all over again. Did I mention he absolutely loves watermelon?

Every single moment of this experience, this life, the waiting, the pain, it's all anything but typical. Don't forget.

YOUR WORLD IS OVERFLOWING WITH OPPORTUNITY. IF YOU WOULD ONLY LOOK.

MASHED

I started making more interesting observations during my second glass of scotch.

The tumbler in my right hand was filled to the very brim with fresh ice. The booze sloshed back and forth as I gestured. I stood for a while, sipped often. I shouted out into my microphone when I had something interesting, inspired, timely or witty to say. I smiled as well, because the first observation was, "Fuck, I'm working right now."

I never planned for this. I couldn't have planned for it. The microphones were a play thing at first. We did it because we wanted to do it, because it would be fun, because we had things to say. There was no grand plan, only a commitment to keep doing it, and doing it, and doing it. When our friends and families laughed at us, we did it. When we got too busy, too tired, burned out, doubtful, or distracted we just kept doing it, and because of that we can now professionally drink and talk shit with inspiring people. This blows my mind on a daily basis.

Lesson #1: I think miracles can happen. The world is a big mysterious place, so there's certainly room for anything. But please understand that you cannot bet your life on a miracle, which is precisely what most people do when they sit around and hope for some grand change or shift in their lives. Stumbling upon anything like that is an improbable thing.

Think about the athletes, personalities, artists that you admire. Realize that they didn't win your attention and affection, they earned it. They just kept doing what they were doing, no matter what. They spent so much time doing it that they became it. The change took over in time. So give your change time. Don't wish for it, just earn it.

My second interesting observation had to do with our inspiring guest, Travis Mash. My admiration and surprise were shared through those microphones.

"I have to say, Travis, I never saw any of this happening."

"Ah, what's that?" Travis replied, curious.

"This, right now, what we're doing. You know, I first met you a decade ago?"

"Really?"

"Yeah, it was backstage at the Arnold Classic. I was still a young powerlifter, and this was the first time I had been to a world championship meet. I was pretty star-struck. You know, you were one of the lifters I looked up to."

Travis' face just lit up with this big grin. "Oh yeah?"

"Yeah! I remember mumbling under my breath, 'Oh shit, there's Travis "Fucking" Mash warming up for the squat, just over there!' That experience changed the way I approached competition and training. It changed my expectations for how strong I could be. It changed everything."

Maybe I went a little hard on the praise, but hell, by this point we had all but drained that bottle of scotch. There was no sense in trying to hold back the emotion. I finished what I had to say.

"I never would have guessed that ten years later we would be standing here as good friends, a little drunk, talking shit together on the radio. That's an amazing thing."

Lesson #2: If you do nothing else, do this: quit worrying about whether or not you're good. I know, you are average at best, right? Wrong. You're just human, and to be human is to be a bit of a maniac sometimes. Like now, when your ego-driven monkey mind feels like it's not capable of more, or deserving, or smart enough. In those times, all you need to know is that every human feels that exact same thing, including your heroes. So, raise your expectations. Cool shit will happen, trust me.

My final observation had to do with a shirt. Travis' shirt, to be specific. He brought a bunch to share so we were all wearing this fucking thing. The color, a bright Incredible Hulk-green. On the front you have a silhouette of Travis' squatting, and I quote, "A whole shit-fuck ton of weight." Indeed, it looks heavy.

Across that black stamp you get Travis's motto in bright white font. It couldn't be more fitting, and is everything I need to say to myself in the mirror over and over again as I sip my morning coffee, at 10:00 a.m., in my home bathroom, because I am a free man. "I do what I want."

Lesson #3: That five-word chunk of philosophy will make you happy. For me, it's been a bit of a personal revolution. It doesn't matter what you stand to gain, or what you might lose in the short-term. It doesn't matter at all because, you have your wants. You might be paid to be somewhere else. You might be struggling to drum up the confidence. You might be thinking of quitting. But you have your wants. You will always have those wants. So do it. Right now, do it. Don't risk regret down the line, because one day you will regret time misspent.

I sat down at the dinner table and finished off the last little bit of scotch. The tumbler dry, it occurred to me that there was nowhere else I'd rather be. Then it occurred to me that there were so many places left to go, and inspiring people to meet, amazing stories to experience and share. That's what I want most from my life, and for my family. That's what was on my mind as I put my headphones back on to record another show at 1:00 a.m.

"Here I am, I feel good, mostly on account of the booze and stuff. So what am I to do? Go to bed, or do what I do for a little bit longer? It's an easy decision to make."

Whenever there is doubt, there is no doubt. Do what you want to do. Keep doing it, no matter what, and you might find yourself standing alongside your heroes.

DO WHAT YOU WANT. SACRIFICE AND GET FREE.

MATCHA

I love my coffee, but there's something really fantastic about a proper tea ceremony. It's an opportunity to slow down for a little longer and go all Zen and shit, for lack of a better phrase.

To do it right is to be present, which is the power of ritual to begin with I think. The homie CTP has this ritual down already. The record player behind us helps dial down time by pouring out ambient tunes by this extraordinary, experimental Japanese metal band called Boris. Discovering music so new and so different is a delight that powerfully enhances the experience. I fucking love it.

We settled on the ground around the small black coffee table. I'd like to tell you that my posture was perfectly straight, and that my legs were crossed into something (sort of, kinda) like the lotus position. But that's not so. In all honesty, I just take whatever position seems most comfortable, which is a tougher thing to find over time.

On the table top we had all of the essential elements. A very nice, very Asian cast iron teapot holds water just off the boil. The cups, the tea whisk, the pungent matcha tea itself. The incense was optional I guess, but I love the stuff. Smell is an incredibly powerful, stirring sense, so why not stoke it with penetrating smoke. It can only add to the enhancement.

The first step was to sift a small amount of the bright-green powder into a large cup. From there, you make a paste by pouring in a bit of the hot water, then

whisking it all around in capital N's and W's until
you get something smooth and free of little lumps.
Then you add a bit more water and whisk hard once
again, creating a hot and frothy tea that can then be
immediately slurped down.

I'm told you really should slurp. If the act
has anything in common with eating noodles,
then slurping is simply the best way to show
your appreciation for the effort that went into the
preparation. Slurp, almost always.

I took the cup into my hands, raised it to my
face and drew in a deep breath through my nose. With
my lungs comfortably full, I exhaled, then slurped
down the potent fluid. You might guess the flavor,
actually. Matcha is said to contain approximately three
times more antioxidants than the traditional sort of
green tea you might have shoved into the far back
corner of your pantry right now. It's also as bitter and
as "mean green" as any gnashed juice preparation that
you might pay an arm and fucking leg for over at your
local Whole Foods.

All in all, you can't help but feel healthier by the
end. The mind expects a therapeutic effect from the
green tea, which in turn likely provides one. Belief and
expectation are powerful, and that's only accentuated
by the ritual itself.

I lay flat on my back, content, calm, as open-
minded as I can possibly be. Over the music, we
played a slightly louder lecture by the great Alan
Watts. This guy was a philosopher, lecturer, author,
and rose to fame in the 60s and 70s as possibly one
of the first great popularizers of Eastern religion and

thought. Maybe the first gray/white guru, whatever. We love the guy because he had an incredible knack for talking endlessly, hour after hour, absolutely blowing your fucking mind with sharp insight into existence, ethics, meaning and everything in between.

For the most part I followed Alan's advice, I meditated properly. Not in any contrived or prescribed way. I needed no guru methodology of chanting. The only point really was to just be. The whole idea was to first recognize each sound in the room as only a noise, external auditory stimulus to be acknowledged without response. The thoughts are no different. The aim is to let them happen, only with heightened awareness. "There it is, that thought over there." Just as you acknowledge the sound, you learn to acknowledge the thoughts without response. Breath, thoughts, sensations, they all happen on their own.

For the most part the lecture was chill, but one particular part poked a hole straight through my little meditation bubble, compelling me to whip out my iPhone and take down a note pronto. Alan, with his proper British accent, was commenting on the topic of karma. I know, I know, that's hardly anything new. It's a word everyone has heard a thousand times, but I had never heard it defined so. From the top, "When Buddhists talk about karma, they mean action, and when something happens to you, be it good or bad, they say it is your karma. That means quite simply, 'It is your doing.'"

I can't quite pin down the emotion. It might have been a relief that all the effort and risk and good intentions might actually pay off. That energy might be coming back to you. But there was also judgment, not from without but from within. I felt instantly that most of my struggles have had little to do with misfortune, bad timing, or lack of skill. They've actually got everything to do with my stubborn self. It's my doing, which is fair.

So this is why we take the time. We slow down and sit quietly. We let the answers come to us for a change. And today, the answer is this. You have nothing but the present moment and the very next decision of whether or not to act. You could do nothing and, of course, you would get nothing.

Further, you might decide to do something shallow, expected, unimaginative, contrived, half-hearted, boring, or whatever, but you shouldn't be surprised with what you get in return.

It's Zen, it's karma, it's action for reaction, as in physics. Forget the rules, if your fate is your doing, then for fuck sake, at least do what you want. With any luck you'll become just what you want to be.

YOUR WORLD IS YOUR DOING. KARMA, BABY.

GET FREE

One of the very best moments of my life came in between breaststrokes.

Let me just say my swimming technique is nothing pretty, baby, believe me. But I've been working at it with a smile on my face. I'm getting better. Like anything worth pursuing, I give it some time whenever I can. I make it an important thing, which really is the only thing that progress requires.

That's lesson enough all on its own. If you are struggling to get what you need, the response you expect, then you really should ask the questions, "How important is this to me, really? It's easy to ask for the return, but how much have I really given?"

I flipped over after my fifth lap, kicking off the back wall with all the leg power I could possibly muster. While I'm sure I must have looked like a concussed manatee reversing its course in confusion, in my mind's eye I was a fucking nuclear torpedo coming off that wall. Thankfully, that feeling really counts for something.

It took some time but I eventually settled into a rhythm. My early crude strokes were dialed in, giving me the best feeling of efficiency and propulsion that I could manage. My heart and lungs pumped away because swimming is hard work when you're built more like Shrek than Jaws.

It took one kick and three strokes to hit peak speed, to get the timing right. With a flick of my troll feet and a rapid row I was able to shoot forward and out of the water just high enough to get a good full look at the perfectly blue sky hanging above my head. The moment was just long enough for one clear thought, itself the emotional shiver that I expected a few months prior.

"Holy shit, I'm free!"

The shiver gave way after another five laps, right as the fatigue began to set in deep within my lungs. More lessons still, you have to get comfortable with letting those peak moments pass. You have to smile when the good times go hard, fatiguing, frustrating, or painful, because well, that's just the way it is.

Let it all pass, baby. Nothing's worth holding onto too tightly. If you stand to learn anything from taking an Eastern point of view it's that everything changes. Moments will pass. All you have is right now and the decision of what to do with it. "Chris, the sooner you embrace this the happier you will be." This is the singular lesson that life keeps trying to beat into my stubborn primate mind.

I fished myself out of the deep end and made my way over to the umbrellas, where my family was parked and enjoying the shade. The little boy stood eating a popsicle, his trunks still wet from his last dunk, arms bound up in the green floaties he was still wearing. It's the cutest goddamn thing you'll ever see.

My honey sat with her long hair pulled back into a loose knot. Her beautiful dark eyes were hidden away under those big ass alien-eye sunglasses she loves to wear. I told her what I always tell her, even though she never believes me. "Hey, you're sexy, baby. Do you know that?"

She blushes, smiles and replies, "No, come on."
"It's true, whether you think so or not."

She held the brand new little girl in her arms. Oh Mae, I have to tell you. I had no idea how much you were going to change my life when you came along those few months prior. I was prepared, so I thought, but I had no idea how much my view would change.

At first you had me absolutely terrified, way down into the deepest part of me. The thought of letting you down was the most chilling thought I had ever known. But in hindsight I see that fear for what it was. I wasn't in danger of letting you down or losing anything, I was just freaking out. I had never known that kind of love before, darling. You drew the breath right out of my lungs. Your little furrowed eyebrows melted my heart right from the beginning. What's a Daddy to do, Mae? That big change took time.

My mid-day family swim would have been one of many missed moments had I not made the decision to get free. I could have been locked away in some building, wedged between generic cubicle walls, waiting on the moment to arrive when the conditions for change would be ideal. I looked around, I waited and waited, and all I ever did was say no. Over and over again, "No, not yet."

But never again. No more missed moments, no more passed opportunities, no more deferral or delay. No more fear over what the future might hold, or what might be lost. There's no time for that. Not anymore. The only thing that matters now is looking for every possible opportunity to say yes. Inside this pool and out, I'm ready to kick hard.

THERE IS NO PERMANENT YOU. EMBRACE THAT.

DIVINE

Imagine that you're walking along a stone pathway. With each step your weight displaces and shifts tiny bits of gray and pearly white stone underfoot. Your gait creates a steady, repetitive, soothing noise, not unlike the sound of shifting and cracking marbles in an all-leather pouch.

It doesn't take long for the outside world to fade out. A slight smile alights on your face. You start to breathe through your nose into the very deepest parts of your belly. You slowly begin to get a sense that you are indeed something much greater than your day-to-day commitments. You are separate, a witness to your desires, your thoughts, your worry, your dreams, everything.

You are just "I" for now, which is all there really is anyhow.

You can't help but notice a bold green filling up your peripheral vision. The greenest of greens, building and building all the way up to the tree line ahead. You notice the top of the hill, but it's not your target. You get there exactly when you should, based on that constant rhythm, the shift, the crack of each step. You are carried forward all on your own, just as you are breathing.

On that hill is a lake, crystal clear. Despite that clarity, you peer forward and see no bottom. No stones, no mud, only darkness, the unknown. But this is nothing to fear.

You approach the water line and dip your toes. Cold, very cold, but that just takes some getting used to. You step forward, step, step, splash. The chilled water feels like pins and needles as it climbs up the calf, to the thigh, your hips, your chest. Your heart flutters and goes fully electrified as your head dips under.

The sinking requires no effort. You don't resist, you just slip further and further into the deepest part of your lake. With every inch of the descent you notice that the water is growing warmer and warmer, brighter and brighter. Your presence is lighting up these depths. Your focus is intense, peaking, it's emitting an intense energy that fills and simmers in this place.

There is no noise, no pain, only solitude. Perfect quiet. Peace. Clarity of thought. Your unique genius is easy to spot here. It screams out. It thrills your soul. It...splashes over you like a thousand little cold slaps.

"Fuck! That's cold!!!"

That's the only word left to use in moments of invigorating or stressful surprise. The wave felt like a thousand gallons of iced tea splashing over my neck and shoulders. In a flash, I was ripped from my conjured pond and dropped right back into reality. There we were, a group of fifteen-some-odd new friends locked arm-in-arm in the cold surf just off the coast of Huntington Beach.

My legs quivered and stiffened quickly under the weight of my body, which was the result of a brief but surprisingly tough Warrior Yoga and SEALFIT WOD that we completed on the beach only minutes before. "What an easy day, gentlemen. Here we are under this beautiful sun. Enjoy it!"

Mark was our anchor out in the water, the wise warrior and former Navy SEAL who couldn't have looked any more at ease during the entirety of our training session. Immediately after meeting him, I could recognize the energy that he was emitting, his smile, the confidence. I only thought of what I stood to learn from the man. He's also masterful at leading meditation sessions and visualization drills, which probably has something to do with the sheer amount of positivity and force that he packs behind each and every word. "Be a witness," he reminded us. "To your discomfort...the sounds...your thoughts. You are in your pond. Nothing can get to you down here."

After a few minutes, the water all around seemed perfectly warm and still. I could no longer tell that I was locked arm-in-arm with anyone. I was just at my bottom, cozy and secure, fully present, glowing with an energy that was feeling more and more distinct and radiant.

This visualization lasted maybe fifteen to twenty minutes, but it was an amazing experience. It's hard to say, but I don't recall ever feeling so clearheaded, so optimistic, so freed of worry, hopeful and capable. In a word, divine. "Nothing can get to me here. I am a witness. We really are powerful."

We communicated with wide smiles and tiny chunks of sentences as we made our way back up to the waterline. "Wow. Intense, right? I know, dude. Incredible." Everyone took a seat on the firm, wet sand in the typical lotus style, or at least the closest that the quiver would allow. I sat adjacent to the group, facing the stunning Pacific Ocean, hunched over for a better view of the shimmering sand below. My heightened awareness of the present moment and acute surroundings made it the most-important, illustrative thing. The angle of the noon sun was just so. It caused certain grains of sand to shimmer like bright little stars, as far as my vision would extend. Bright, bright little diamonds.

The first thing to cross my mind was Neil deGrasse Tyson's statement that the number of stars in the universe is greater than the seconds that have passed in all of history. All at once, I felt free of the expectation and weight that can so often cripple my creativity, spirit, and joy. In a world where things can be so complex, mind-blowing, and virtually limitless, this was a vivid reminder of scale, and that it is always best to not take yourself too seriously. "Let go for good, Chris. There is nothing to fear. There is no limit. Let it be."

The occasional strong wave would wash all the way up over my feet and into my lap. By that time, I was witnessing everything for what it was. A distinct sensation, cold ocean water spilling over into my lap. Coarse wet sand under my ass. The perfect Southern California sun pouring down all over me. A sound, and then Mark Divine began giving a culminating guided meditation.

He encouraged us to imagine what we could be in a year's time, from business to relationships to family. To push the limitations of what we believe possible. To see ourselves as wise and accept that there are no limitations to what we can do. He told us to fold time up and visualize pushing that energy into our hearts and let it radiate.

I must admit, I cried. The moment was too freeing, too reassuring, too intense. It was one of the most profound moments of my life, because it was when I first believed that anything was actually possible. No shit. My soul was all stirred up, my heart ran over, my mind hummed with new possibilities. "There are no limits."

All moments pass, even the divine ones. We stood, stretched, grabbed all of our shit and made our way back up the beach to the street where we had parked. Walking, I was reminded of a story from the previous day. I was chatting with my buddy AJ Roberts over dinner about life, relationships, change, his accent even. AJ was one of the strongest men in the world for a time. He's also one of the few human beings that I know who has undergone the same kind of change as me. His accent is mostly faded out now due to travel and the heavy SoCal influence, but you can still tell he's British. I asked him if that accent still pops up from time to time.

"It depends. When I'm home, I can just slip right back into it no problem. You feel the tone, the rest just happens. It's a geography thing, you know. Your accent and affect are just the result of the people you're hanging around with. It changes with location. It shifts the way you see this world. When I'm home in England, the old voice returns. But when I'm here I talk differently. I think differently. My expectations are expanded. I'm brand new."

I made up my mind by the time we had crossed back over the Pacific Coast Highway. There would be no turning back now. The path ahead looks more and more clear. To get to the highest levels of awareness and possibility, I would need to keep changing, forever, always. There would be no end, no easy time. My accent would change, no doubt, but that only makes sense. As of today I'm speaking an entirely new language.

LET GO FOR GOOD.

THERE IS NOTHING TO FEAR.

THIS IS POSSIBLE.

HEAT

Summer has its up and downsides. Early morning conditions and quality of life are just about perfect. Everyone and everything is in a relaxed, cool state. There's the common knowledge that, yes, conditions will soon go fucking nuclear. Why not be cool for a little while longer?

My first recommendation is to live like a big, sexy jungle cat, baby. Stay up late, run around hard, but still manage to get your ass up at a reasonable hour in the morning. You've got shit to create, right? There's value you have to deliver to this world. It's payment for your borrowed, infinitely powerful, unimaginably rare, and beautiful, and subjective consciousness. Reality is reality, emotion is emotion, and we all have our low moments. But you are still that jungle cat, dear. Why pretend otherwise?

You have no idea how powerful you are, you just know that it feels really fucking good to dig your bare claws deep into bare wood and stretch. To chase your prey, to smack lips at the site of a sexy, curvy, vicious lady panther, this is the stuff of happiness, and better still, it takes zero voluntary thought. You just do what seems awesome and best, right now. Just do it before the full heat sets in. It's hard for anyone to look good in the heat, darling. There's no need, wait it out.

Around Memphis, things are practically baking by noon. The heat requires precautions. Drink up a few five-dollar bottles of oxygen-enriched super water, because, well, hydration comes first. Also, wear a flat-billed cap coupled with branded shades to protect your dome and photon absorbing orbs from the harsh cosmic rays. You know, to protect your skin, and to look cool and bitchin' and what not. Better still, just wait until the heat breaks, and then get outside and run. Or don't. Maybe just go for a long walk. Spend an hour sitting quietly on your freshly mowed back lawn to read, imbibe, think it over, align with nature, if only on a small, cultivated scale. It remains one of the best possible uses of your time.

The heat has clear upsides when dished out in proper doses. If nothing else, getting hot mobilizes, purifies, and resets the point of view. This is my thirty-fourth Memphis summer, so I'm more than qualified to lead you through this visualization exercise. Don't get nervous, you don't have to do anything but read. The feeling will happen all on its own.

Right now you are cold, too cold. You're very stiff, especially throughout your hips and back. These are common symptoms of the keyboard monkey, don't fret. It happens all the time when you chain an otherwise healthy and vibrant creature to a desk. Imagine yourself pushing away from that big gray desk. You stand, albeit slowly, arching up slowly one vertebrae at a time until your frame is fully erect. You stretch, you breathe, you feel at least three inches taller than you did just a few moments ago.

You turn and exit through a very plain, very ordinary door and find yourself in a small yard. For maximal effect, imagine that this is your grandparent's house, or someplace dear. Reach far back for a memory from your childhood. The foggier the better. Right there in the middle of that space there's a dense shade tree, maybe twenty steps from where you stand. You walk, slowly, mindfully. The green grass is shaggy and cool under your feet. The sun presses down and does its thing, which is a nearly orgasmic sensation against your chilled flesh. Tiny pulses of tickling electricity race across every inch of your skin. Above your head and all around leaves rustle with the passing breeze. Cicadas holler in waves, their crackling screech is unmistakable, unpleasant, and yet, very comforting. Unlike a lot of unpleasant things in this life, at least they are comforting.

A few birds are broadcasting half-hearted love calls from the deepest parts of the shaded tree canopy. I can't fault them at all, it's a winning, energy-saving strategy in time. Sooner or later, a tired little sparrow will pass by, fatigued and wilted. She will be vibrant and beautiful, and you might be one lucky son of a bitch bird. Maybe she settles on your branch. Let this be my second official recommendation, friend. If nothing else, be clean and polite. That right there will amplify your chances of getting lucky.

Be careful, because you know how it goes. All pleasures fade, that's true. Even canopy love, sugar. Just as the sun's warm press begins to feel more like a hot grind you settle down underneath your dense shade tree. The ground is very comfortable, spongy and soft. Sitting with your legs crossed just comes naturally. You lean forward, right, left, outward, gently, much further than usual thanks to that intense heat that's limbering you up now. The stretch feels amazing, freeing. Your mind slips into a very calm state. You are blending in. The penetrating heat is renewing; it's intense, and you are now the sweatiest thing I've ever seen.

Just as the squirm and discomfort begging to set in, a giant rain cloud pushes through overhead shoving away the heat, rapidly cooling your surroundings and making everything go gray and cool. This is the flip-side of the morning Zen. Your world all around breathes a collective sigh of relief and unwinds, exhales, breathes deep. The sharp contrast now makes perfect sense. Everything now shines lush and emerald green as a show of thanks. The first and only thing you manage to notice is that the cool breeze is worth every single second of red hot scorch. You are elated, bubbly and effervescent, fully present and in general, Zen as fuck.

How do you feel? Did you notice the room go cool on you? Maybe, maybe not, but for me just the word "cloud" is enough. I have a powerful love of shade and overcast skies which reaches all the way back to my football days. At the start of my playing, I was a vibrant but lazy fat kid who badly needed a little roughening up. Let me be honest, I never enjoyed playing football. It was often terrible, at times merciless, but it was also necessary, and I knew that. The countless, brutally hot August suns must have had a curing effect on my psyche. It toughened me all over, in places big and small – that and the dirt, the weight of the gear, the repeated impact, the deep relationships. It all happened in that heat, I remain thankful for that.

The lessons are endless, but there is one in particular that brims and bubbles with the most blood. It's also the single most important, transformative experience of my life. We're out in full daylight here so I might as well share.

I was never much of an athlete. To say I was a football player would be false. I played football, which sounds far more accurate. I'm pretty good at sport, in much the same way that I take to rhythm easily. I love to drum, for instance, but I'm no drummer. I've never sacrificed anything for the drums. I've never poured myself into them fully, expressing myself through the skins, working the craft, all that, so I wouldn't dare attach to the tribe. The same thing is true of football. I was never fully there, never fully committed to it. I think that's what Big Joey hated so much about me at first. He knew I was faking it.

Joe wasn't exactly pleasant when I first met him during pre-season training, but I didn't mind it at all. This is expected. Out of a team of 100 dudes, a few are sure to be raging assholes. These are just the odds. My misfortune was that the one who happened to hate me was also around six-foot-four and weighed about 290 pounds. The situation only worsened after a pre-season strength testing session. We were bench pressing with the aim of doing the most possible repetitions with 315 pounds. Yes, I might have been a poser ballplayer, but I was always a pretty good lifter. I managed 15 reps, which Big Joey immediately bested with his beastly 17-rep effort. I could tell he really wanted to beat me, and he wasn't satisfied with the bench press. "Fuck me," I thought. "I have a feeling this is going to be a very long season."

The heat and pressure peaked during the start of

football camp in August. For three weeks, practice was full contact, in the full sun, twice a day. The field was beyond bright, beyond hot, fast-paced, intense, reformative, bruising, and then there was Joey, every day, waiting on me. The worst of it came during the half-team scrimmage drill. Imagine a football field cut in two, starting with the offensive center (that was me). Only the offensive and defensive players to my right were included in the drill. Everyone knew where the action was happening. There was going to be a run to the right, followed by a massive collision that would be observed right up-close by the overly-eager, bizarrely aroused coaching staff. "Let's see what you boys got, alright?!" (Whistle.)

Joey was lined up directly in front of me as a defensive lineman. Again, we both knew where he was going. His job was to rush the gap, knock me on my ass, and then completely demolish the poor bastard holding the ball. Sometimes he would do just that, which hurt on my end. Other times I would win. Maybe he would underestimate me, miss the timing, get cocky, tired, whatever. Maybe I would get a jump, popping him under the chin with my helmet and jamming him in the ribs with my hands. He wasn't ever hurt by that move, but he sure as hell didn't appreciate getting blocked by said poser.

In the end, this was the far more painful outcome. The play would usually end in a pile-up, and Joey would often throw a few solid punches into my kidneys just to even the score out. So it went.

This was pain, frustration, anger, punishment, forging, hardening, awakening. I could have quit, but didn't. It wasn't exactly right, but in hindsight, I don't mind the fuss. By the end of that very long season there was no more punching, no more aggression of any kind really. We just played our best, and we both did alright. That was it until one icy February evening some two months after the season's end. We were drinking and bullshitting with some of the guys at Joey's place one evening. After an hour or so, everyone was ready to go out to the local bar, the only one that would serve the lot of us, regardless of age. Joey waited back as the rest exited, grabbing me by my right trap meat on top of my shoulder, drawing me in. I wasn't afraid of what he might do, but at the same time I wouldn't have been surprised by a quick gut shot for old time's sake. But that was all uncalled for, needless worry. Once he had my attention he just let me know what was on his mind. "I like you, Sluggo." That was it. I won that guy over, somehow.

I still didn't feel like much of a football player, but for better or worse I was no longer that poser in Big Joey's eyes. I might have started out fake, but at least I was tough, and apparently too dumb and stubborn to take a hint and quit. It does count to be clean and polite, and if you really want to win the respect, find something that strengthens your spirit and be tough in the face of whatever comes your way. The acute heat and pressure is not all that bad, especially when you consider that the reward is far more validating and empowering than anything you could have previously imagined, before the painful parts, before the sun went extra bright on you.

If I might make a final recommendation, don't worry so much about your discomfort. There is always a contrast. Heat always breaks and gives way to cooler conditions. In much the same way pain, boredom, the bummer vibes, they all break with time. You just have to wait it out. Maybe start this next part out by first finding a nice spot in the shade.

HEAT AND PRESSURE ARE ONLY UNPLEASANT AT THE START. HOLD ON AND SEE.

HUNTING TREASURE

I can hear the delivery truck's engine roar and groan as it climbs the hill around the corner from my home. This is a great sound, a comforting sound, because 98 percent of the time there is a delivery with my name on it.

I lean back in my study chair just enough to see the big brown vehicle lurch to a stop. Next, there's a quick peak in tension. "What's he got for me today? Is it *Mo' Meta Blues*, *Waking Up*, or that best-reviewed translation of *The Pali Canon* that just seemed like a must have for the shelf?"

The delivery guy pops out from his cabin like a hyper-energized and timely meerkat in little freshly pressed and cuffed brown shorts. His box is book-shaped. He knocks and leaves, and I scoop up my parcel, open, flip, feel, inspect, admire, skim, and all-around just smile about as hard as I ever smile, because nothing beats the feeling of a new book in hand.

It's not all high. Part of me feels guilty. Maybe my wife is right about this. "How could you possibly ever read all of those books you buy? You are so weird." For anyone that might feel like rushing to my defense, let me admit now that she's right. I cannot read all of these pages, which bums me out. It means admitting that some pearls will always remain unknown…dang.

Also, I feel guilty that maybe I'm rushing through many of these volumes, or maybe just giving up before all of the nuggets are found. That plays on a common misconception, actually. One that I hold. Those books should be absorbed fully, one at a time, single file. You should feel bad about not finishing a piece, even if you are honestly bored to fucking tears and fantastically disinterested in the topic.

I remind myself of the lesson that Christopher Hitchens shared years ago. If I may paraphrase, "When you find yourself feeling less than, be reminded that even those you admire and envy are only mammals. They are identical to you in every way, so take your shot."

There are readers out there. They get lost in the story, in the plot. They immerse themselves fully into the pages, living it, crying over it, reinventing themselves thanks to it. But that's not me. I'm nothing more than a treasure hunter. An antique collector. An ever more talented and inspired salvage artist. To me, every book is a new field of junk that I've stumbled upon. I didn't plan it. I simply took a recommendation, or maybe I got lucky enough to find it all on my own. But I'm here, and I'm looking for anything that catches my eye.

Not pretense. No expectation. No plan. That's not how any prospector worth his weight finds anything unique and valuable. You stumble around with skill, friends that's the key. You get a feel for it with repetition. You dig in, flip around, get lost where you naturally want to get lost. You will remember what counts, but you make your notes. If the pages do not inspire, you move along. There will always be empty fields.

That's just the point. Some days, there will be too many ideas, too much to learn, too much stuff that you could make and share. It's terribly overwhelming in the best sort of way. Other days you get just enough to keep you busy. Sometimes, the looking gets so tough that you feel like you might never have a decent idea ever again. It's all the same, because here's the great secret to wisdom. Are you ready?

It doesn't matter what you find, or how much. The only thing that matters is that you search. Every day. At every opportunity. Look around for something worth remembering. Move along if you have to, there's plenty to find. And when you do find it, take it in fully. Even if it's heavy. Even if it needs some work. Take it in. The feeling you'll get goes beyond what the words can describe. Give it a try.

No, I don't need this latest book. There are hundreds of other things I could have spent that 26 dollars on, believe me. But here's the way I see it. This book might only have one nugget, one pearl, or one jewel in the entirety of its 282 pages. I'll take that deal every time, because for 26 dollars, I just found a jewel that might sit atop of my latest scrap reading lamp. When I hit the power, the room and my mind is going to shine. Talk about money well spent.

What else are you looking for out there?

ALWAYS SEARCH FOR SOMETHING WORTH REMEMBERING. YOU ARE SURROUNDED BY PEARLS AND CLUES. LOOK AROUND.

STROKE

I've made this morning swim a daily habit. It started with clear intent – "I'd be better off if I weren't so large. For happiness, career, health, mobility, there's plenty of evidence. Why not start by moving around more?"

For now, I'm large, some two-hundred and seventy-five pounds. Gravity rides my ass pretty hard. Against hot pavement, I begin to wear away like cold cheddar against a grater. The tissue below can't take the pounding, baby. I need the water.

For me, swimming is a rare moment of physical freedom. After some twenty-three years of heavy lifting and sport, this is the only time I am fully mobile and without joint pain. That's just the truth. Free of restriction, I can be something else for a little while, something much lighter.

The exercise itself has always felt ideal. I stroke comfortably, shooting my hands forward like a spear into still water ahead. I grab what I can, making sure to get my giant head as far forward and down between my shoulders as possible. That might sound excessive, but keep in mind that while this motion is the goal, the reality is that my shoulders have very high mileage. They barely move at all, which is the second reason I love the water so much. I can really work on myself here, protected.

Maybe the safety and freedom of the water is what supports the magic. The rhythm of the strokes and the continual cool of the water. It's easy to go Zen because of the lack of gravity. Maybe your mind becomes primed.

Burdened with less, it's free to consider more, which would explain why I seem to get so many ideas between laps.

Not all are noteworthy, but some are good enough to make me forget what I'm doing. Just today, I pondered away ten minutes whilst chewing on one particular random thought nugget. Just there are the end of the lanes, bobbing, starring off to the far wall.

"Holy shit, everyone is special and powerful, to one degree or another."

I know that sounds cliché as hell, but it's true. Let me explain my view. We tend to wonder if we're all that unique, capable, smart, durable, what have you, but we almost always choose to believe that we are not. We just don't feel that way, so it must not be true. "How divine could I be if I feel so average, or worse?"

For years, I wondered those things, but always fell backwards against fear and doubt and my naivety. That caused a lot of damage. It's probably the real reason that I allowed myself to pack on so much weight. If you asked me at the time, I would have brashly told you that, "Hey, I have a goal of being as strong as possible, okay? I know that I'm not the best physical specimen around, but I've been training very hard for a very long time. I'm close. If this is the price, it's the price."

The truth is that it's easy to create a character that you can hide behind or deep within, but it's really hard and heartbreaking to face yourself, your fuck-ups, inherited limitations, wounds, insecurities, social imprints, parental baggage, self-image skew, you fucking name it. For me it took many years to get around it, it's taking time now to peel back the big, loud guy. He was a great shield, I have to admit.

I'm trying my best. I'm doing it, very slowly. I'm not worried because I now believe that I'm super-talented, and driven, and very smart. How else could I spend so many years out in my wilderness? You might share that experience. Have you ever had a job that you were really good at, but that you hated? Every day felt at least a little bit wrong. Sometimes it would be cool, just enough to make you push back your departure. I've spent a lot of time right there in that spot, at various stages here and there. At the time, I felt trapped and without opportunity, but looking back I'm fascinated with how dumb and talented I was!

Can you imagine getting good at something you fucking hate? Enough to do it for a career, to somehow keep that gig till you pop up sixty-five and well-done? That's a hard thing. It's so hard, in fact, that I decided that I wouldn't do that sort of work anymore. I was working harder and harder and harder to pretend, at each and every stage. To be the football player, researcher, powerlifter, the teddy bear big guy. For a time, it was fine, but the literal and figurative weight is hard to carry around forever. And that's when it hits me.

"If I'm going to pretend, why not do the easy thing and imagine that I'm whatever I want to be? I've been doing it so long, I must be incredibly good at this game by now. I've received paychecks in the past, so you could even call me professional.

"The skill is there, so I should make this choice final – I'm done working hard to be something, anything, that I'm not. Not more creativity will be spilled. It's too tough of a thing to keep up. Instead, I'll be something that I haven't been in a very long time. Something much lighter, free and mobile enough to become whatever I want."

I won't hide it. Whatever's hiding down under the big guy is about as beat-up and sore as these shoulders. It's going to take time to see real movement, but that's fine. At least I'm working on myself.

AS LONG AS WE'RE PRETENDING, WE MIGHT AS WELL PRETEND TO BE WHATEVER WE WANT TO BE.

PICK IT UP

You have a fear. It's held close and tight, well out of view.
What is it? It could be something natural and common,
like snakes, jury duty, injury, fire, or pain. Everyone fears
the potentially venomous biting things. No one believes
that they have what it takes to survive the toughest tests
in life and still bounce back. It's so hard, and it's scary as
hell to know that you will hurt plenty, and lose quite a lot
along the way.

Don't fret, don't let it sour the mood. Remember
instead that life is a drama that requires these tough
moments. It's the key to the whole show. You need it, or
else you can have no punch line or satisfaction afterward.
You don't have to go around it. You cannot avoid it. And
you don't have to stay here any longer. The best way
forward, as Robert Frost would say, is straight through.
You have to deal with your shit in this life. Work straight
through your fear. Do not run; you can't anyway. It's too
sticky and durable, a heavy shadow at your back.

Reach out and touch what you're afraid of. Go
on. Just start slowly. Think about what would go down
in a clinical setting. The snake of choice would be right
over there in the corner of the room. You would start by
getting the nerve together to walk through the door, then
a few more steps to the table, to sit in the chair, you inch
forward until you are within reach. You stick out your
heavy gloved hand and touch it. Your fear. Your dread.
And in that instant you will realize that this "thing" you
fear is anything but a murderous viper-beast. The thing is
really no big deal.

Beyond the common anxieties, there are also fears that feel way more personal and unique. They are *our* faults, shortcomings, errors that we mumble underneath to ourselves. "I'm not capable, smart, tough, or creative enough for this." In your mind, the blooper reel plays on repeat, and all you notice around you are the highlights. Snakes are kind and goddamn cuddly compared with this sort of venomous perspective. You have to remove it from your life. You have to move away from it right now because you will get numb. You'll accept it. You will eventually become it. The fear will rule you forever.

Reach out and touch it just the same. Start by getting in the same room with your snake. You aren't clever, creative, durable, fast, handsome, smooth, funny enough? Prove it. Stick out your hand and see if you get bitten. Go on, do it! But just be advised, you'll get bitten every so often. Accept that some level of pain and risk is baked into this drama. You must have it. You wouldn't want to live in a world without it. But the bite is never all that bad. Despite the fuss, you move on. You remain undeterred. You did not die, as it turns out, nor did your world instantly implode. If you can get that far, you might finally believe that all fears are the natural and wholly uncommon type. Every primate has been blessed/cursed with this divine mind. The difference is a matter of voluntary action. Some will make a habit out of facing their fears and giving lift to their perspective, and some won't.

I don't want to downplay the pain. Unlike fear, pain is always around in some form or another. Like a tide rolling in and out, pain gives way to joy. It's the fundamental pump that drives everything in the cosmos. Build, then tear down. Get born, then pass away. Crush the ice cream, spoil your dinner, then spend the remainder of the evening pinching at your muffin top. One moment gives rise to the next. But that doesn't mean that all types of pain are fundamental. We can and should avoid it when we can.

So, what's the biggest pain of all? What could be causing the suffering, unhappiness, and dissatisfaction most of the time? I think it comes from a heaviness that accumulates with time. Like little barnacles on a ship, your heart can get heavy with expectations, the fears, the wounds, critique, failure, desperation, hope, excitement, you name it. It gets really hard to carry that all around. The pumping stops. You lay the heart down eventually. "This is where I am, and what I am. This is what I do." But that's not true.

Your heart will only get heavier and heavier, and harder and harder to lift. The flow of life will go on, of course it will, and you will be pulled in the current. You will want to go, you'll know the calling, but your heart will remain anchored. It will stretch, it will ache. That'll never change; please know that. At best you will go totally numb. You'll just forget what you love. Don't ever let that happen. Heavy or light, pick it up. Hold it high for all to see. Drift along with the current of life. Remain present. Don't ever be driven by external expectations. Just let the next thing you do also be the most-important thing you could do. You are divine, so don't waste a fucking moment of your time. Let the pain accumulate with the drift, but keep it wiped clean. See the shiny polished finish underneath, a clearer view of what matters most.

See for yourself that there's really nothing to fear. The hurt can be bad, the resources scarce, the pain very real and very heavy, but you are not powerless. You can still act, you can still reach. You are still capable of picking your heart up and carrying it wherever you want, really. So, what's stopping you?

PLEASE, PLEASE, PICK IT BACK UP. SEE FOR YOURSELF JUST WHERE YOU COULD TAKE IT.

MORNING

"It is perfectly true, as the philosophers say, that life must be understood backwards. But they forget the other proposition, that it must be lived forwards."
– Søren Kierkegaard, 1845

Anything worth knowing is all there the instant your eyes open. If you're looking.

In a flash, I see a square, perfect, off-white little ceiling. And there's the feeling of a tiny limb stretched out and over me. This boy is growing like a weed, and now the rest of his panting, sweaty puppy dog body is wedged right up against me, which makes me insanely happy.

I also see, over this tiny frame, the little mess of frizzy hair and perfect cherub cheeks. And my love, my cause to be, together we are all curled-up tightly and I cannot help but ask the question: given the pace of this change, how did I rush past the sight so many mornings?

I unwedge and rise, both in body and mind, and I start the conversation.

"Brain's a bit foggy, eh? I must not have slept very well. What is this, sweat, or did the puppy piss all over me last night?...Lord, my glutes feel like two freshly plucked and pummeled veal cutlets. Those fucking sandbag squats really are merciless, aren't they? Tell me, do you really want to be strong again? Is it worth it?"

It's all reflection of varying scale, good questions that give rise to good actions that will inevitably shape my day in good ways. Voltaire said it: to know somebody, you should ignore their answers, and instead, take a look at the quality, edge, and intent of their asking. Are they curious of the world, of themselves?

This is the principal thing: you're talking about cutting the shit and changing your life. Those that can't ask won't change, baby. Look and see.

In this pre-caffeinated state, I have all the grace of a drunk bull in a pitch-black china shop. Stumbling, mumbling those questions, I step straight through to the bright-green room, our perfect little apartment kitchen. A chill meets me there, its wind pouring in from the cracked, rectangular window that's just above the back patio door.

That air now whips over the stove burner, it pushes the muted flames all around the bottom of my water kettle, and I cannot help but be fascinated, thinking over more rushed times. For a very long time, I was no different than this flame, burning plenty hot but struggling to heat all sides of the pot at once. I close the window, still the room and then watch that flame go vertical and bright blue.

"Now we're cooking."

I'm happy to get older, mostly because lessons like this only seem to bloom and peek out from the nooks of life more and more often. It seems you don't have to look online or in any book for what can always be felt and noticed here and right now. Especially in the four-minute gap that exists between boiling your water and then pouring it over freshly ground coffee beans.

"Anything and everything, it's all right here underneath my feet."

I sip down that first cup of coffee, shower and offer inspired, grateful thoughts to the universe. For water heaters and high-pressure shower heads. For hoodie jackets, trusted books, clean paper, my Lamy fountain pen. I take it all out back with me into the morning chill, out on to the dawn lit patio where the next part of this meditation begins.

I lay the tools and coffee number two down onto the small, circular glass table in the middle of the mostly moss yard. There are ferns and bright flowers back here, which are beautiful. They are rooting themselves down through loose gray stones and into rich, black soil.

I'm really only doing the same, drilling down, but by sitting down. On my pummeled cutlets, with crossed legs, with an interest in feeling whatever there is to feel. And in breathing belly-deep, in sets of ten, to rev and heat up this biological engine.

I lie flat now on my back, with legs still crossed and looking up to the sky. I move more and more air, and I now see my mind go from foggy to still and bright blue. Just like the sky above me. This is where the coffee is made, so to speak. Where getting still is a chance to notice your own patterns. What you might be addicted to, what it is you really should be doing with your life. Root, root and dig down. You'll start to understand.

My well worn grooves, my own patterns – it's easy to see and feel from down here on wooden deck slats. When I was really young and chose to do nothing, blissfully oblivious to life and its opportunities, the blades of grass and nooks all around my feet. And more pointedly, I see my recent rushed history. There's all this stuff to see in the morning, but you miss that when it's inner heat and pressure that pops your eyes open every morning. Those rushed and red eyes were always looking ahead to the next thing. A more accomplished and worthier version of myself to be.

Finally, I see the past fears. I come face to face with those fears, little voices with really big questions.

AFTERWORD BY THE PUBLISHER

I feel I know Chris Moore. But I don't, sadly, in the sense of having ever met him. Almost unbearably, he died just days before he was going to come and visit me in London, to talk about how Eyewear would be publishing his writing. I was excited to show him around Maida Vale, and the famous track where the historic training for the four-minute-mile took place. So I never got to meet him, in the flesh.

But in a way that Chris would I think appreciate, despite it being dreadful and sad, I have come to know, and even love, this big "reformed meathead" because of, and through, his writing. And, to be blunt, that is a rarer thing to achieve than one might think. I say this because Chris announces at the start of his first book that he will be true to his own rough-and-ready voice; and while many young writers lay claim to finding their own voice, few achieve that, ever. Chris did. His words pour out of a real presence. With Chris Moore you know where you are; you know where he is; he has become himself in his writing, and that is rare and beautiful.

Reading the over 500 pages of Chris' brief essays, rich with anecdotes, stories, wisdom, advice, quotes, what comes across is: his sense of humour, his passion for life, his love of his family, and coffee, and books, but, beyond everything, his helpfulness and generosity. *Barbell Buddha* is one of the most generous books you will ever read. And, deceptively, it is one of the wisest.

I say deceptively, because though Chris did not see it this way, because he had not yet envisaged his writing gathered in one hardcover book, this is a classic in the making. It feels canonical. It feels like a keeper. It is a treasure trove of wisdom.

Chris' gift was to have experienced a lot of very physical activities, and then to project that outwards, into exponential realms of self-development. Without ever being overtly political, or capital R religious, his ideas, and suggestions, and guidance, come across with a sort of Jack Black sensibility one gets from *The School of Rock* – Chris was a teacher, like all founders of movements and faith systems – but he was also a larger-than-life, fun-loving, comedian, as in touch with beer and rock, and porn, and guy stuff, as he was with Zen, mindfulness, and family life and the need to be a good father and husband.

Reading, editing (with Kelly Davio, who did a brilliant job of fact-checking, correcting errors, and making this already great book near perfect) and proofing this massive book, I can only say, Chris Moore's life has not been a story of failure, but a story of success, that Seneca would recognize.

His dream was to have a family, and to become a great writer. Few people can be as blessed as Chris was – for he has many friends who love and admire him, and, though he died tragically young, in the midst of doing so much – he also died *after* having completed what is now *Barbell Buddha*.

And what a book it is. You could say it was like a strange fusion of *Zen And The Art Of Motorcycle Maintenance* meets Marcus Aurelius, by way of Napoleon Hill – but that is not to give full credit for the alchemy

that is all Chris' own. I have never read a book of
advice or self-help so authentically human, humane,
and genuinely funny. Not funny because someone
tried to be – but funny because the author was
bursting with a love of the world, and was able to
convey a rich sense of things, from high to low.

Chris was not Shakespeare, of course, but this
book is way bigger than the sum of its parts (it started
often as posts) – it is a universal book of hope and
change – whose fragments, assembled, present one
man's vision of how to live a better life – not a morally
superior life, but a better one. I am very proud to be
the publisher of this book, and to have helped it come
into the world in this proper way. I hope that even
those who think they know all that Chris Moore had
to say will return to these pages, rediscover their
massively appealing and entertaining guide, and
continue to encourage others to buy and read and
love, these pages.

The greatest testament to Chris Moore would
be to dog-ear and mark up this book, even with coffee
or beer stains, and lug it around the world with you
on an adventure. Help make this book travel, as widely
as the spirt of its author did.

TODD SWIFT, PHD
MAIDA VALE, SEPTEMBER 2016